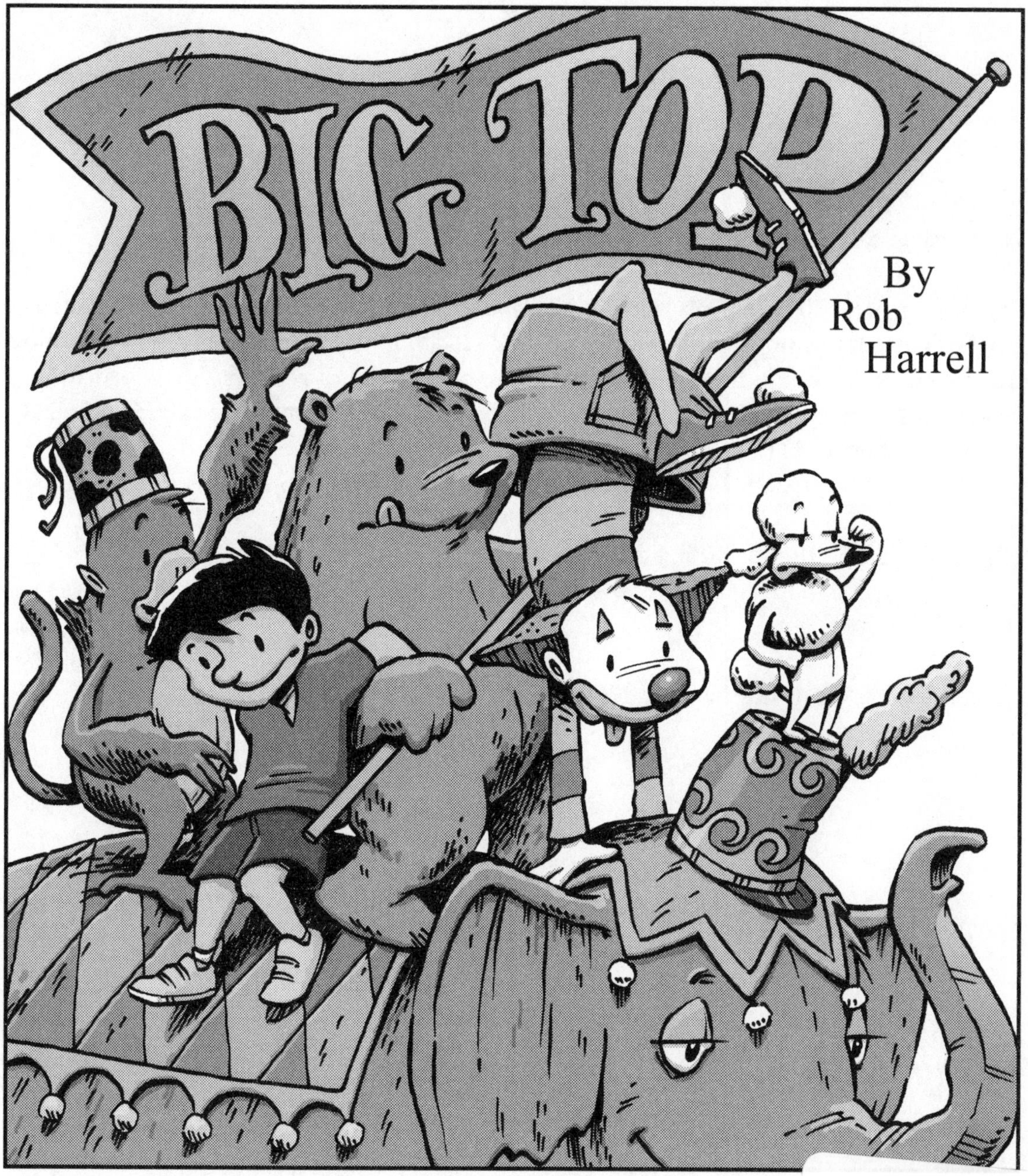
BIG TOP
By
Rob
Harrell

Andrews McMeel
Publishing
Kansas City

05 06 07 08 09 BBG 10 9 8 7 6 5 4 3 2 1

ISBN: 0-7407-5004-6

Library of Congress Control Number: 2004112531

──────── **ATTENTION: SCHOOLS AND BUSINESSES** ────────

Andrews McMeel books are available at quantity discounts with bulk purchase for educational, business, or sales promotional use. For information, please write to: Special Sales Department, Andrews McMeel Publishing, 4520 Main Street, Kansas City, Missouri 64111.

Foreword

By Dusty Poodle

I've been asked to say a few words about our little circus, and I have to say I'm not surprised. Sure, Manfred is the literate one, but if you want someone to cut through the hoity-toity stuff and give you the dirt, I'm your dog. Or dawg, depending on your disposition.

In a word, our show is a disaster. A big, dirty, traveling disaster. But then that's what makes us who we are. Would you really want to read about some well-oiled, spit-shined, professional entertainment machine? Of course not. Think of us as the next big Mark Burnett reality show ratings-buster: *The Circus*. Or, if you hate reality TV, don't think of it that way at all . . . it's no skin off my tail.

What follows are the initial stages of what we hope will be a long, long journey. In some ways, it already feels like those young high school yearbook photos that won't go away. The hairstyles have changed a bit (in those early shots I look like a wet pile of popcorn), and we were still finding our acting legs, but again . . . you get the good with the bad. It was a young, heady time, and I wouldn't trade it for the world.

So sit back and get ready for the show. Pop some popcorn and play some circus tunes if you can. The circus is in town, and it's gonna be a hot mess, baby. Send in the clowns . . .

**Dedicated to Amber and my parents
for their amazing feats of love and support.**

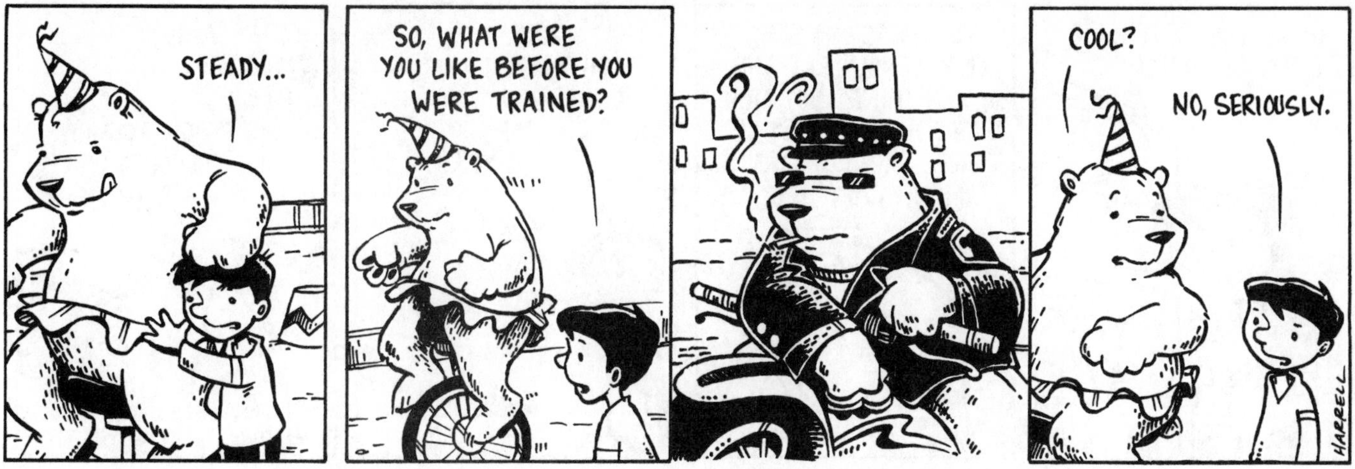
STEADY...
SO, WHAT WERE YOU LIKE BEFORE YOU WERE TRAINED?
COOL?
NO, SERIOUSLY.
HARRELL

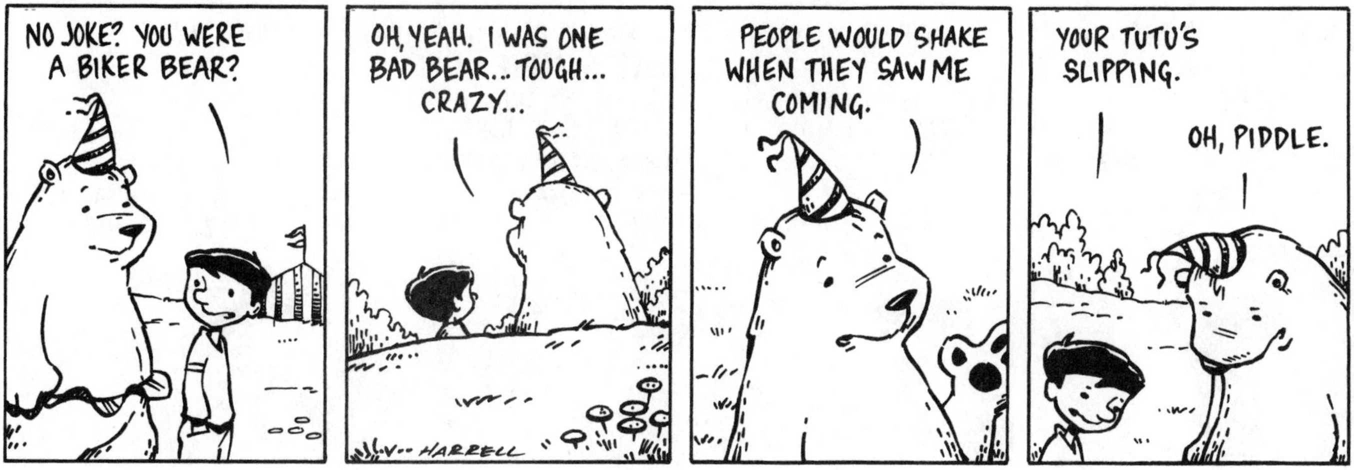
NO JOKE? YOU WERE A BIKER BEAR?
OH, YEAH. I WAS ONE BAD BEAR... TOUGH... CRAZY...
HARRELL
PEOPLE WOULD SHAKE WHEN THEY SAW ME COMING.
YOUR TUTU'S SLIPPING.
OH, PIDDLE.

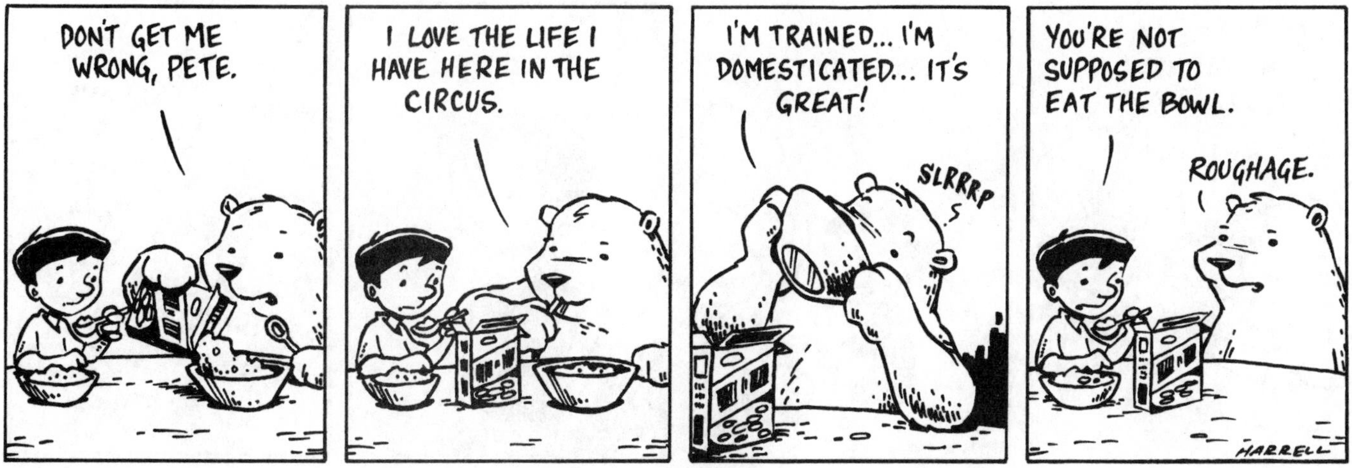
DON'T GET ME WRONG, PETE.
I LOVE THE LIFE I HAVE HERE IN THE CIRCUS.
I'M TRAINED... I'M DOMESTICATED... IT'S GREAT!
SLRRRP
YOU'RE NOT SUPPOSED TO EAT THE BOWL.
ROUGHAGE.
HARRELL

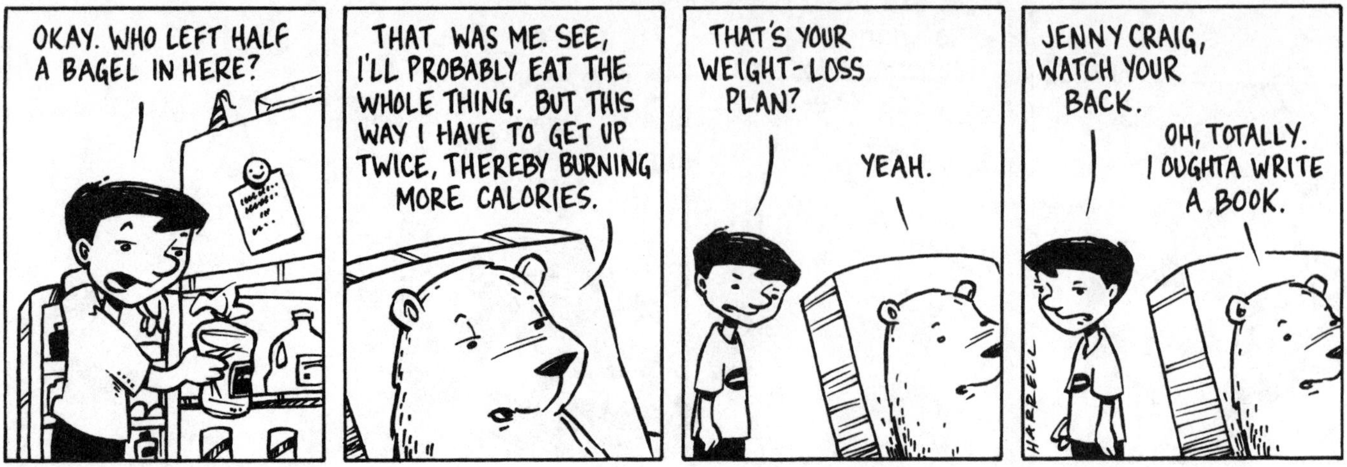
OKAY. WHO LEFT HALF A BAGEL IN HERE?
THAT WAS ME. SEE, I'LL PROBABLY EAT THE WHOLE THING. BUT THIS WAY I HAVE TO GET UP TWICE, THEREBY BURNING MORE CALORIES.
THAT'S YOUR WEIGHT-LOSS PLAN?
YEAH.
JENNY CRAIG, WATCH YOUR BACK.
OH, TOTALLY. I OUGHTA WRITE A BOOK.
HARRELL

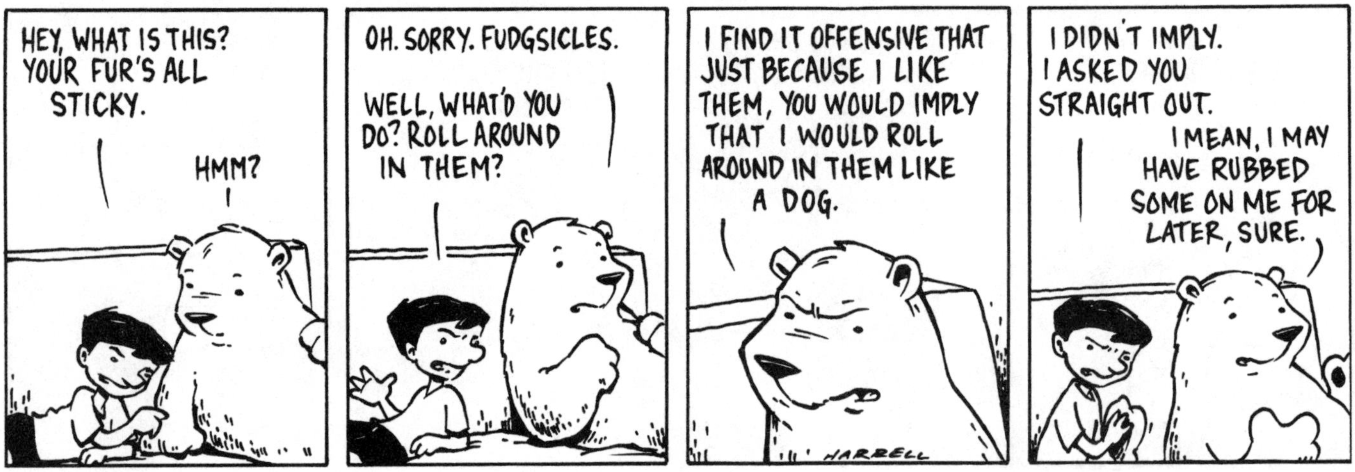
HEY, WHAT IS THIS? YOUR FUR'S ALL STICKY.
HMM?
OH. SORRY. FUDGSICLES.
WELL, WHAT'D YOU DO? ROLL AROUND IN THEM?
I FIND IT OFFENSIVE THAT JUST BECAUSE I LIKE THEM, YOU WOULD IMPLY THAT I WOULD ROLL AROUND IN THEM LIKE A DOG.
HARRELL
I DIDN'T IMPLY. I ASKED YOU STRAIGHT OUT.
I MEAN, I MAY HAVE RUBBED SOME ON ME FOR LATER, SURE.

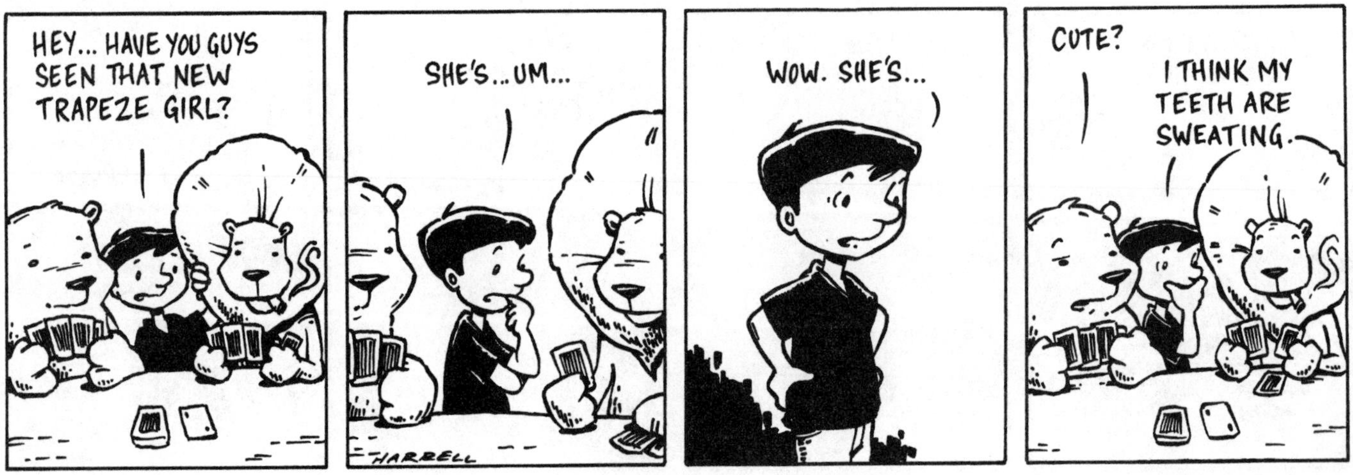
HEY... HAVE YOU GUYS SEEN THAT NEW TRAPEZE GIRL?
SHE'S... UM...
HARRELL
WOW. SHE'S...
CUTE?
I THINK MY TEETH ARE SWEATING.

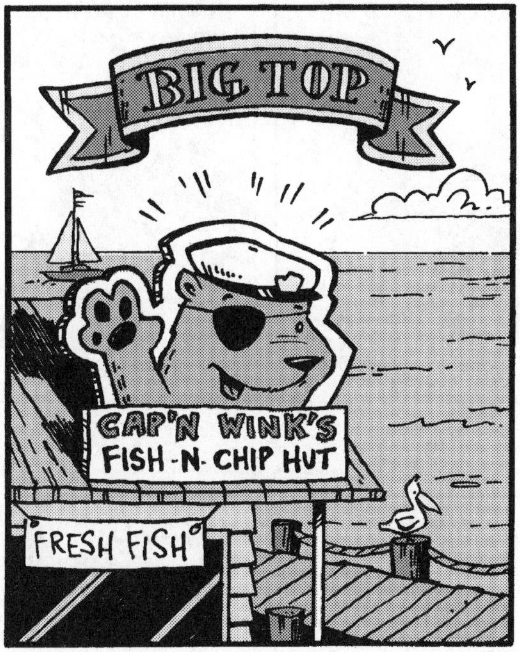
BIG TOP
CAP'N WINK'S
FISH-N-CHIP HUT
FRESH FISH

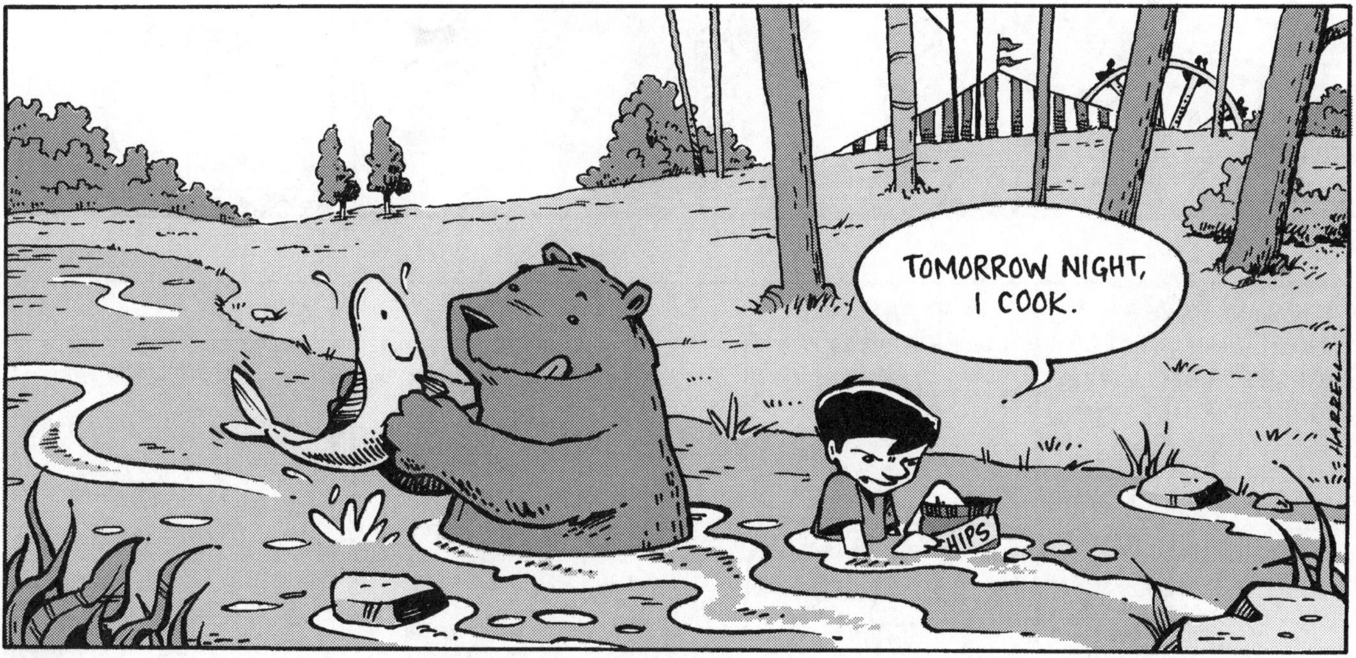
TOMORROW NIGHT, I COOK.
HIPS
HARRELL

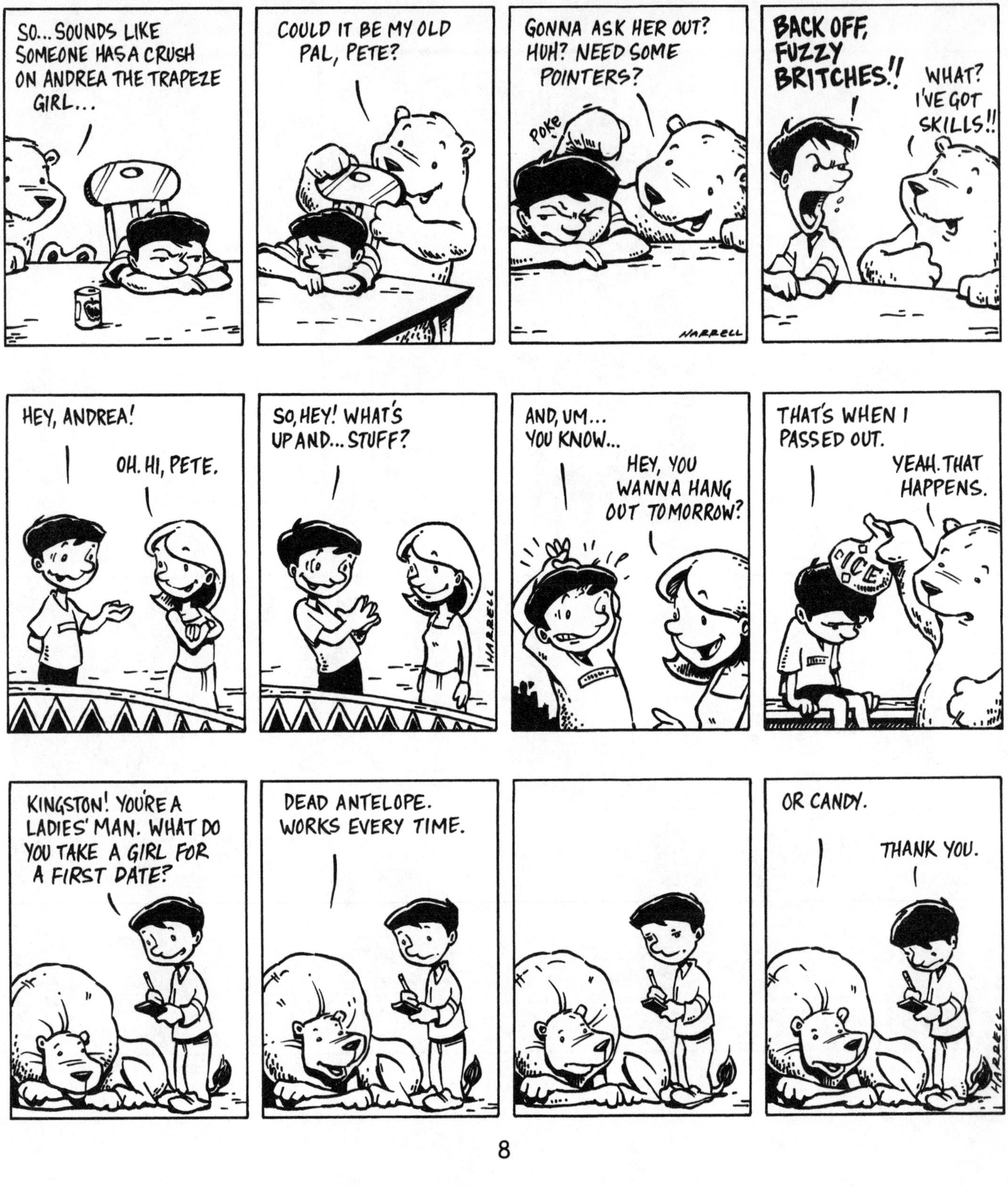
SO... SOUNDS LIKE SOMEONE HAS A CRUSH ON ANDREA THE TRAPEZE GIRL...
COULD IT BE MY OLD PAL, PETE?
GONNA ASK HER OUT? HUH? NEED SOME POINTERS?
POKE
BACK OFF, FUZZY BRITCHES!!
WHAT? I'VE GOT SKILLS!!
HARRELL
HEY, ANDREA!
OH. HI, PETE.
SO, HEY! WHAT'S UP AND... STUFF?
AND, UM... YOU KNOW...
HEY, YOU WANNA HANG OUT TOMORROW?
THAT'S WHEN I PASSED OUT.
YEAH. THAT HAPPENS.
ICE
KINGSTON! YOU'RE A LADIES' MAN. WHAT DO YOU TAKE A GIRL FOR A FIRST DATE?
DEAD ANTELOPE. WORKS EVERY TIME.
OR CANDY.
THANK YOU.

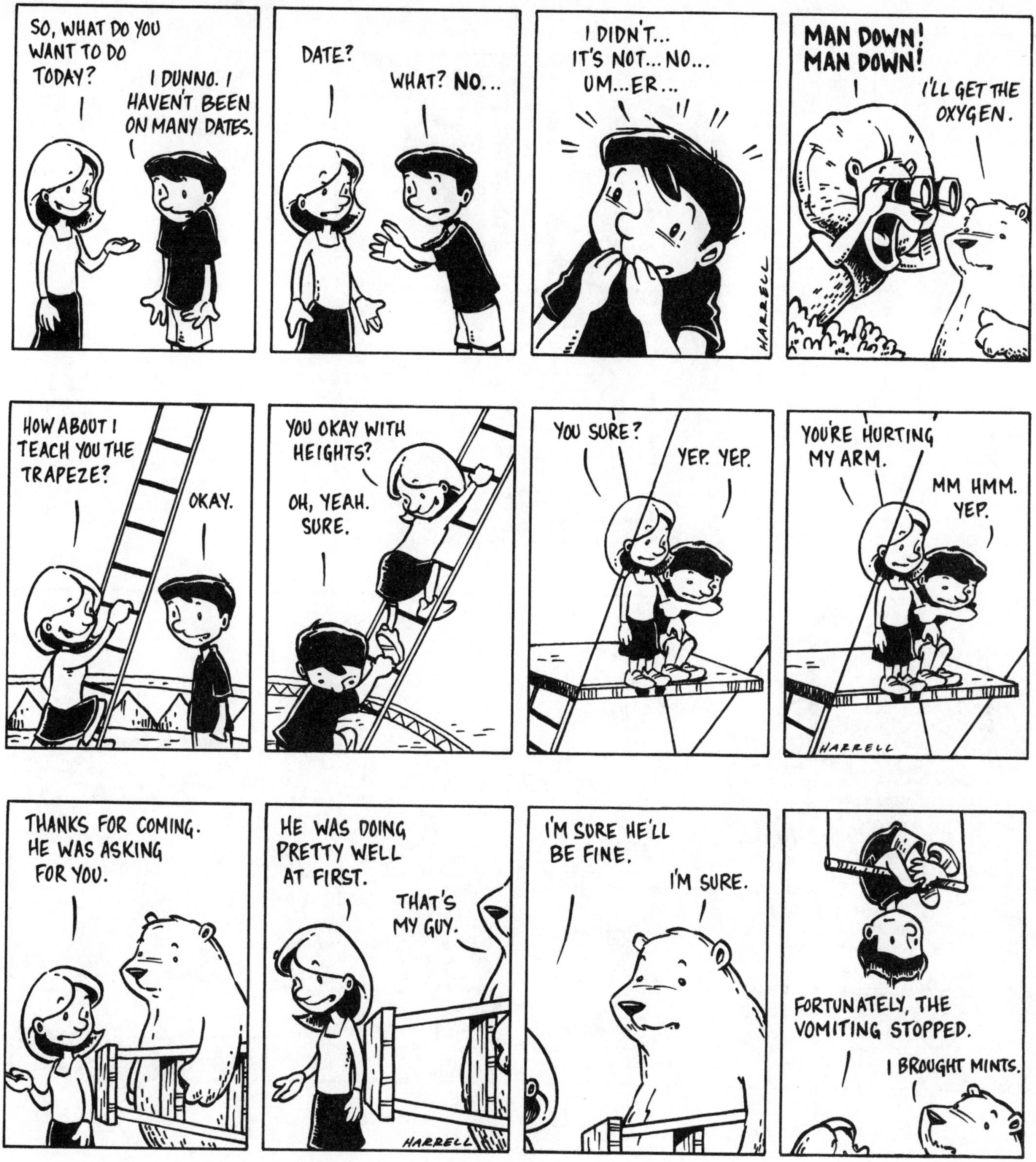
SO, WHAT DO YOU WANT TO DO TODAY?
I DUNNO. I HAVEN'T BEEN ON MANY DATES.
DATE?
WHAT? NO...
I DIDN'T... IT'S NOT... NO... UM...ER...
HARRELL
MAN DOWN! MAN DOWN!
I'LL GET THE OXYGEN.
HOW ABOUT I TEACH YOU THE TRAPEZE?
OKAY.
YOU OKAY WITH HEIGHTS?
OH, YEAH. SURE.
YOU SURE?
YEP. YEP.
YOU'RE HURTING MY ARM.
MM HMM. YEP.
HARRELL
THANKS FOR COMING. HE WAS ASKING FOR YOU.
HE WAS DOING PRETTY WELL AT FIRST.
THAT'S MY GUY.
HARRELL
I'M SURE HE'LL BE FINE.
I'M SURE.
FORTUNATELY, THE VOMITING STOPPED.
I BROUGHT MINTS.

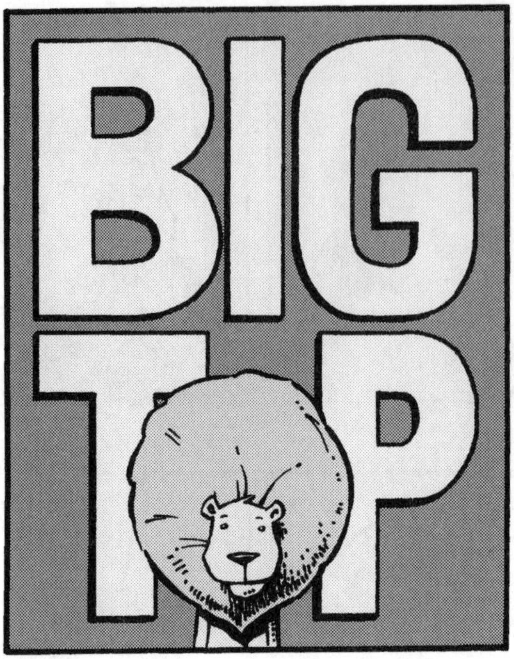
BIG TOP

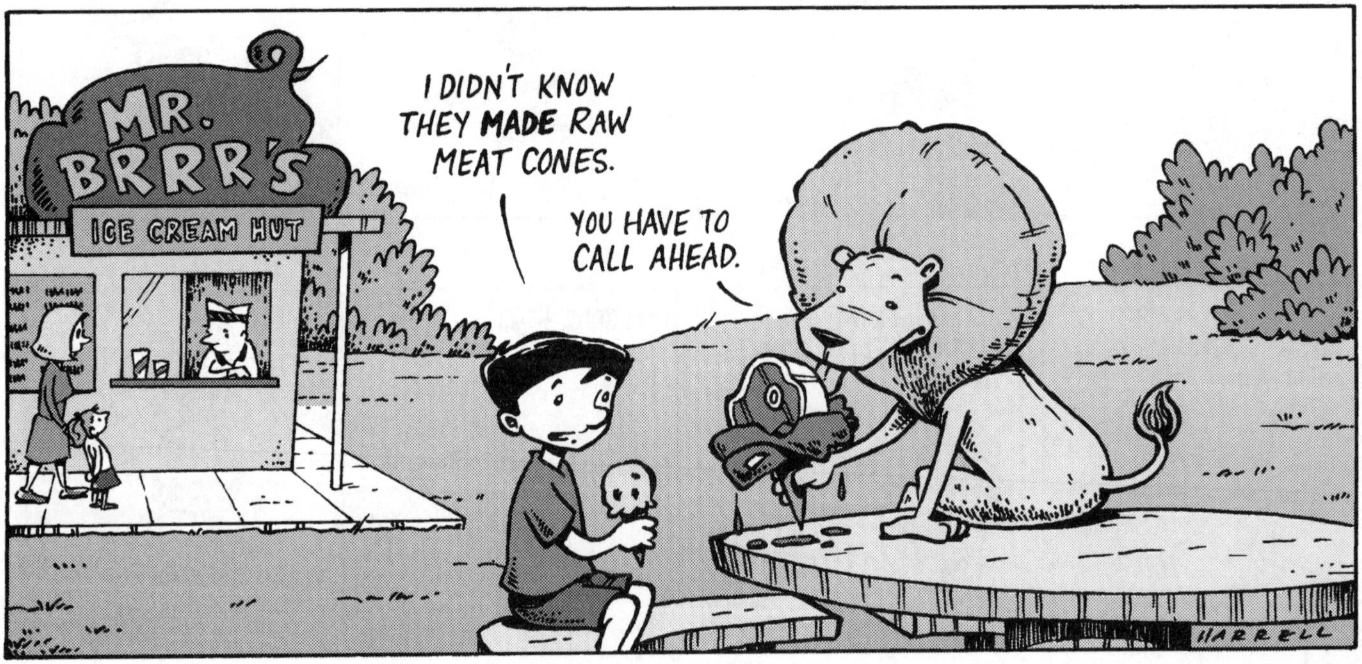
MR. BRRR'S
ICE CREAM HUT
I DIDN'T KNOW THEY MADE RAW MEAT CONES.
YOU HAVE TO CALL AHEAD.
HARRELL

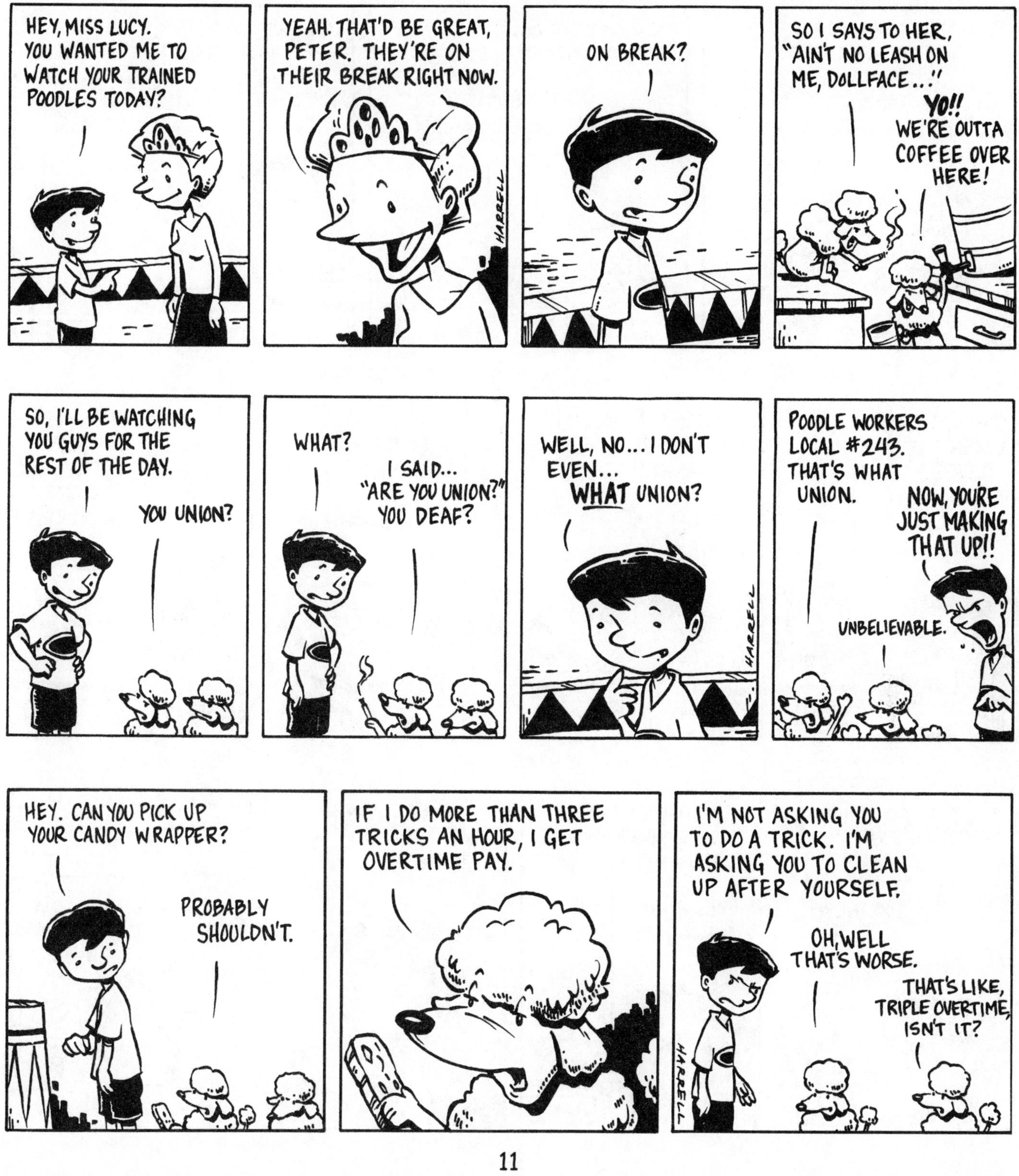
HEY, MISS LUCY. YOU WANTED ME TO WATCH YOUR TRAINED POODLES TODAY?
YEAH. THAT'D BE GREAT, PETER. THEY'RE ON THEIR BREAK RIGHT NOW.
HARRELL
ON BREAK?
SO I SAYS TO HER, "AIN'T NO LEASH ON ME, DOLLFACE...!"
YO!! WE'RE OUTTA COFFEE OVER HERE!
SO, I'LL BE WATCHING YOU GUYS FOR THE REST OF THE DAY.
YOU UNION?
WHAT?
I SAID... "ARE YOU UNION?" YOU DEAF?
WELL, NO... I DON'T EVEN... WHAT UNION?
HARRELL
POODLE WORKERS LOCAL #243. THAT'S WHAT UNION.
NOW, YOU'RE JUST MAKING THAT UP!!
UNBELIEVABLE.
HEY. CAN YOU PICK UP YOUR CANDY WRAPPER?
PROBABLY SHOULDN'T.
IF I DO MORE THAN THREE TRICKS AN HOUR, I GET OVERTIME PAY.
I'M NOT ASKING YOU TO DO A TRICK. I'M ASKING YOU TO CLEAN UP AFTER YOURSELF.
OH, WELL THAT'S WORSE.
THAT'S LIKE, TRIPLE OVERTIME, ISN'T IT?
HARRELL

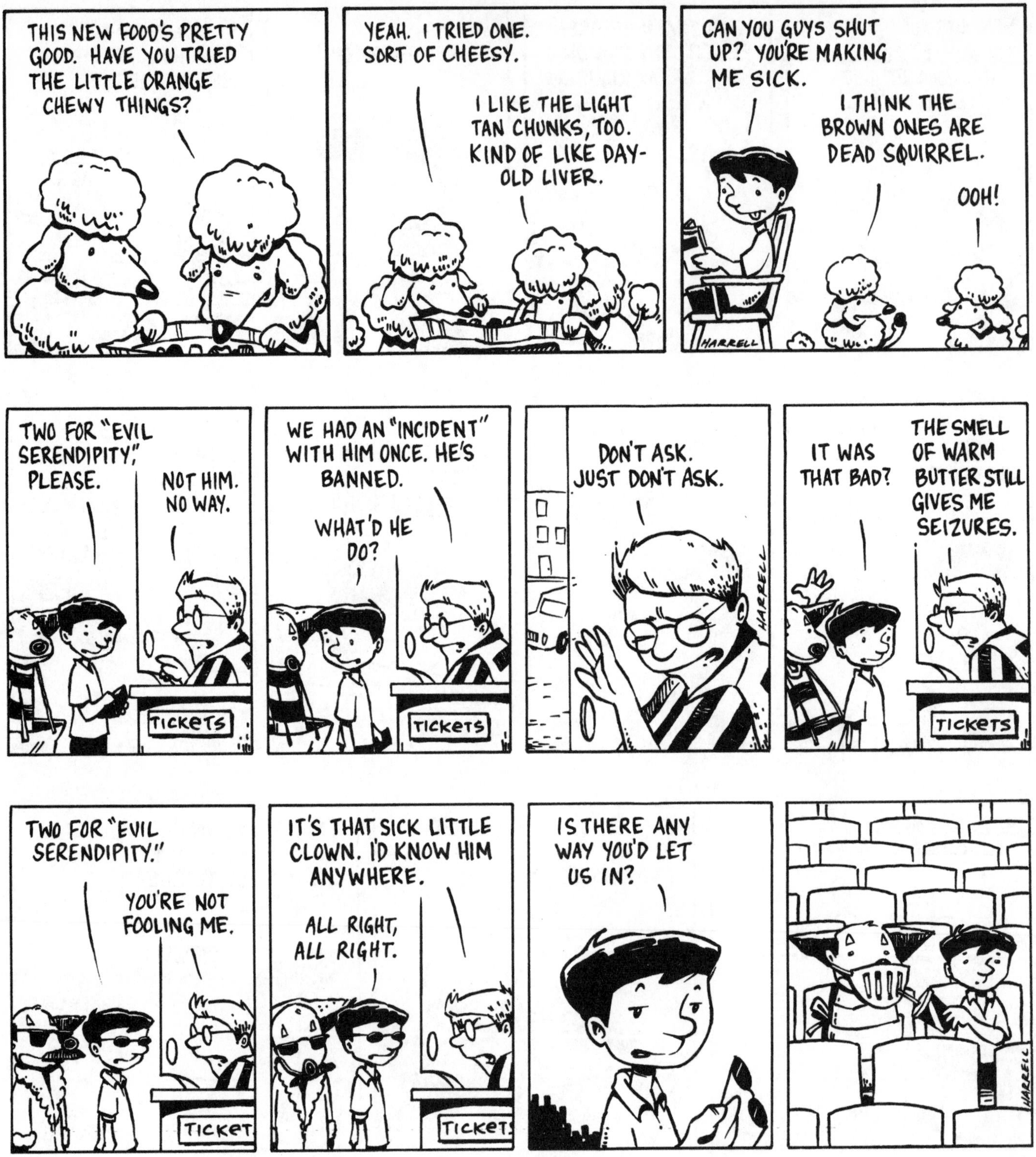
THIS NEW FOOD'S PRETTY GOOD. HAVE YOU TRIED THE LITTLE ORANGE CHEWY THINGS?
YEAH. I TRIED ONE. SORT OF CHEESY.
I LIKE THE LIGHT TAN CHUNKS, TOO. KIND OF LIKE DAY-OLD LIVER.
CAN YOU GUYS SHUT UP? YOU'RE MAKING ME SICK.
I THINK THE BROWN ONES ARE DEAD SQUIRREL.
OOH!
HARRELL
TWO FOR "EVIL SERENDIPITY," PLEASE.
NOT HIM. NO WAY.
TICKETS
WE HAD AN "INCIDENT" WITH HIM ONCE. HE'S BANNED.
WHAT'D HE DO?
TICKETS
DON'T ASK. JUST DON'T ASK.
HARRELL
IT WAS THAT BAD?
THE SMELL OF WARM BUTTER STILL GIVES ME SEIZURES.
TICKETS
TWO FOR "EVIL SERENDIPITY."
YOU'RE NOT FOOLING ME.
TICKET
IT'S THAT SICK LITTLE CLOWN. I'D KNOW HIM ANYWHERE.
ALL RIGHT, ALL RIGHT.
TICKETS
IS THERE ANY WAY YOU'D LET US IN?
HARRELL

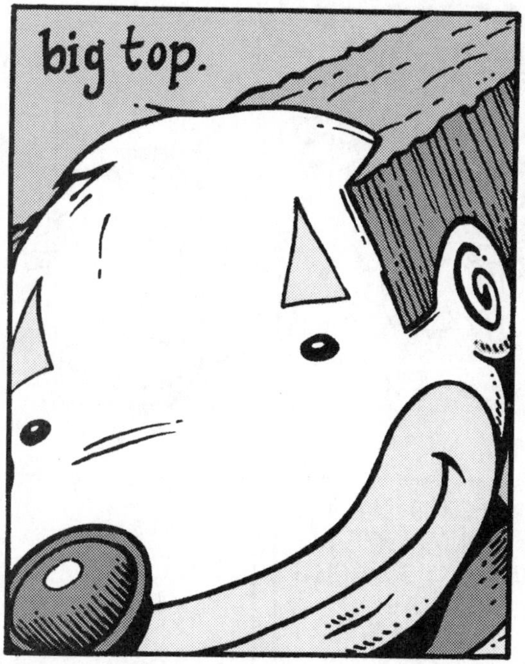
big top.

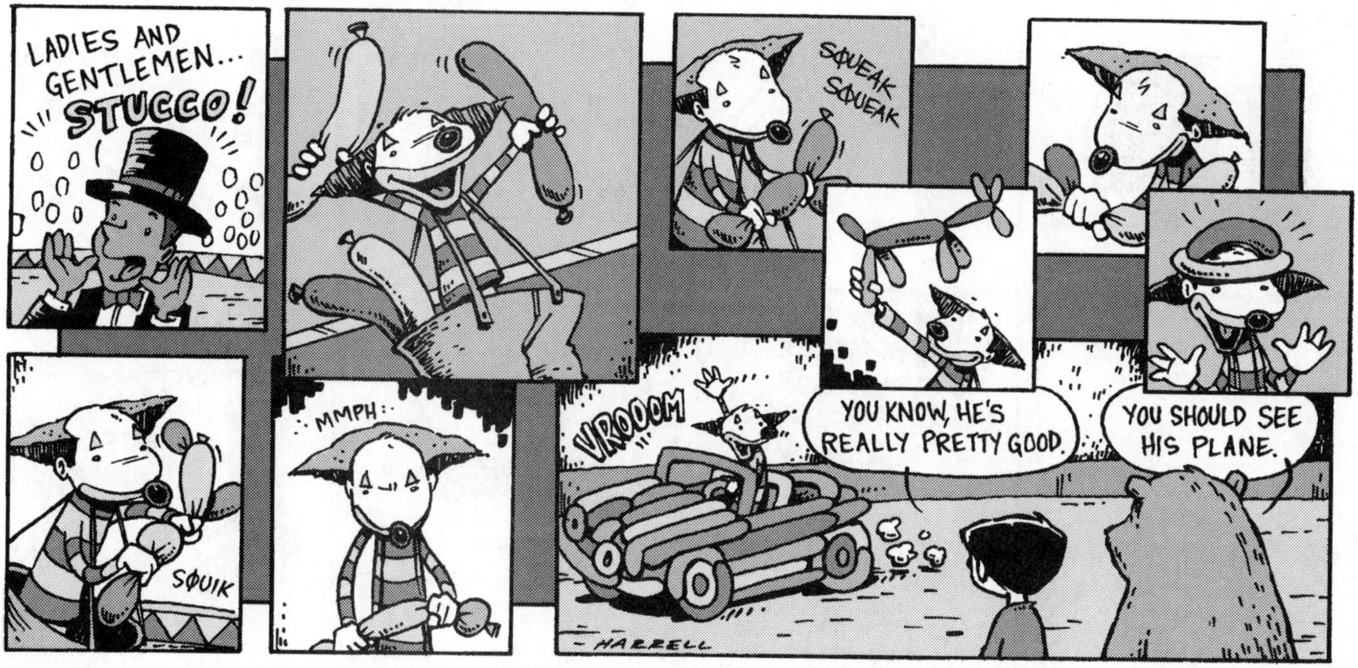
LADIES AND GENTLEMEN...
STUCCO!
SQUEAK SQUEAK
SQUIK
MMPH
VROOOM
YOU KNOW, HE'S REALLY PRETTY GOOD.
YOU SHOULD SEE HIS PLANE.
-HARRELL

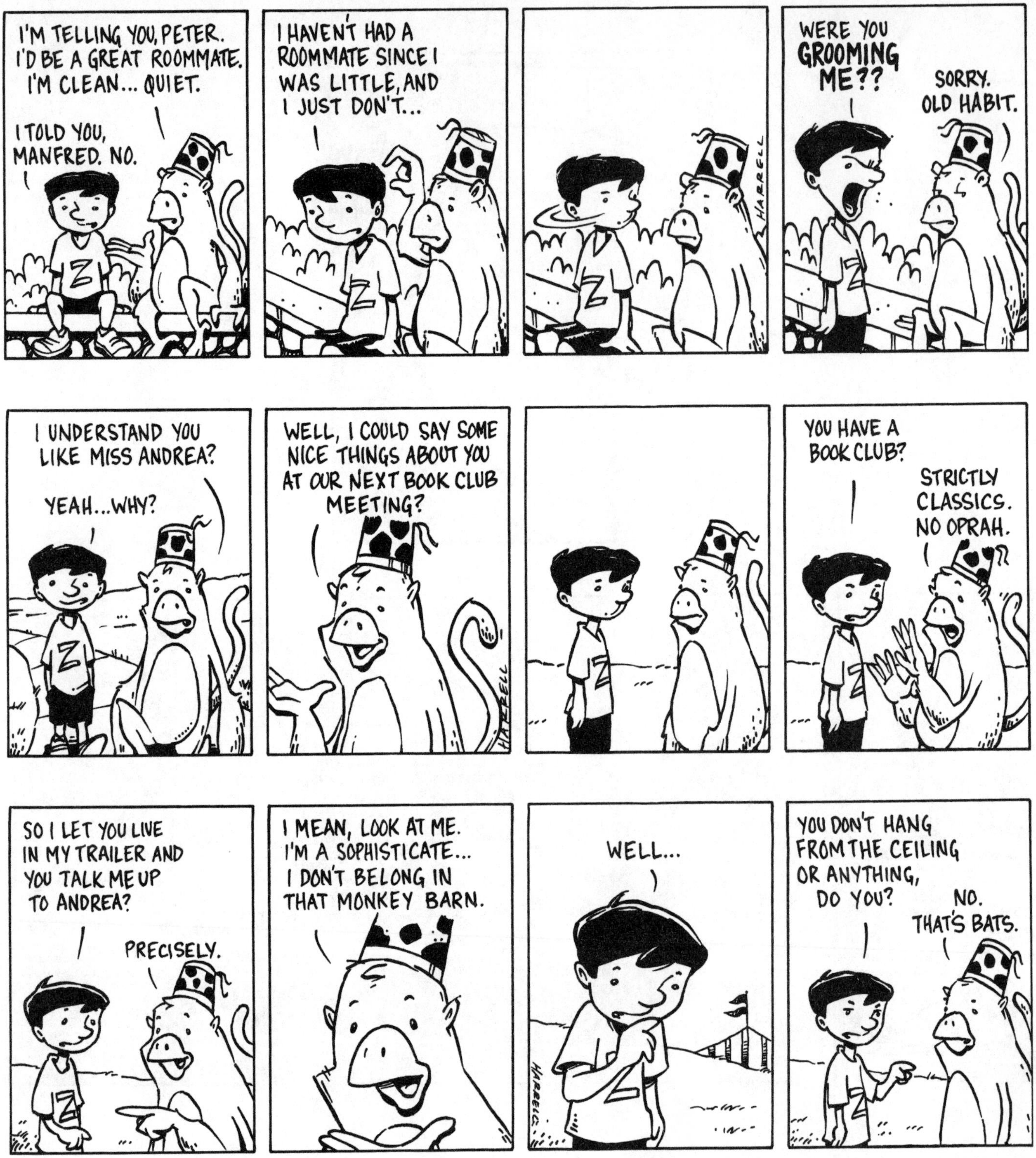
I'M TELLING YOU, PETER. I'D BE A GREAT ROOMMATE. I'M CLEAN... QUIET.
I TOLD YOU, MANFRED. NO.
I HAVEN'T HAD A ROOMMATE SINCE I WAS LITTLE, AND I JUST DON'T...
HARRELL
WERE YOU GROOMING ME??
SORRY. OLD HABIT.
I UNDERSTAND YOU LIKE MISS ANDREA?
YEAH...WHY?
WELL, I COULD SAY SOME NICE THINGS ABOUT YOU AT OUR NEXT BOOK CLUB MEETING?
HARRELL
YOU HAVE A BOOK CLUB?
STRICTLY CLASSICS. NO OPRAH.
SO I LET YOU LIVE IN MY TRAILER AND YOU TALK ME UP TO ANDREA?
PRECISELY.
I MEAN, LOOK AT ME. I'M A SOPHISTICATE... I DON'T BELONG IN THAT MONKEY BARN.
WELL...
HARRELL
YOU DON'T HANG FROM THE CEILING OR ANYTHING, DO YOU?
NO. THAT'S BATS.

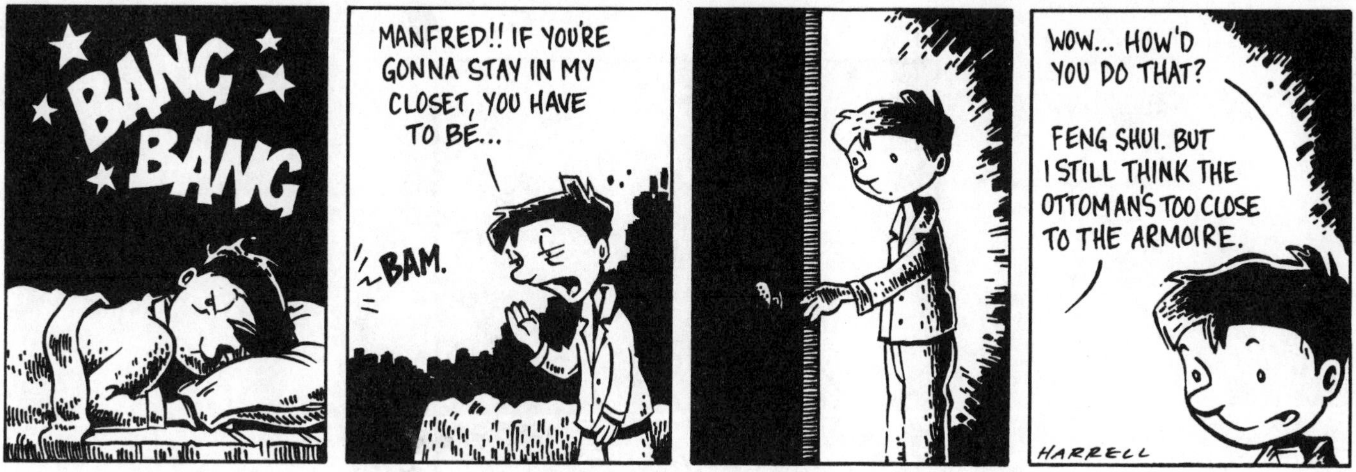
BANG BANG
MANFRED!! IF YOU'RE GONNA STAY IN MY CLOSET, YOU HAVE TO BE...
BAM.
WOW... HOW'D YOU DO THAT?
FENG SHUI. BUT I STILL THINK THE OTTOMAN'S TOO CLOSE TO THE ARMOIRE.
HARRELL

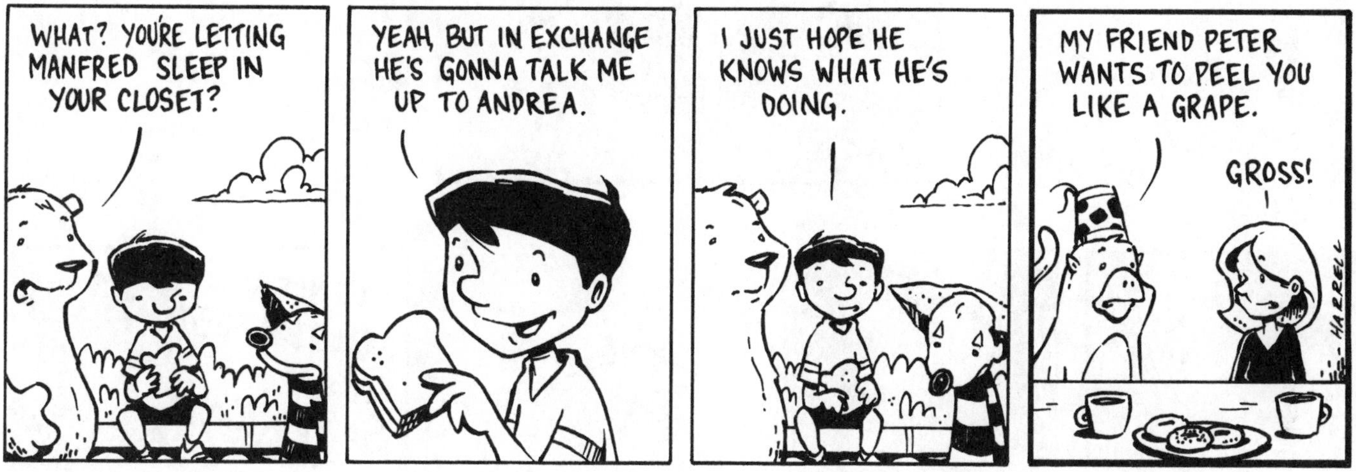
WHAT? YOU'RE LETTING MANFRED SLEEP IN YOUR CLOSET?
YEAH, BUT IN EXCHANGE HE'S GONNA TALK ME UP TO ANDREA.
I JUST HOPE HE KNOWS WHAT HE'S DOING.
MY FRIEND PETER WANTS TO PEEL YOU LIKE A GRAPE.
GROSS!
HARRELL

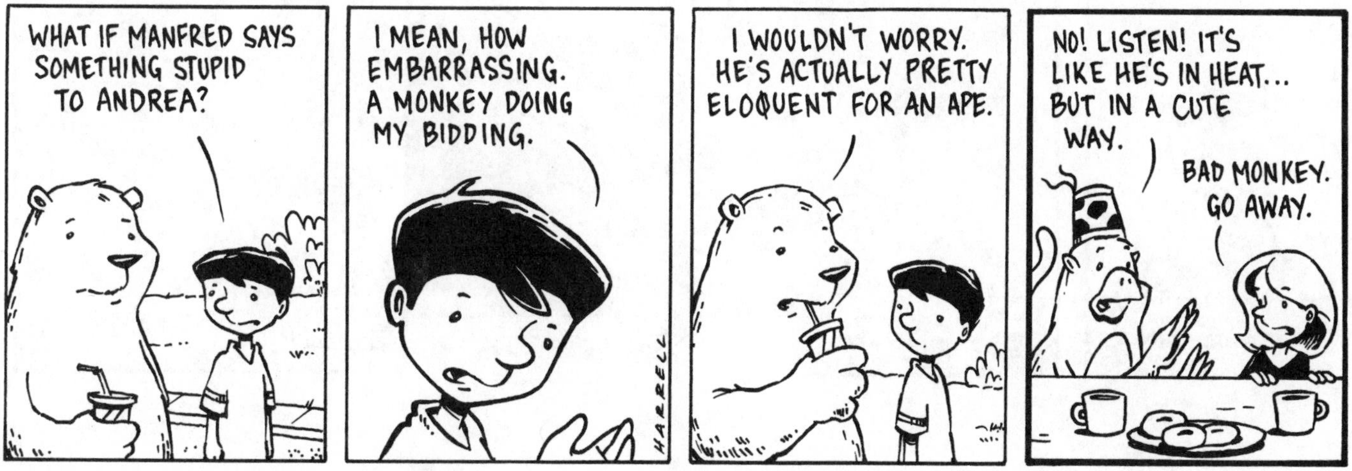
WHAT IF MANFRED SAYS SOMETHING STUPID TO ANDREA?
I MEAN, HOW EMBARRASSING. A MONKEY DOING MY BIDDING.
HARRELL
I WOULDN'T WORRY. HE'S ACTUALLY PRETTY ELOQUENT FOR AN APE.
NO! LISTEN! IT'S LIKE HE'S IN HEAT... BUT IN A CUTE WAY.
BAD MONKEY. GO AWAY.

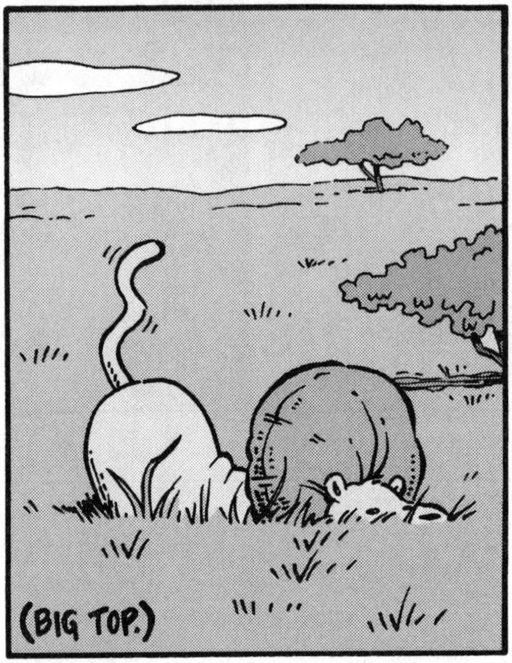
(BIG TOP.)

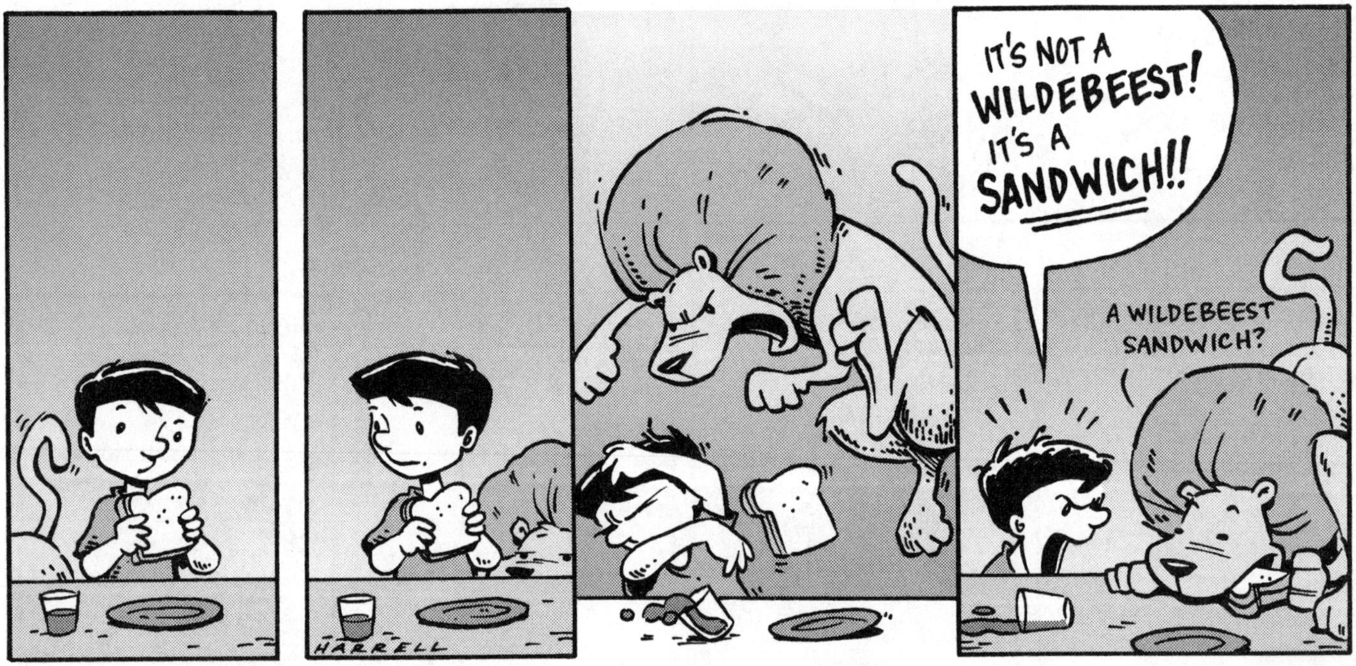
HARRELL
IT'S NOT A WILDEBEEST! IT'S A SANDWICH!!
A WILDEBEEST SANDWICH?

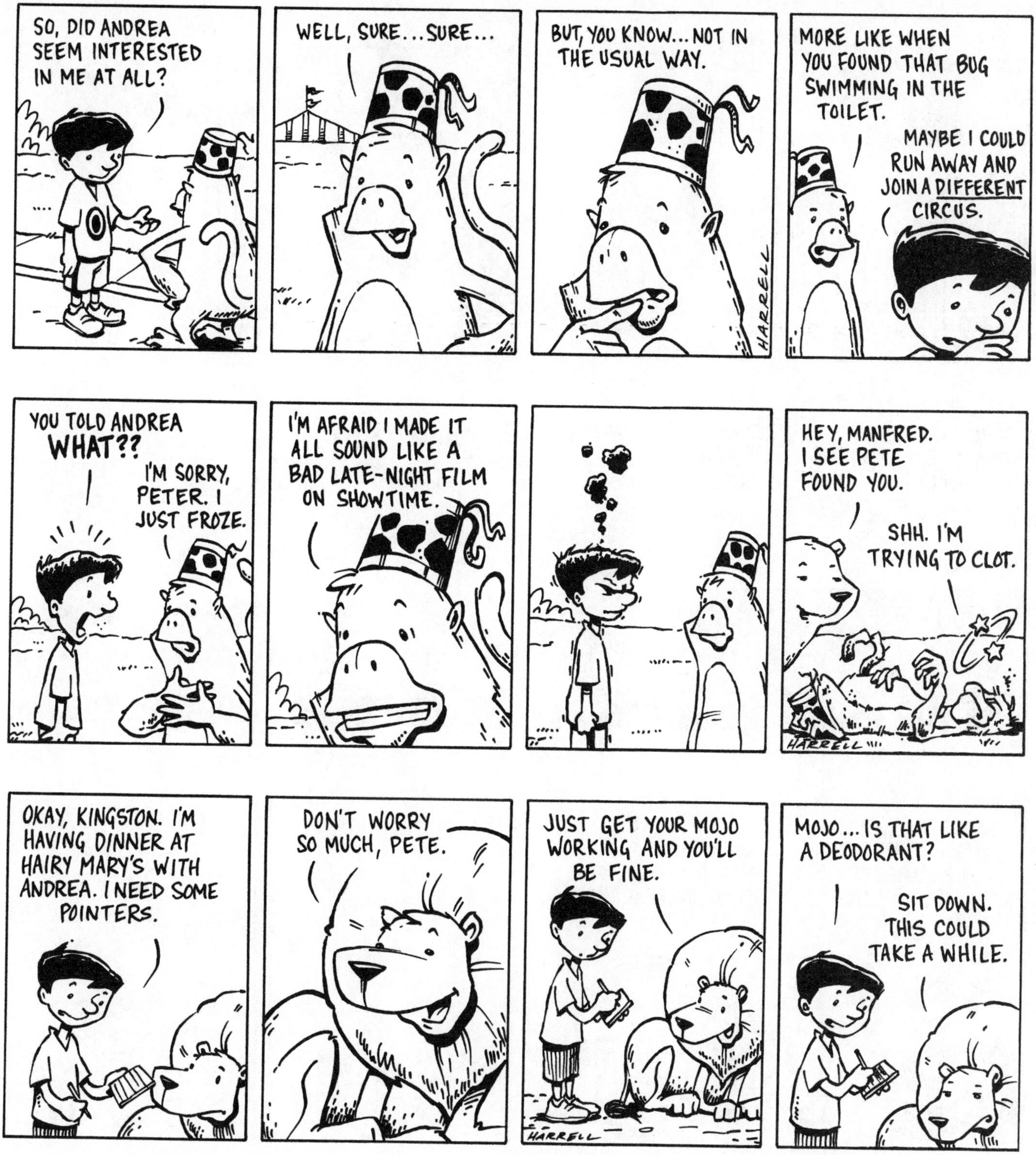
SO, DID ANDREA SEEM INTERESTED IN ME AT ALL?
WELL, SURE... SURE...
BUT, YOU KNOW... NOT IN THE USUAL WAY.
HARRELL
MORE LIKE WHEN YOU FOUND THAT BUG SWIMMING IN THE TOILET.
MAYBE I COULD RUN AWAY AND JOIN A DIFFERENT CIRCUS.
YOU TOLD ANDREA WHAT??
I'M SORRY, PETER. I JUST FROZE.
I'M AFRAID I MADE IT ALL SOUND LIKE A BAD LATE-NIGHT FILM ON SHOWTIME.
HEY, MANFRED. I SEE PETE FOUND YOU.
SHH. I'M TRYING TO CLOT.
HARRELL
OKAY, KINGSTON. I'M HAVING DINNER AT HAIRY MARY'S WITH ANDREA. I NEED SOME POINTERS.
DON'T WORRY SO MUCH, PETE.
JUST GET YOUR MOJO WORKING AND YOU'LL BE FINE.
HARRELL
MOJO... IS THAT LIKE A DEODORANT?
SIT DOWN. THIS COULD TAKE A WHILE.

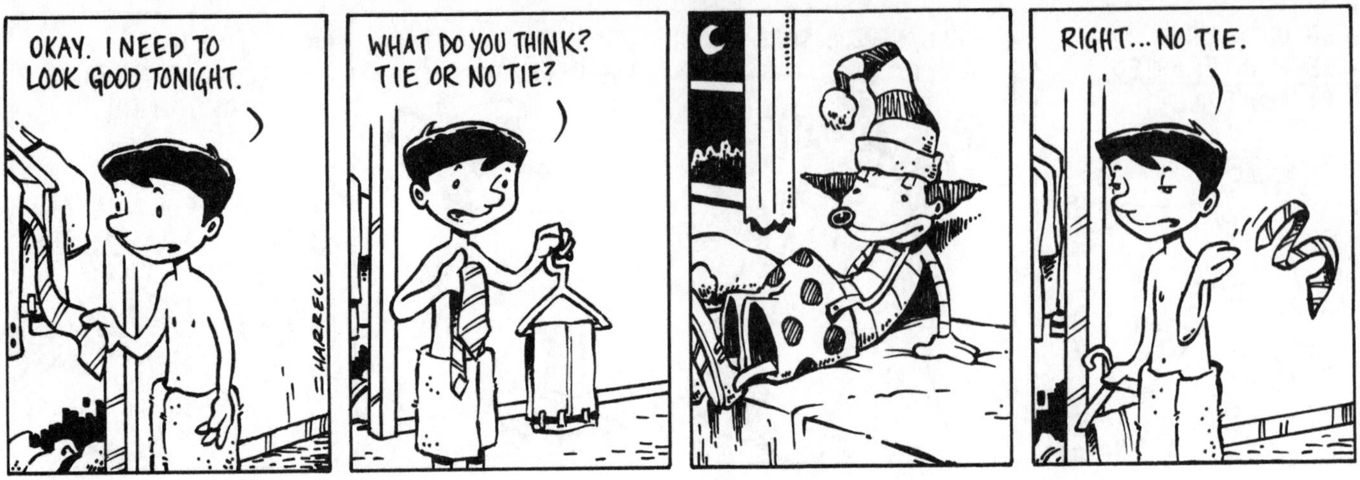
OKAY. I NEED TO LOOK GOOD TONIGHT.
HARRELL
WHAT DO YOU THINK? TIE OR NO TIE?
RIGHT... NO TIE.

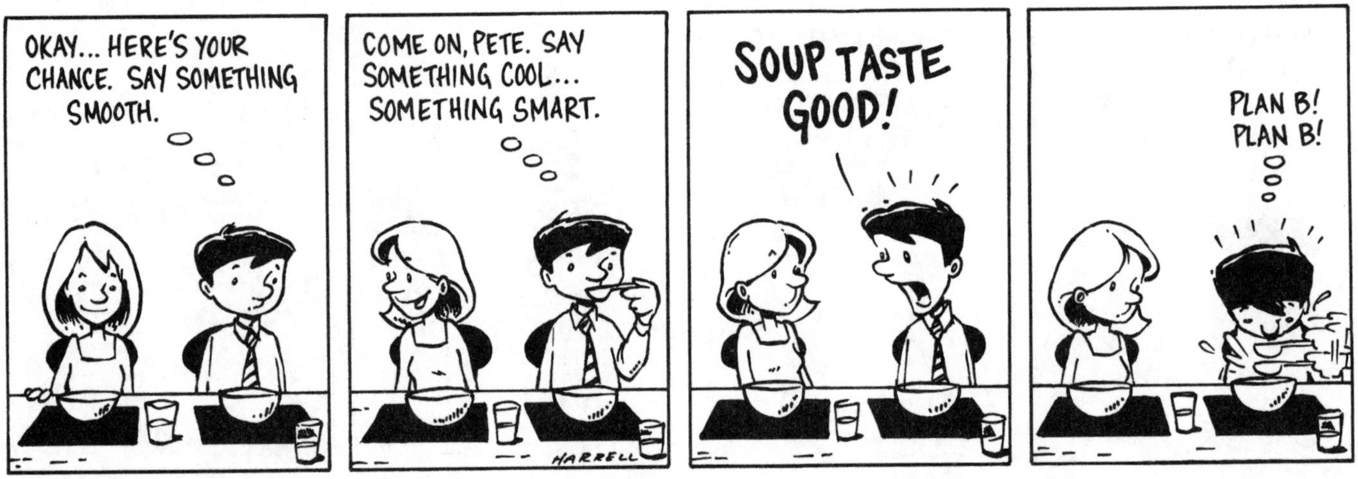
OKAY... HERE'S YOUR CHANCE. SAY SOMETHING SMOOTH.
COME ON, PETE. SAY SOMETHING COOL... SOMETHING SMART.
HARRELL
SOUP TASTE GOOD!
PLAN B! PLAN B!

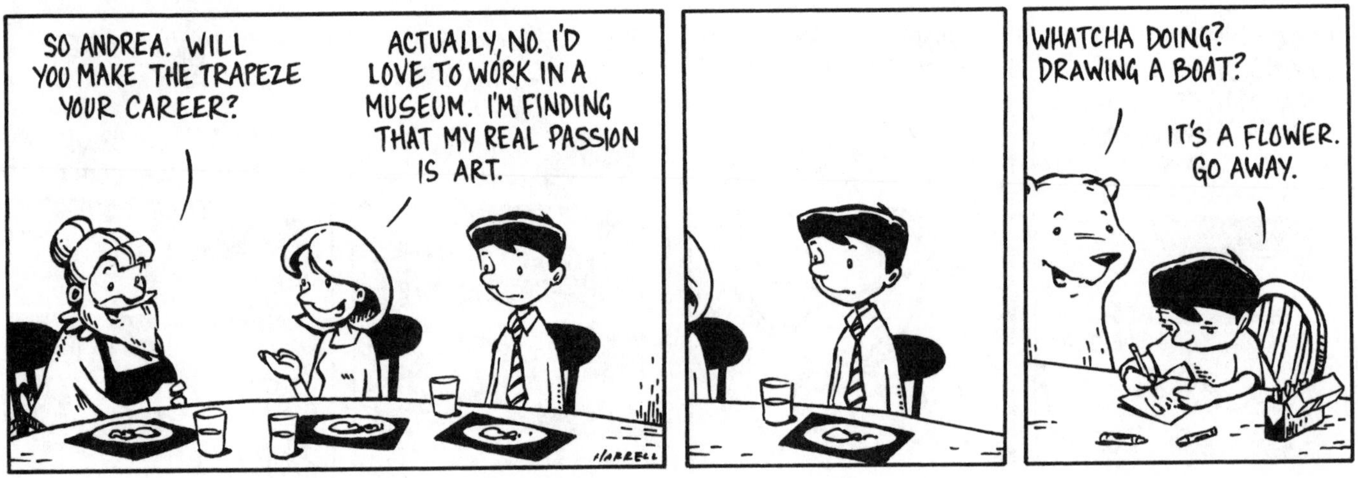
SO ANDREA. WILL YOU MAKE THE TRAPEZE YOUR CAREER?
ACTUALLY, NO. I'D LOVE TO WORK IN A MUSEUM. I'M FINDING THAT MY REAL PASSION IS ART.
HARRELL
WHATCHA DOING? DRAWING A BOAT?
IT'S A FLOWER. GO AWAY.

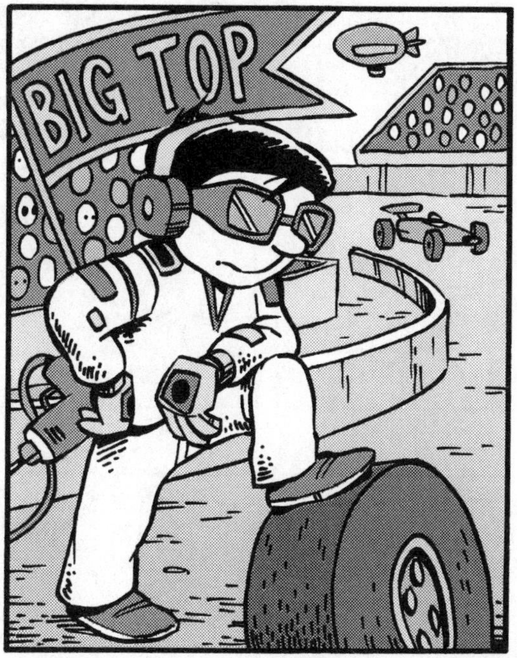
BIG TOP

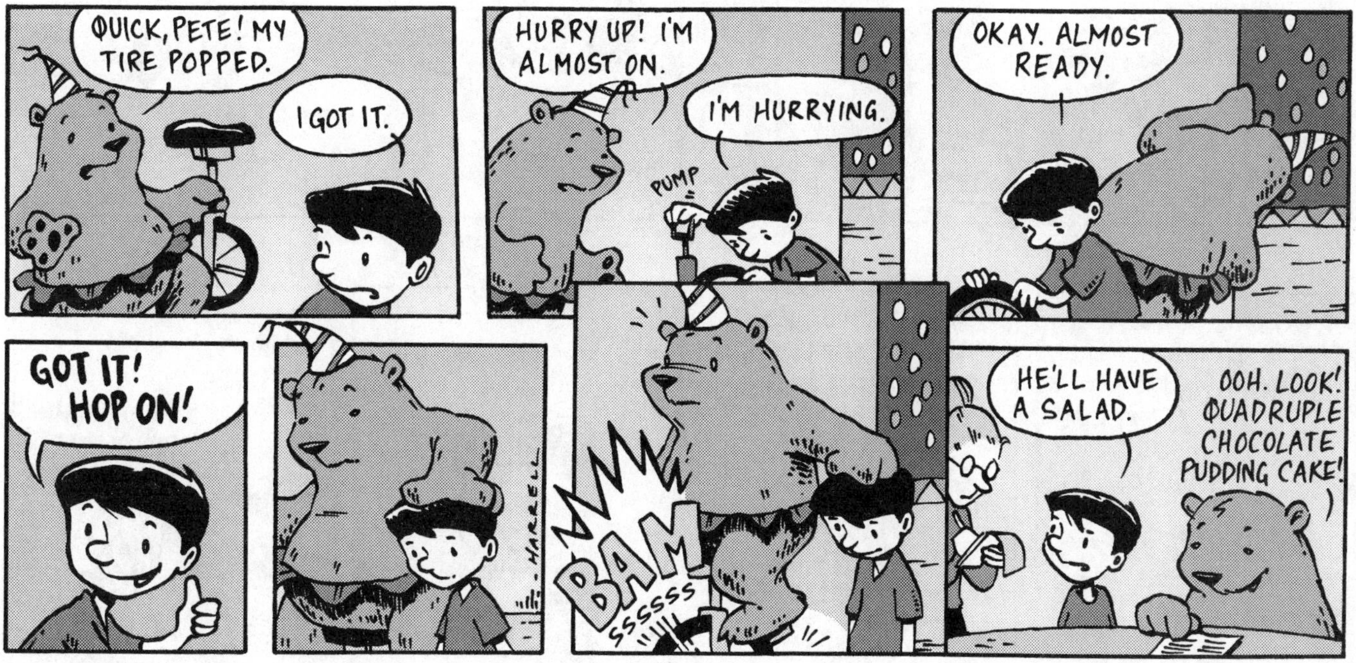
QUICK, PETE! MY TIRE POPPED.
I GOT IT.
HURRY UP! I'M ALMOST ON.
I'M HURRYING.
PUMP
OKAY. ALMOST READY.
GOT IT! HOP ON!
HARRELL
BAM
SSSSSS
HE'LL HAVE A SALAD.
OOH. LOOK! QUADRUPLE CHOCOLATE PUDDING CAKE!

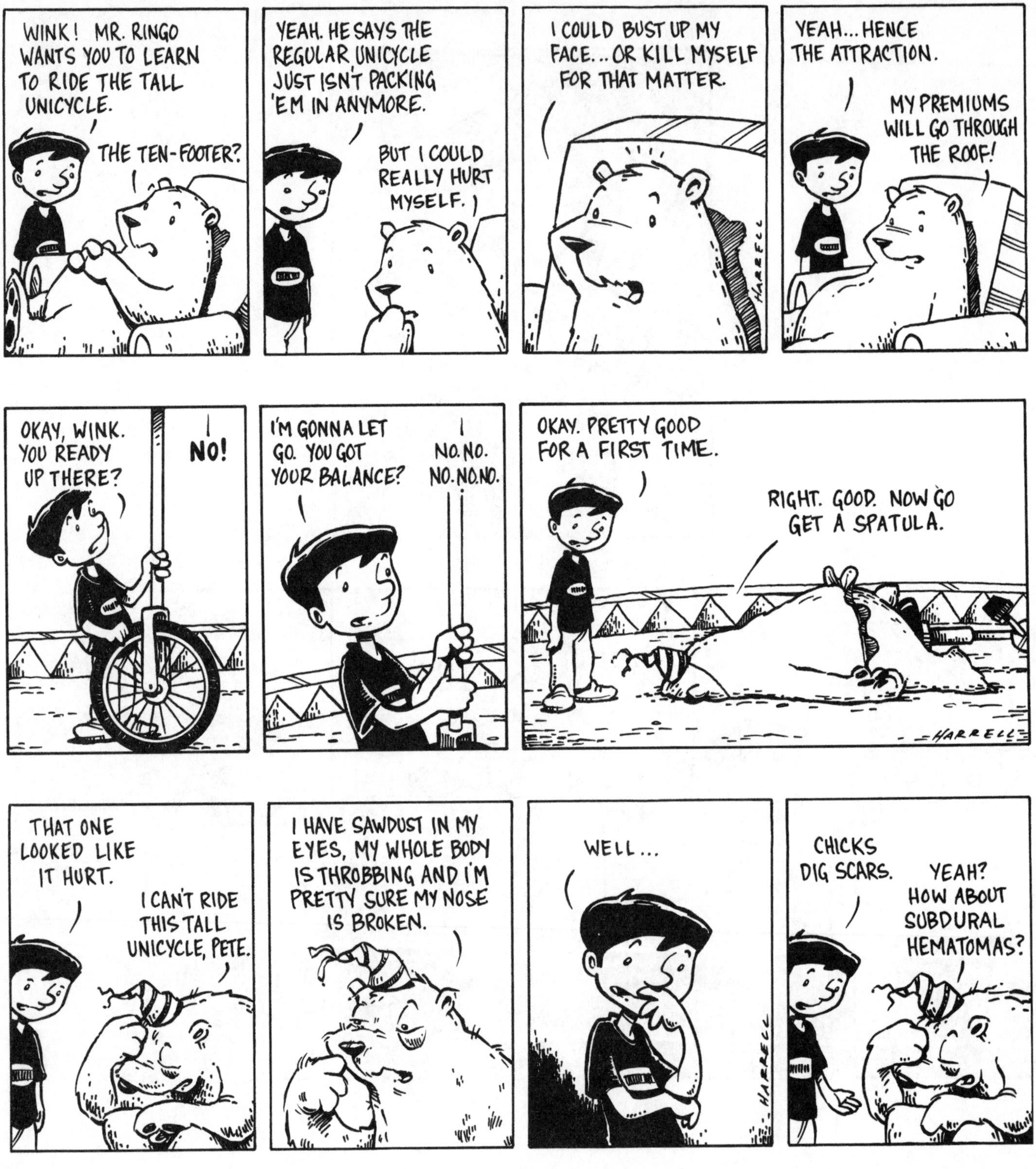
WINK! MR. RINGO WANTS YOU TO LEARN TO RIDE THE TALL UNICYCLE.
THE TEN-FOOTER?
YEAH. HE SAYS THE REGULAR UNICYCLE JUST ISN'T PACKING 'EM IN ANYMORE.
BUT I COULD REALLY HURT MYSELF.
I COULD BUST UP MY FACE... OR KILL MYSELF FOR THAT MATTER.
YEAH... HENCE THE ATTRACTION.
MY PREMIUMS WILL GO THROUGH THE ROOF!
HARRELL
OKAY, WINK. YOU READY UP THERE?
NO!
I'M GONNA LET GO. YOU GOT YOUR BALANCE?
NO. NO. NO. NO. NO.
OKAY. PRETTY GOOD FOR A FIRST TIME.
RIGHT. GOOD. NOW GO GET A SPATULA.
HARRELL
THAT ONE LOOKED LIKE IT HURT.
I CAN'T RIDE THIS TALL UNICYCLE, PETE.
I HAVE SAWDUST IN MY EYES, MY WHOLE BODY IS THROBBING AND I'M PRETTY SURE MY NOSE IS BROKEN.
WELL...
CHICKS DIG SCARS.
YEAH? HOW ABOUT SUBDURAL HEMATOMAS?
HARRELL

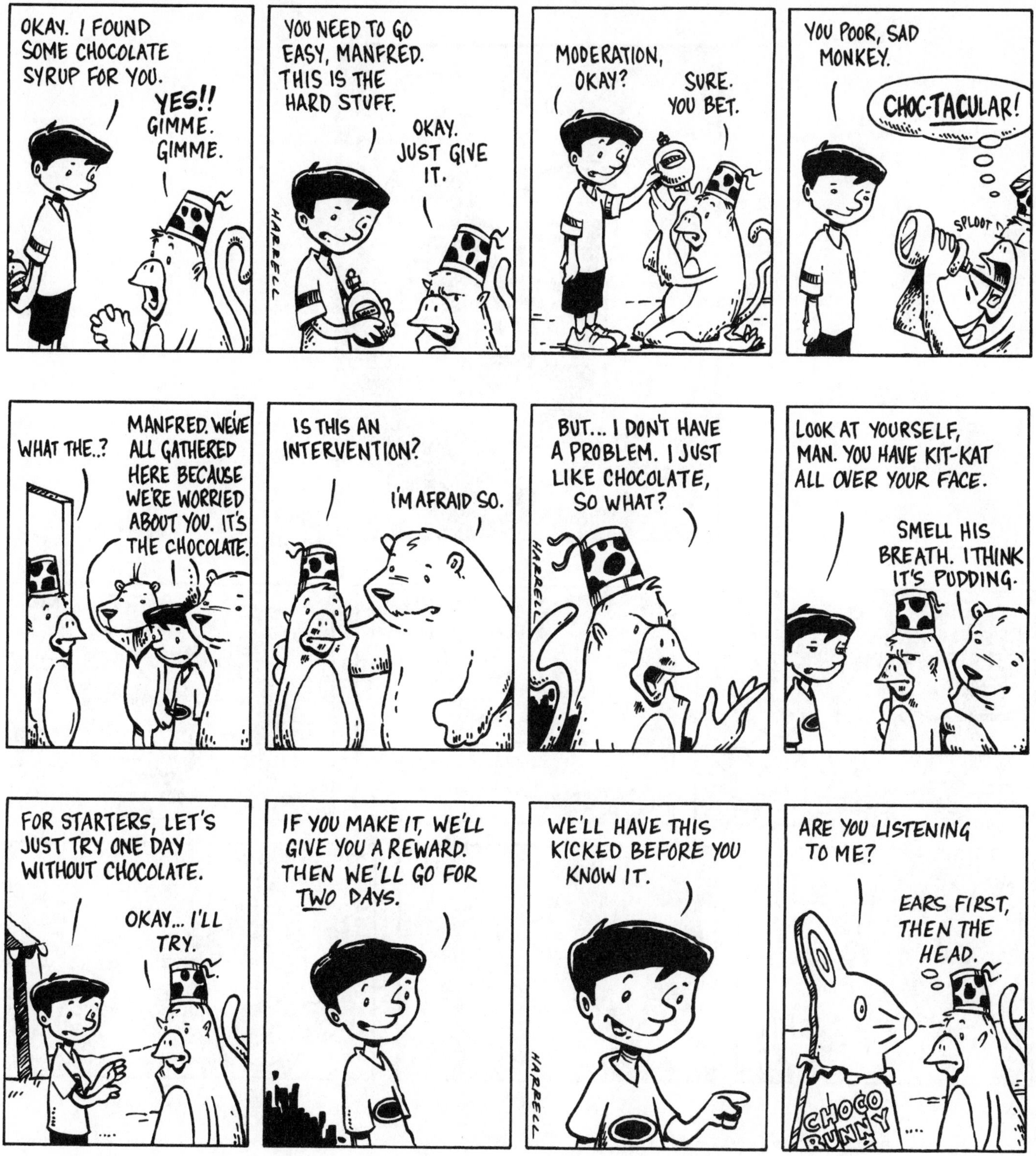
OKAY. I FOUND SOME CHOCOLATE SYRUP FOR YOU.
YES!! GIMME. GIMME.
YOU NEED TO GO EASY, MANFRED. THIS IS THE HARD STUFF.
OKAY. JUST GIVE IT.
HARRELL
MODERATION, OKAY?
SURE. YOU BET.
YOU POOR, SAD MONKEY.
CHOC-TACULAR!
SPLOOT
WHAT THE..?
MANFRED. WE'VE ALL GATHERED HERE BECAUSE WE'RE WORRIED ABOUT YOU. IT'S THE CHOCOLATE.
IS THIS AN INTERVENTION?
I'M AFRAID SO.
BUT... I DON'T HAVE A PROBLEM. I JUST LIKE CHOCOLATE, SO WHAT?
HARRELL
LOOK AT YOURSELF, MAN. YOU HAVE KIT-KAT ALL OVER YOUR FACE.
SMELL HIS BREATH. I THINK IT'S PUDDING.
FOR STARTERS, LET'S JUST TRY ONE DAY WITHOUT CHOCOLATE.
OKAY... I'LL TRY.
IF YOU MAKE IT, WE'LL GIVE YOU A REWARD. THEN WE'LL GO FOR TWO DAYS.
WE'LL HAVE THIS KICKED BEFORE YOU KNOW IT.
HARRELL
ARE YOU LISTENING TO ME?
EARS FIRST, THEN THE HEAD.
CHOCO BUNNY

OH, I HOPE HE'S NOT GONNA PUT HIS HEAD IN MY MOUTH TODAY.

OH, MAN. PLEASE DON'T DO IT. NOT TODAY.

OH, NO. OH, NO. HERE HE GOES.

THE ONE DAY I FORGET...

PASTE

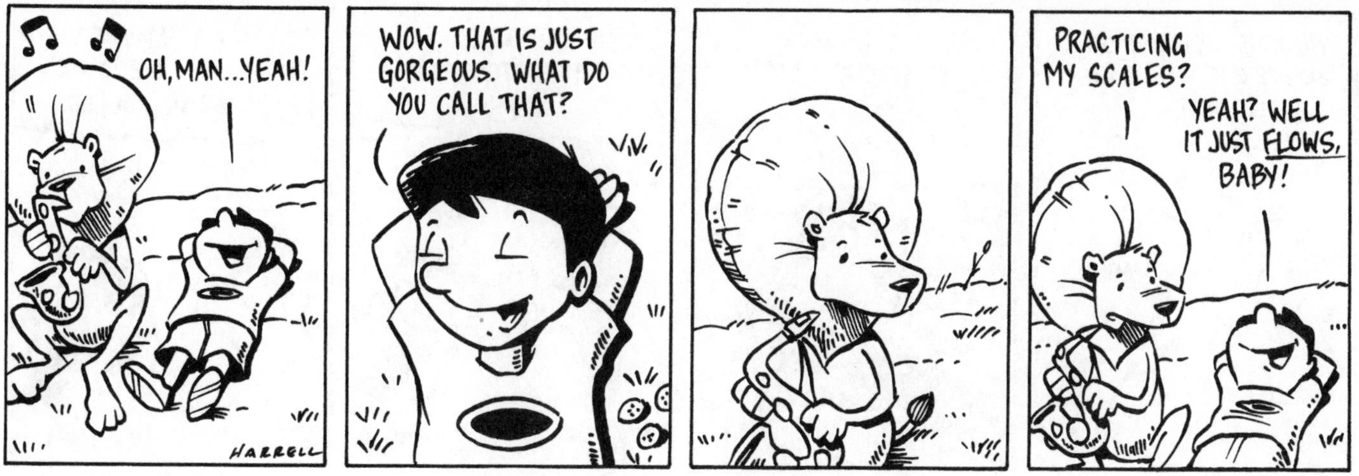
OH, MAN...YEAH!
WOW. THAT IS JUST GORGEOUS. WHAT DO YOU CALL THAT?
PRACTICING MY SCALES?
YEAH? WELL IT JUST FLOWS, BABY!
HARRELL

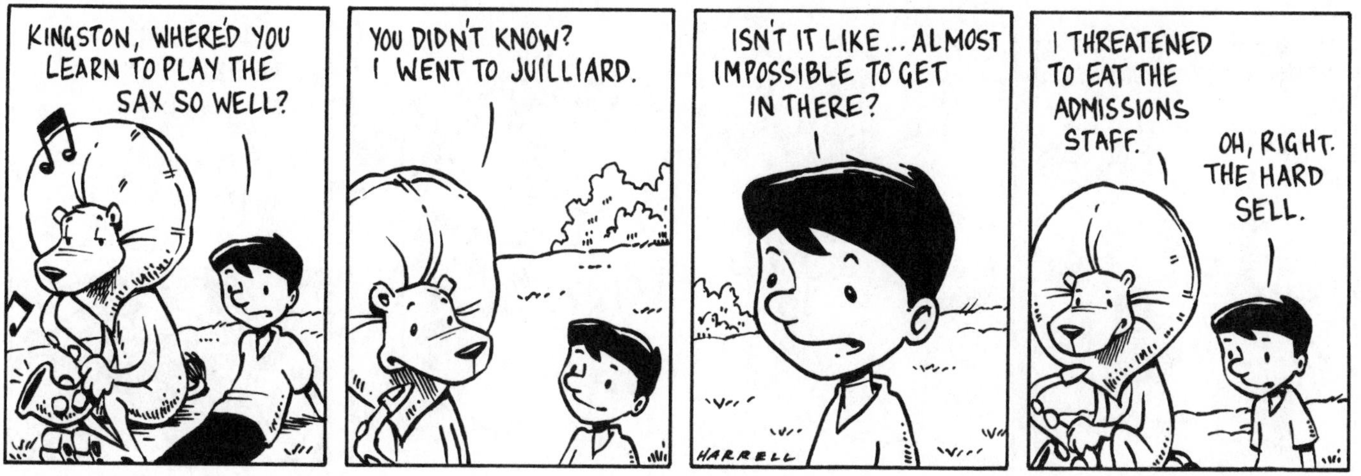
KINGSTON, WHERE'D YOU LEARN TO PLAY THE SAX SO WELL?
YOU DIDN'T KNOW? I WENT TO JUILLIARD.
ISN'T IT LIKE... ALMOST IMPOSSIBLE TO GET IN THERE?
I THREATENED TO EAT THE ADMISSIONS STAFF.
OH, RIGHT. THE HARD SELL.
HARRELL

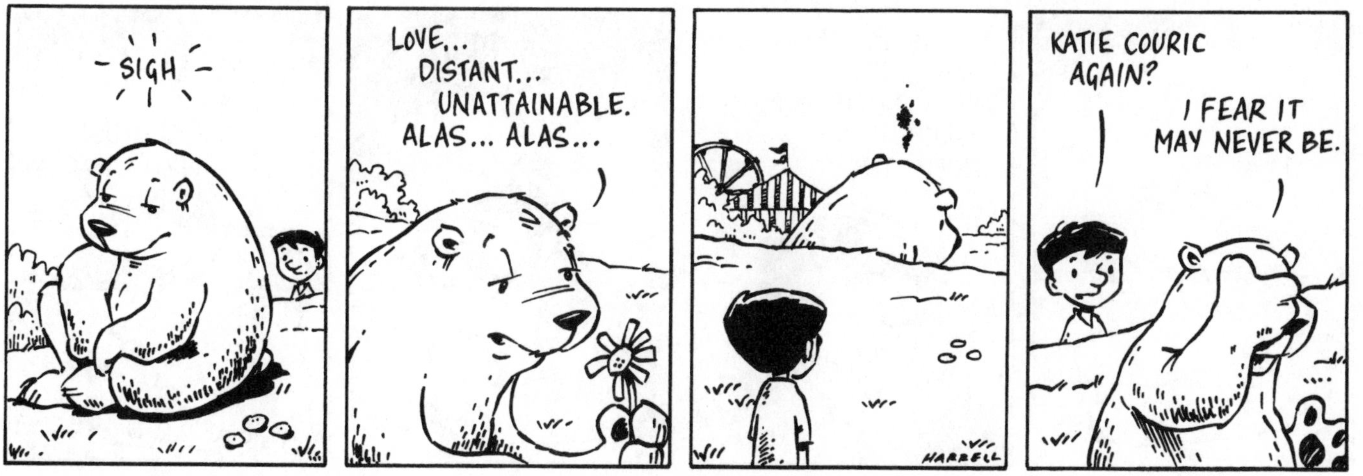
SIGH
LOVE... DISTANT... UNATTAINABLE. ALAS... ALAS...
KATIE COURIC AGAIN?
I FEAR IT MAY NEVER BE.
HARRELL

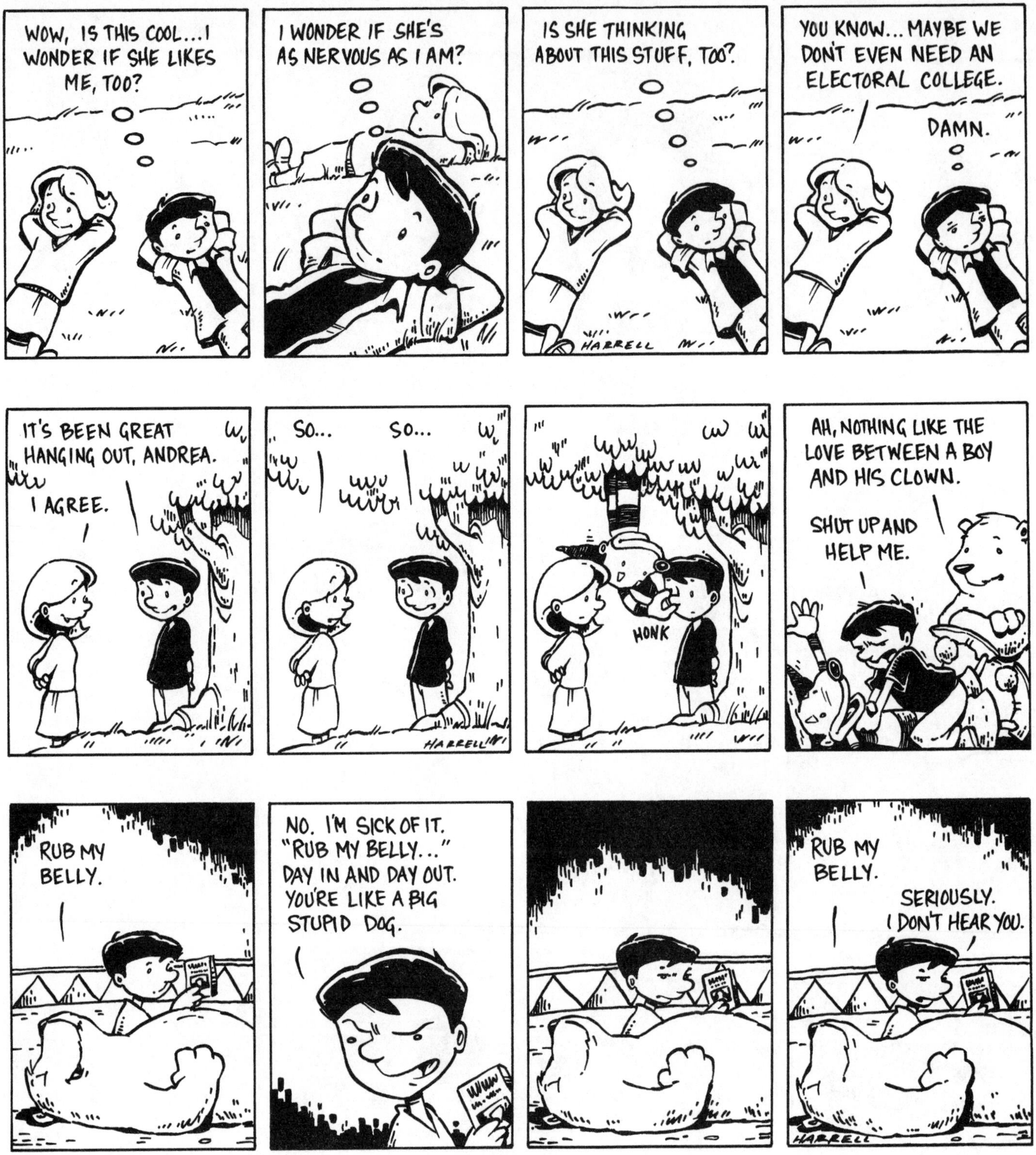
WOW, IS THIS COOL... I WONDER IF SHE LIKES ME, TOO?
I WONDER IF SHE'S AS NERVOUS AS I AM?
IS SHE THINKING ABOUT THIS STUFF, TOO?
YOU KNOW... MAYBE WE DON'T EVEN NEED AN ELECTORAL COLLEGE.
DAMN.
HARRELL
IT'S BEEN GREAT HANGING OUT, ANDREA.
I AGREE.
SO...
SO...
HARRELL
HONK
AH, NOTHING LIKE THE LOVE BETWEEN A BOY AND HIS CLOWN.
SHUT UP AND HELP ME.
RUB MY BELLY.
NO. I'M SICK OF IT. "RUB MY BELLY..." DAY IN AND DAY OUT. YOU'RE LIKE A BIG STUPID DOG.
RUB MY BELLY.
SERIOUSLY. I DON'T HEAR YOU.
HARRELL

BIG TOP

MAN, I WISH I HAD A PREHENSILE TAIL LIKE THAT.
HOW SO?
WELL, I CAN'T DO ANYTHING WITH MINE.
IT JUST WAGS. THAT'S ABOUT IT.
WELL, I'D TRADE YOU ANY DAY.
YOU WOULD?
SURE. THIS THING HAS A MIND OF ITS OWN SOMETIMES.
HARRELL
SLURP.
HEY!! I SAID CHERRY COKE!!
STUPID TAIL.
MAYBE SO. BUT THAT'S STILL PRETTY COOL.

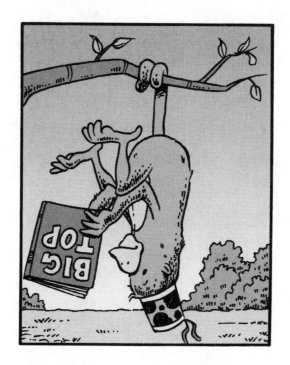

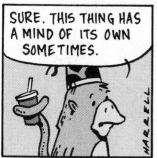

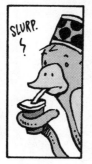

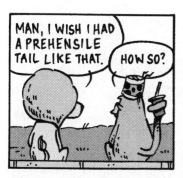

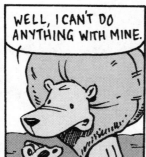

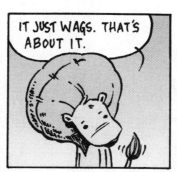

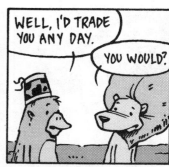

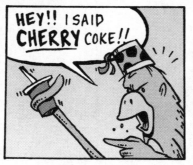

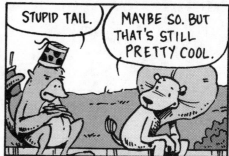

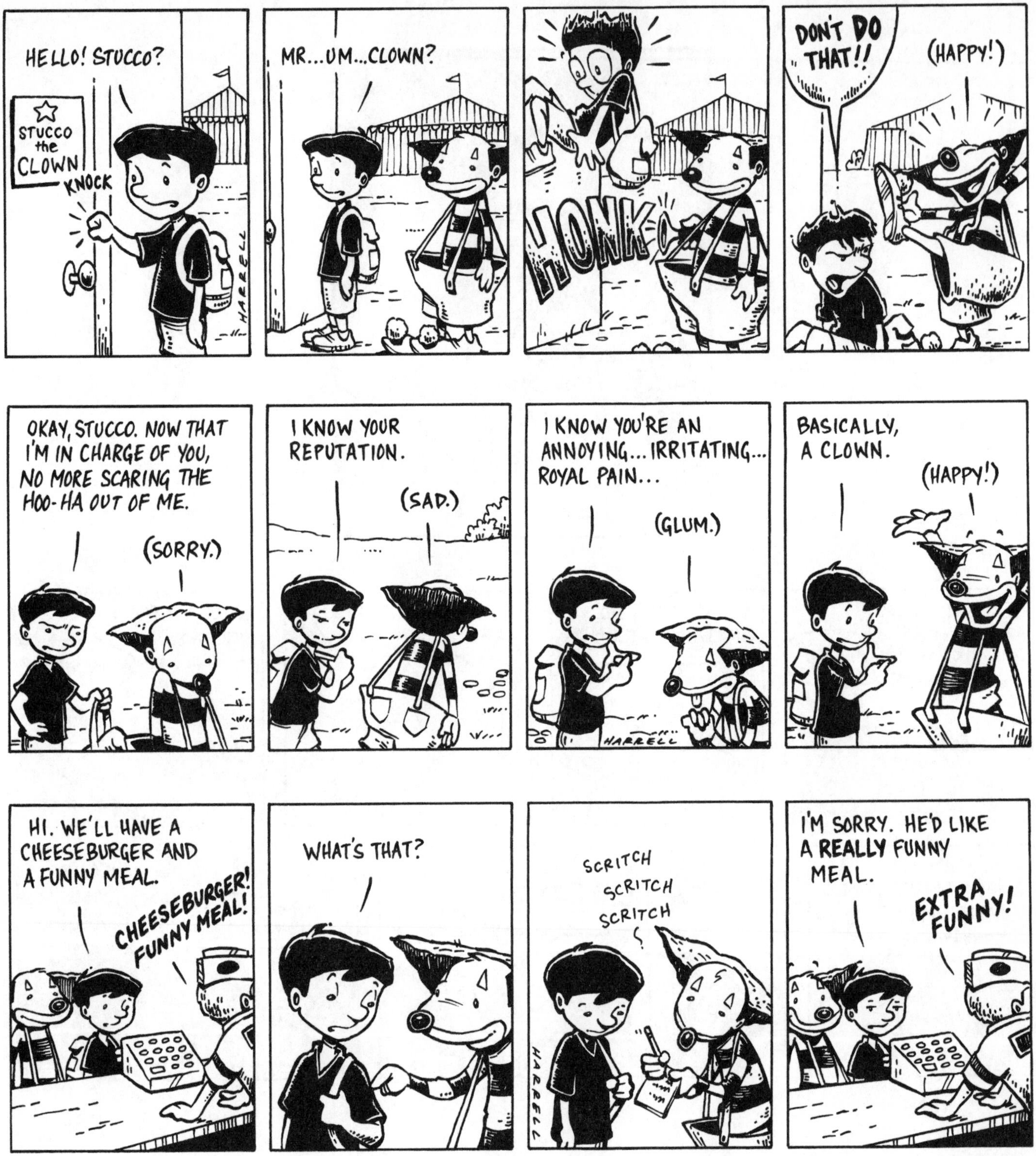

HELLO! STUCCO?
STUCCO the CLOWN
KNOCK
HARRELL
MR...UM...CLOWN?
HONK
DON'T DO THAT!!
(HAPPY!)
OKAY, STUCCO. NOW THAT I'M IN CHARGE OF YOU, NO MORE SCARING THE HOO-HA OUT OF ME.
(SORRY.)
I KNOW YOUR REPUTATION.
(SAD.)
I KNOW YOU'RE AN ANNOYING... IRRITATING... ROYAL PAIN...
(GLUM.)
HARRELL
BASICALLY, A CLOWN.
(HAPPY!)
HI. WE'LL HAVE A CHEESEBURGER AND A FUNNY MEAL.
CHEESEBURGER! FUNNY MEAL!
WHAT'S THAT?
SCRITCH SCRITCH SCRITCH
HARRELL
I'M SORRY. HE'D LIKE A REALLY FUNNY MEAL.
EXTRA FUNNY!

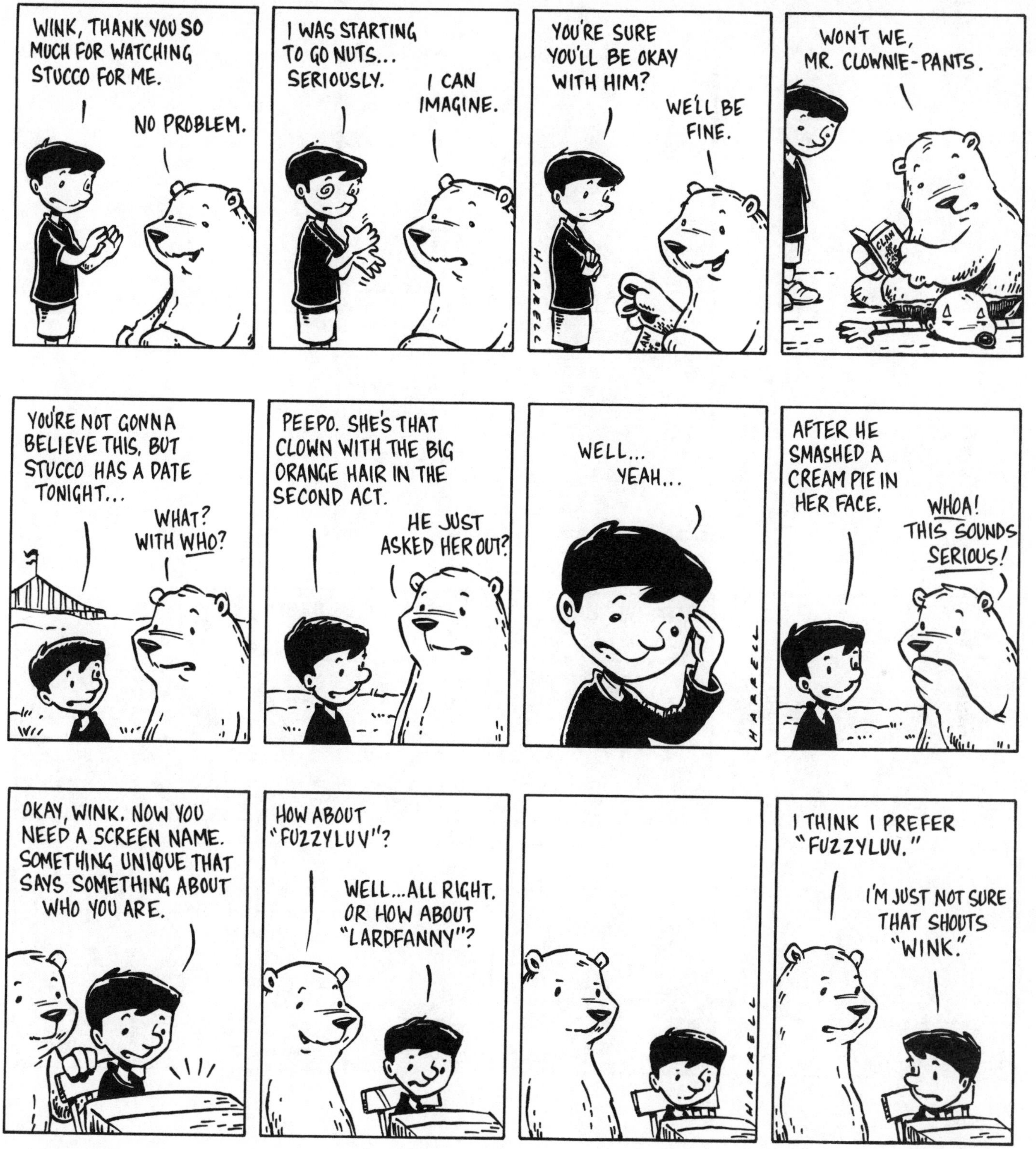
WINK, THANK YOU SO MUCH FOR WATCHING STUCCO FOR ME.
NO PROBLEM.
I WAS STARTING TO GO NUTS... SERIOUSLY.
I CAN IMAGINE.
YOU'RE SURE YOU'LL BE OKAY WITH HIM?
WE'LL BE FINE.
WON'T WE, MR. CLOWNIE-PANTS.
HARRELL
YOU'RE NOT GONNA BELIEVE THIS, BUT STUCCO HAS A DATE TONIGHT...
WHAT? WITH WHO?
PEEPO. SHE'S THAT CLOWN WITH THE BIG ORANGE HAIR IN THE SECOND ACT.
HE JUST ASKED HER OUT?
WELL... YEAH...
AFTER HE SMASHED A CREAM PIE IN HER FACE.
WHOA! THIS SOUNDS SERIOUS!
HARRELL
OKAY, WINK. NOW YOU NEED A SCREEN NAME. SOMETHING UNIQUE THAT SAYS SOMETHING ABOUT WHO YOU ARE.
HOW ABOUT "FUZZYLUV"?
WELL...ALL RIGHT. OR HOW ABOUT "LARDFANNY"?
HARRELL
I THINK I PREFER "FUZZYLUV."
I'M JUST NOT SURE THAT SHOUTS "WINK."

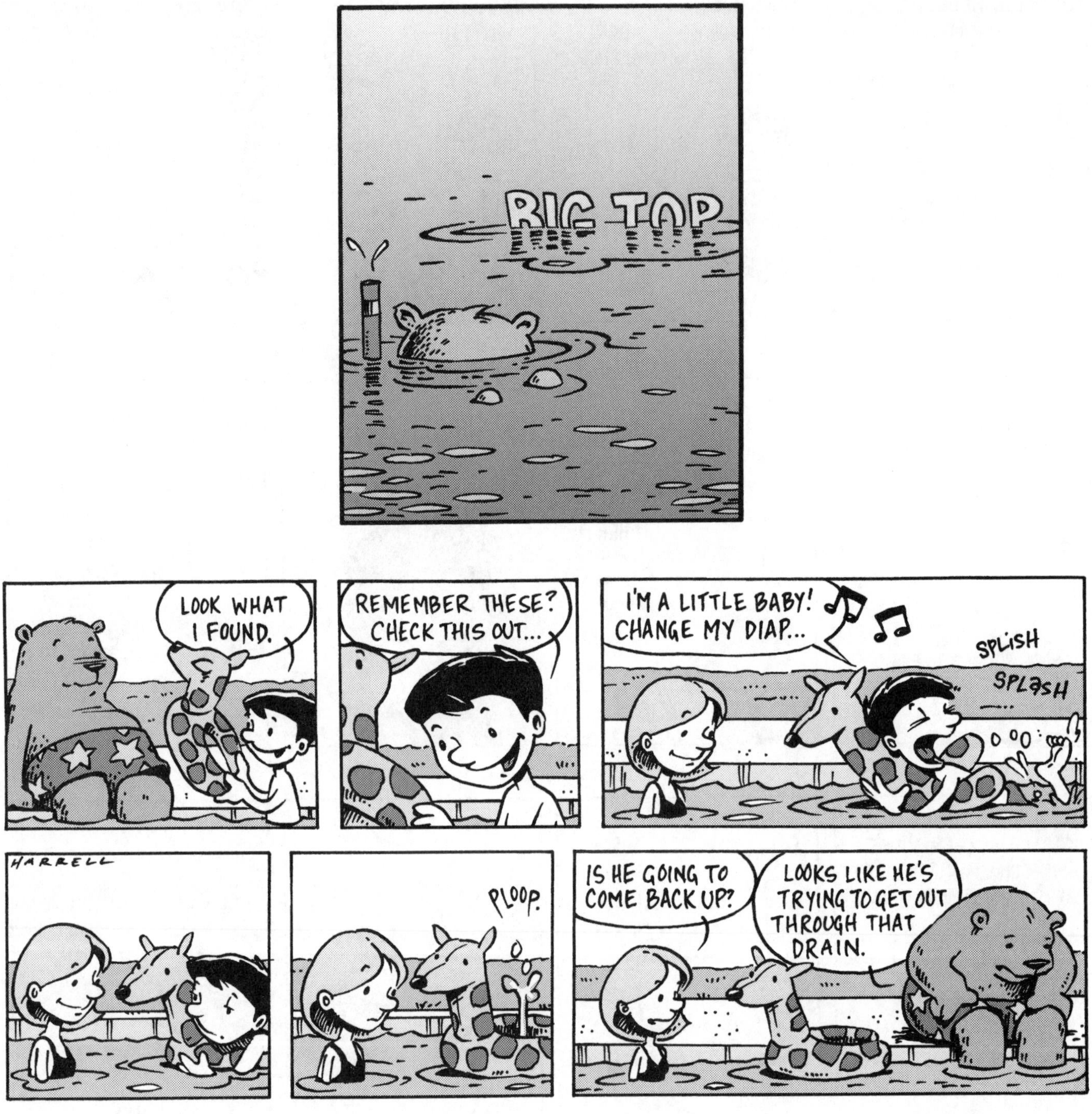
BIG TOP
LOOK WHAT I FOUND.
REMEMBER THESE? CHECK THIS OUT...
I'M A LITTLE BABY! CHANGE MY DIAP...
SPLISH
SPLASH
HARRELL
PLOOP
IS HE GOING TO COME BACK UP?
LOOKS LIKE HE'S TRYING TO GET OUT THROUGH THAT DRAIN.

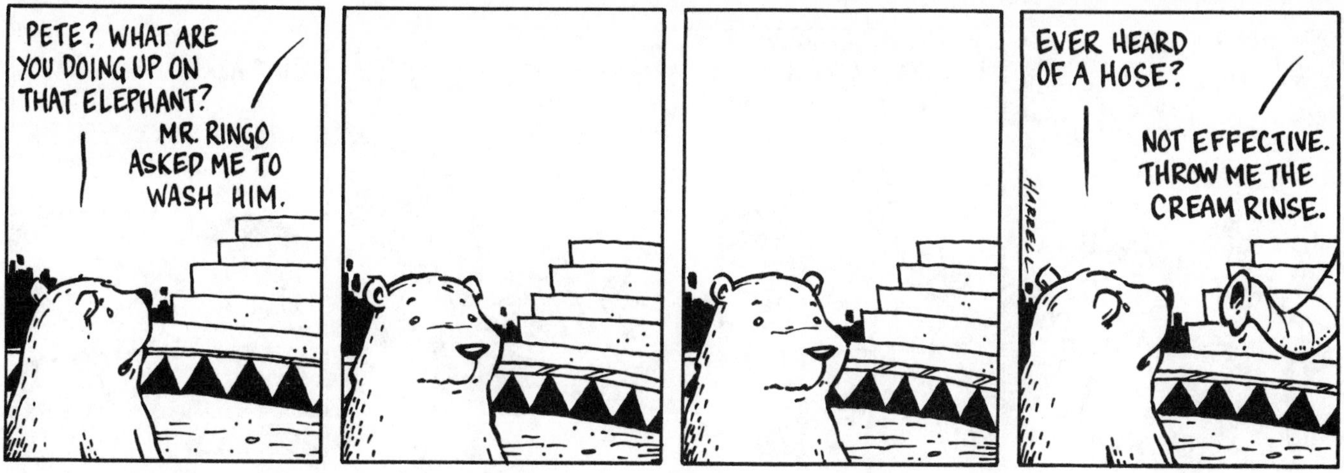
PETE? WHAT ARE YOU DOING UP ON THAT ELEPHANT?
MR. RINGO ASKED ME TO WASH HIM.
EVER HEARD OF A HOSE?
NOT EFFECTIVE. THROW ME THE CREAM RINSE.
HARRELL

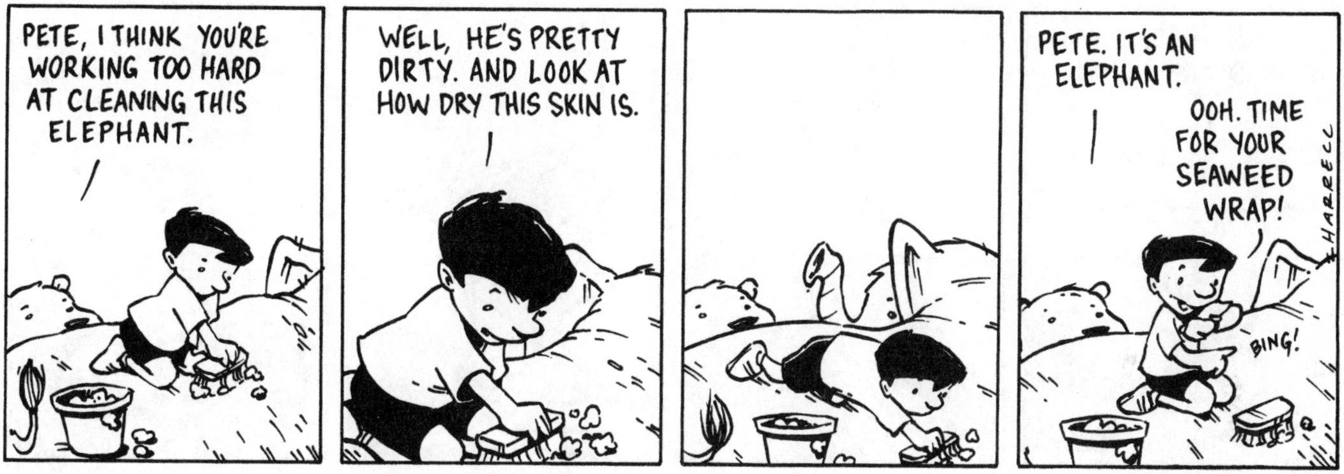
PETE, I THINK YOU'RE WORKING TOO HARD AT CLEANING THIS ELEPHANT.
WELL, HE'S PRETTY DIRTY. AND LOOK AT HOW DRY THIS SKIN IS.
PETE. IT'S AN ELEPHANT.
OOH. TIME FOR YOUR SEAWEED WRAP!
BING!
HARRELL

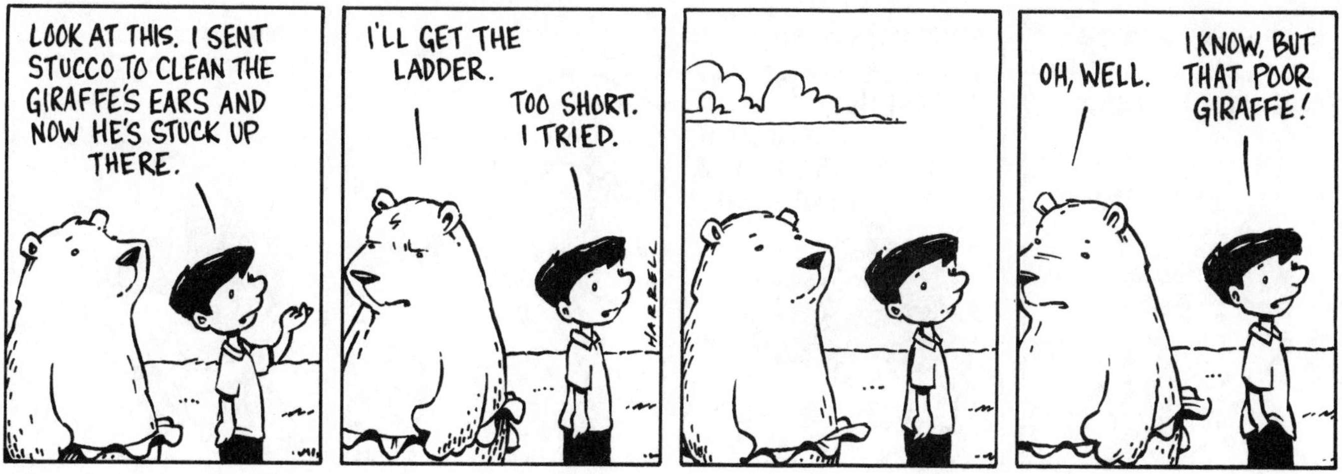
LOOK AT THIS. I SENT STUCCO TO CLEAN THE GIRAFFE'S EARS AND NOW HE'S STUCK UP THERE.
I'LL GET THE LADDER.
TOO SHORT. I TRIED.
HARRELL
OH, WELL.
I KNOW, BUT THAT POOR GIRAFFE!

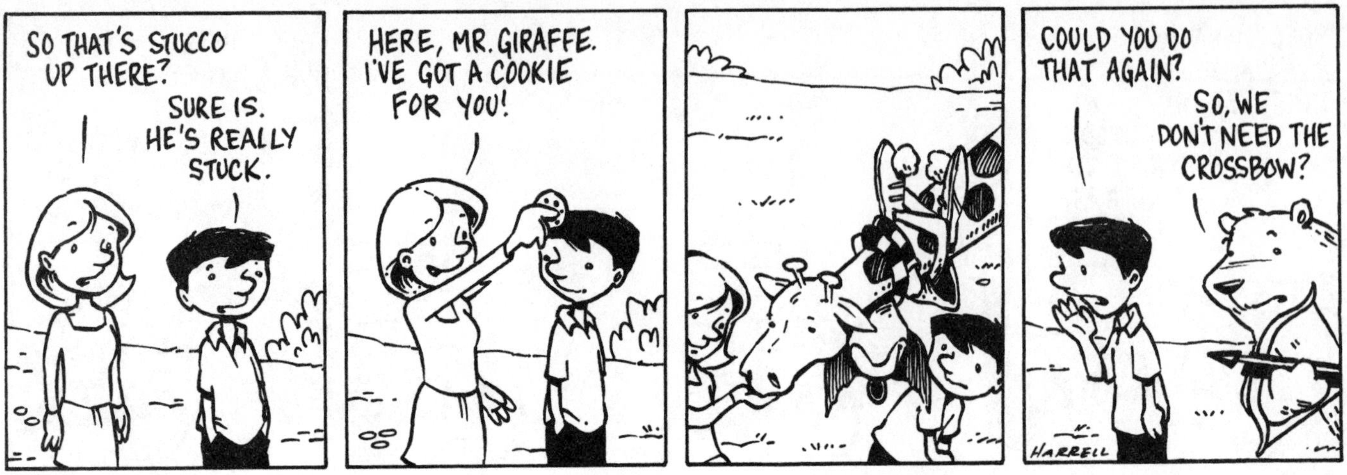
SO THAT'S STUCCO UP THERE?
SURE IS. HE'S REALLY STUCK.
HERE, MR. GIRAFFE. I'VE GOT A COOKIE FOR YOU!
COULD YOU DO THAT AGAIN?
SO, WE DON'T NEED THE CROSSBOW?
HARRELL

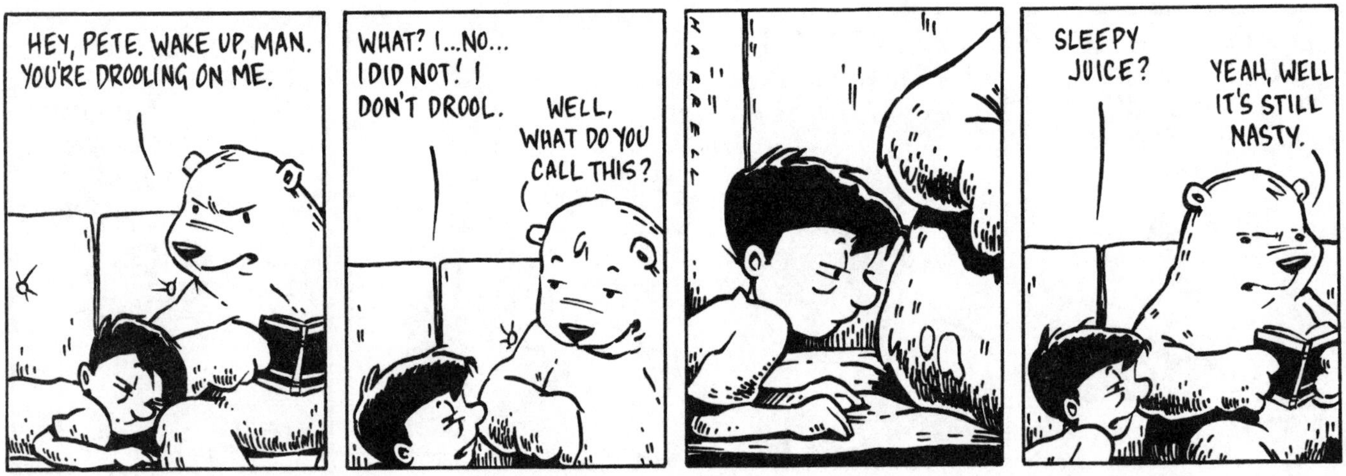
HEY, PETE. WAKE UP, MAN. YOU'RE DROOLING ON ME.
WHAT? I...NO... I DID NOT! I DON'T DROOL.
WELL, WHAT DO YOU CALL THIS?
HARRELL
SLEEPY JUICE?
YEAH, WELL IT'S STILL NASTY.

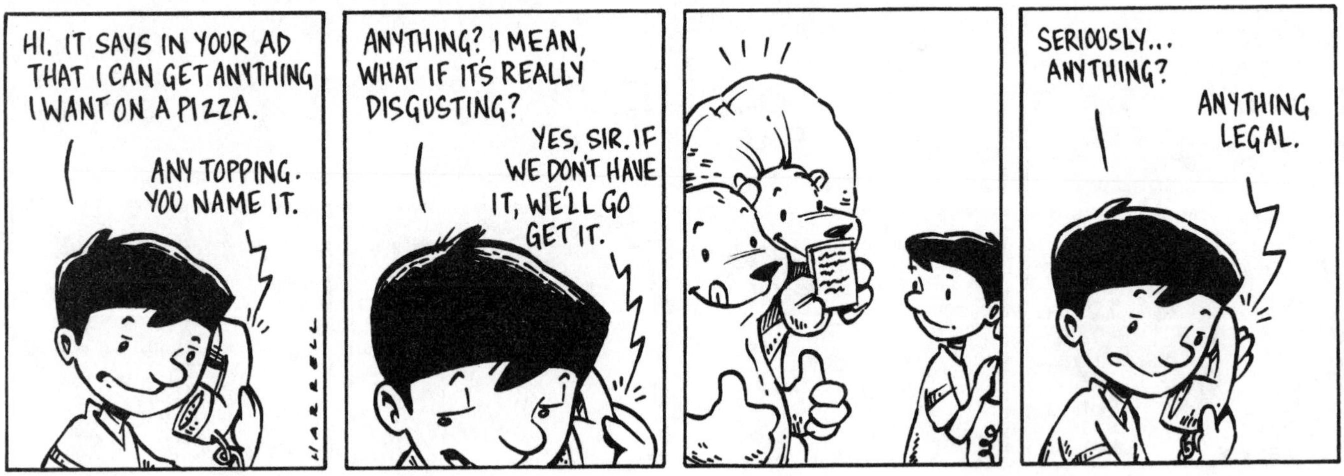
HI. IT SAYS IN YOUR AD THAT I CAN GET ANYTHING I WANT ON A PIZZA.
ANY TOPPING. YOU NAME IT.
HARRELL
ANYTHING? I MEAN, WHAT IF IT'S REALLY DISGUSTING?
YES, SIR. IF WE DON'T HAVE IT, WE'LL GO GET IT.
SERIOUSLY... ANYTHING?
ANYTHING LEGAL.

HEY, PETE. WHERE'S WINK?

OH, HE WENT HOME TO HAVE A LITTLE JAM SESSION.

A JAM SESSION? SINCE WHEN DOES HE PLAY AN INSTRUMENT?

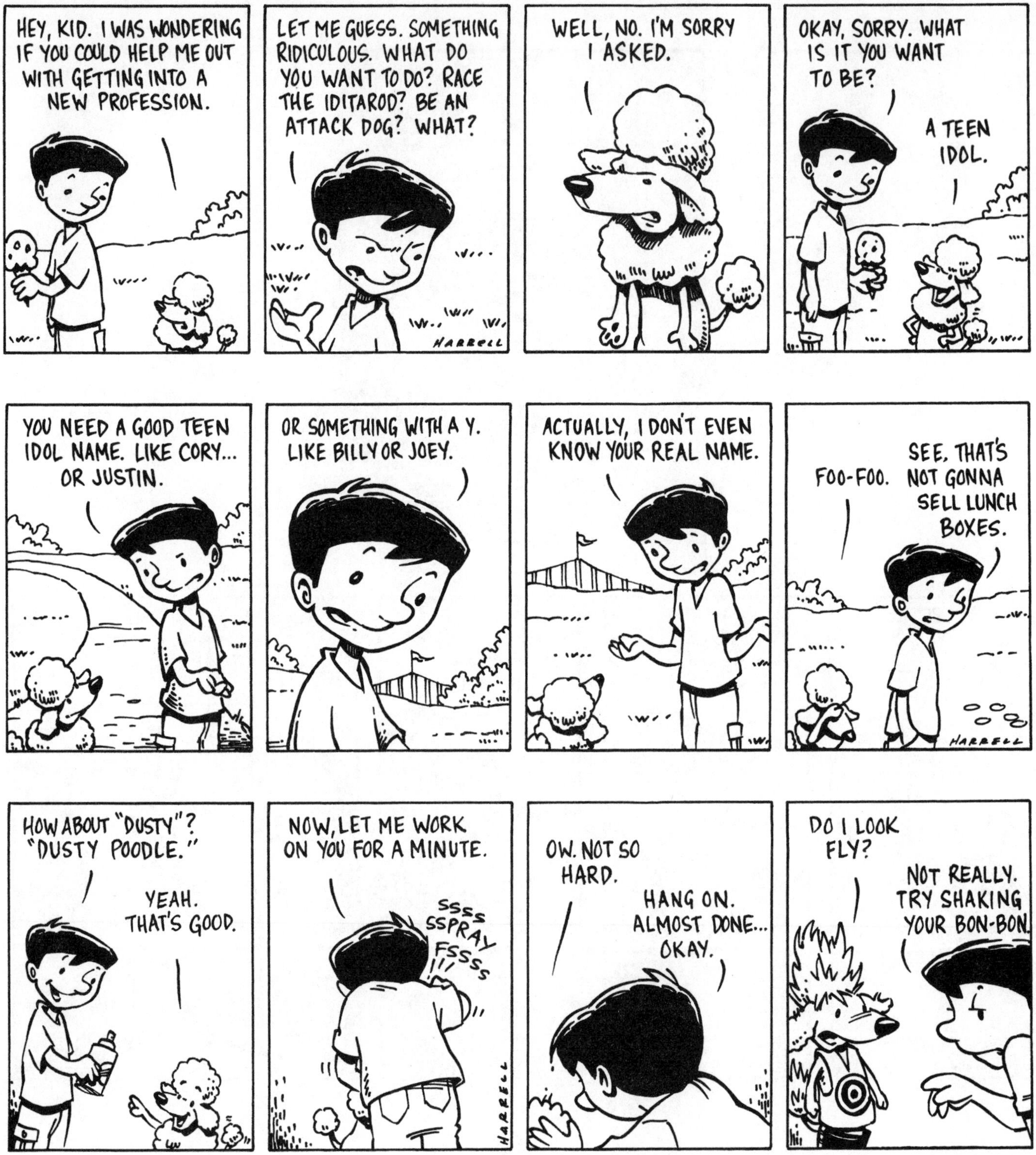
HEY, KID. I WAS WONDERING IF YOU COULD HELP ME OUT WITH GETTING INTO A NEW PROFESSION.
LET ME GUESS. SOMETHING RIDICULOUS. WHAT DO YOU WANT TO DO? RACE THE IDITAROD? BE AN ATTACK DOG? WHAT?
HARRELL
WELL, NO. I'M SORRY I ASKED.
OKAY, SORRY. WHAT IS IT YOU WANT TO BE?
A TEEN IDOL.
YOU NEED A GOOD TEEN IDOL NAME. LIKE CORY... OR JUSTIN.
OR SOMETHING WITH A Y. LIKE BILLY OR JOEY.
ACTUALLY, I DON'T EVEN KNOW YOUR REAL NAME.
FOO-FOO.
SEE, THAT'S NOT GONNA SELL LUNCH BOXES.
HARRELL
HOW ABOUT "DUSTY"? "DUSTY POODLE."
YEAH. THAT'S GOOD.
NOW, LET ME WORK ON YOU FOR A MINUTE.
SSSS SSPRAY FSSSS
HARRELL
OW. NOT SO HARD.
HANG ON. ALMOST DONE... OKAY.
DO I LOOK FLY?
NOT REALLY. TRY SHAKING YOUR BON-BON.

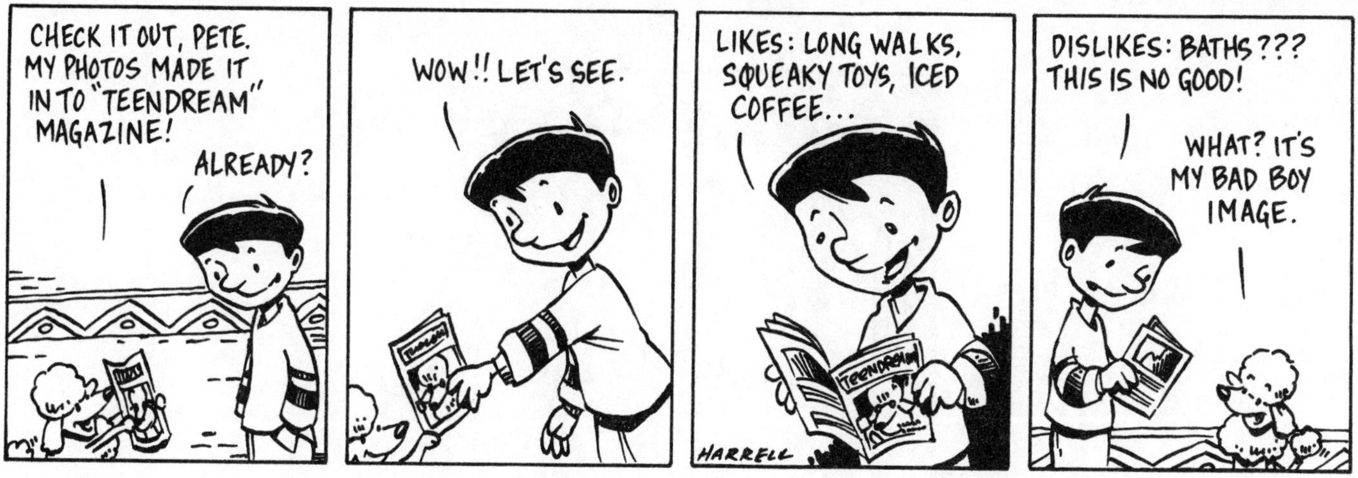
CHECK IT OUT, PETE. MY PHOTOS MADE IT IN TO "TEENDREAM" MAGAZINE!
ALREADY?
WOW!! LET'S SEE.
LIKES: LONG WALKS, SQUEAKY TOYS, ICED COFFEE...
TEENDREAM
HARRELL
DISLIKES: BATHS??? THIS IS NO GOOD!
WHAT? IT'S MY BAD BOY IMAGE.

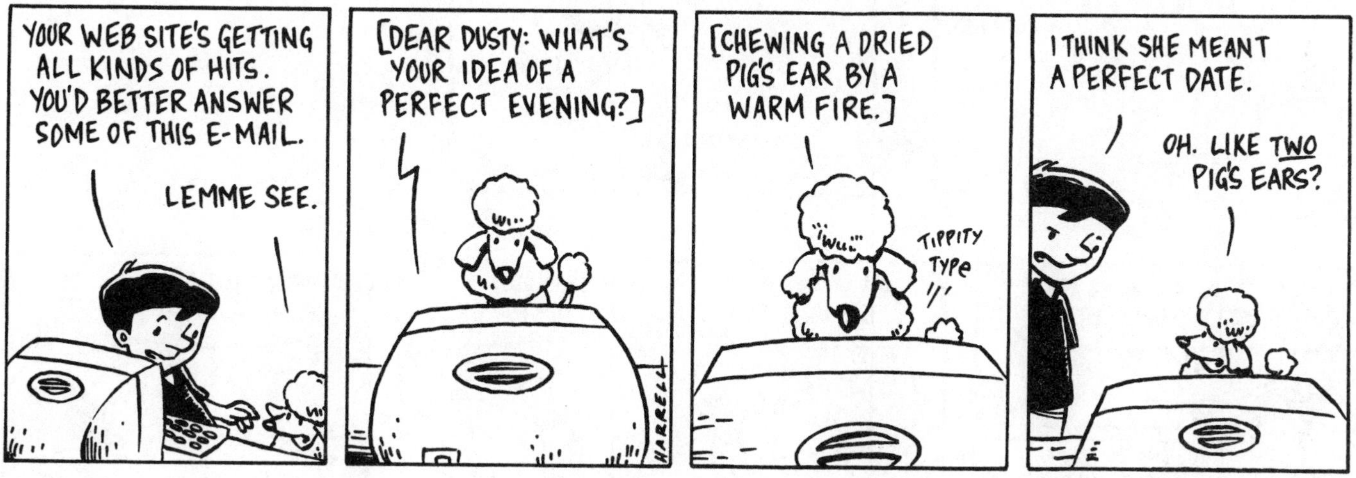
YOUR WEB SITE'S GETTING ALL KINDS OF HITS. YOU'D BETTER ANSWER SOME OF THIS E-MAIL.
LEMME SEE.
[DEAR DUSTY: WHAT'S YOUR IDEA OF A PERFECT EVENING?]
HARRELL
[CHEWING A DRIED PIG'S EAR BY A WARM FIRE.]
TIPPITY TYPE
I THINK SHE MEANT A PERFECT DATE.
OH. LIKE TWO PIG'S EARS?

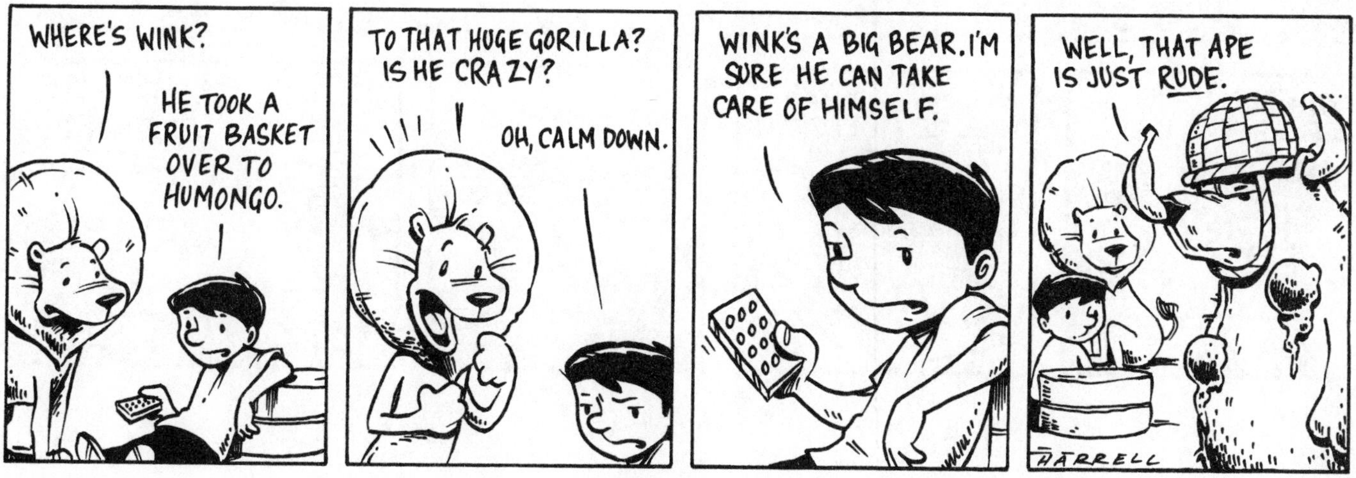
WHERE'S WINK?
HE TOOK A FRUIT BASKET OVER TO HUMONGO.
TO THAT HUGE GORILLA? IS HE CRAZY?
OH, CALM DOWN.
WINK'S A BIG BEAR. I'M SURE HE CAN TAKE CARE OF HIMSELF.
WELL, THAT APE IS JUST RUDE.
HARRELL

BIG TOP
SQUEEK ... SQUEEK...

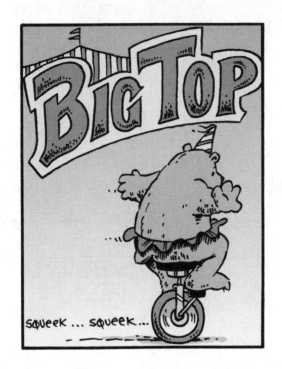

THANKS FOR SHOWING ME HOW TO DO LAUNDRY, MARY.
OH. IT'S MY PLEASURE, PETE.
NOW, LET'S SEE.
THIS ONE HERE IS ABOUT DONE.
HARRELL
SO, WHEN IT SHUTS OFF WE OPEN IT UP...
AND YOUR WHITES WILL BE A BEAUTIFUL, BRILLIANT...
...PINK.
YOUR TUTU?
HEY! IT'S FADED!

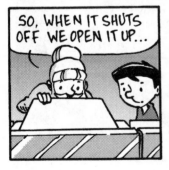

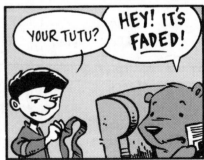

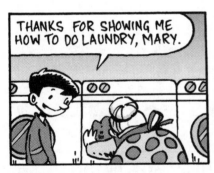

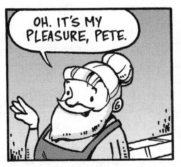

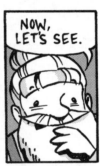

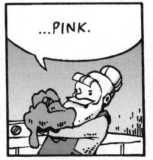

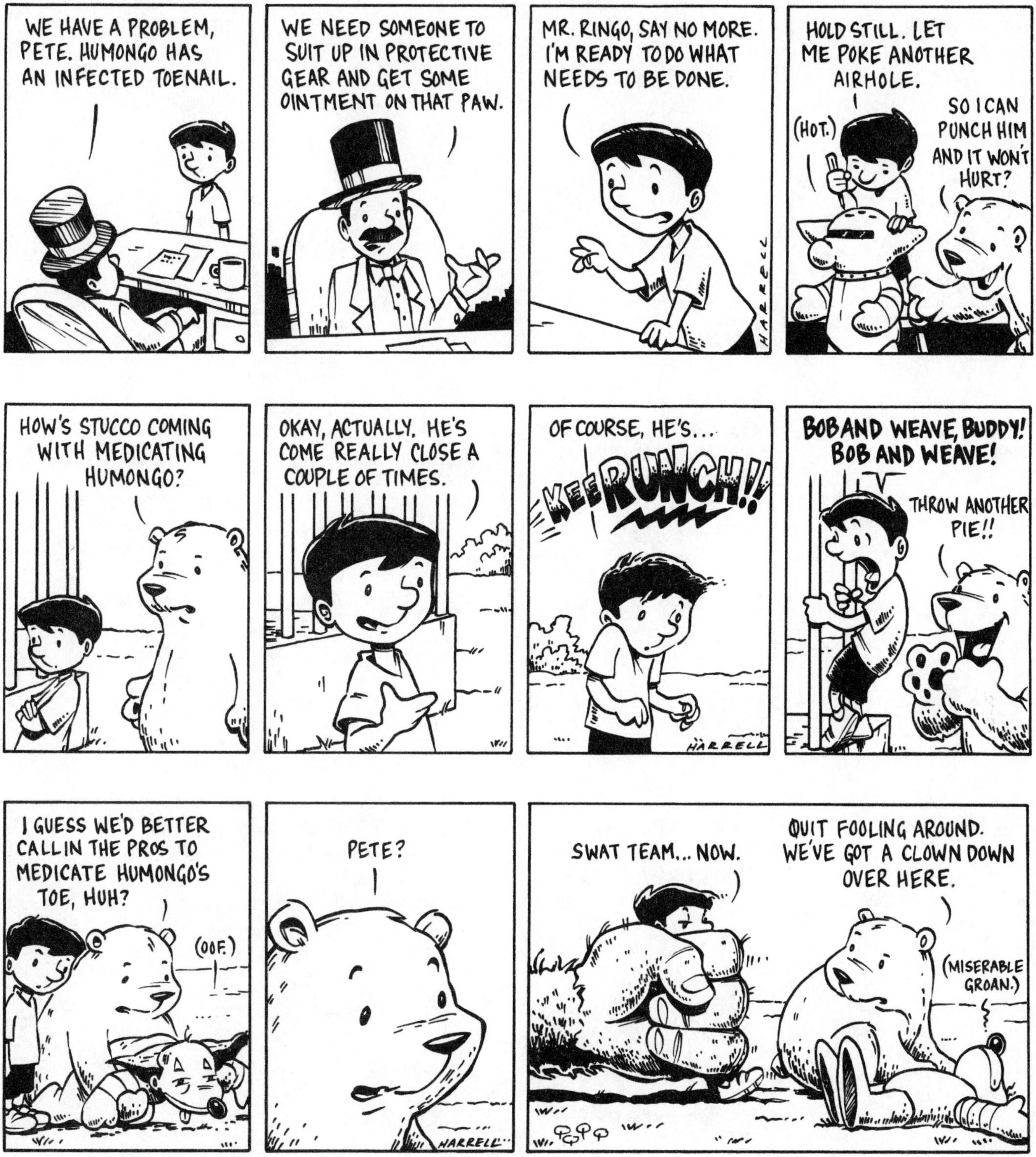
WE HAVE A PROBLEM, PETE. HUMONGO HAS AN INFECTED TOENAIL.
WE NEED SOMEONE TO SUIT UP IN PROTECTIVE GEAR AND GET SOME OINTMENT ON THAT PAW.
MR. RINGO, SAY NO MORE. I'M READY TO DO WHAT NEEDS TO BE DONE.
HARRELL
HOLD STILL. LET ME POKE ANOTHER AIRHOLE.
(HOT.)
SO I CAN PUNCH HIM AND IT WON'T HURT?
HOW'S STUCCO COMING WITH MEDICATING HUMONGO?
OKAY, ACTUALLY. HE'S COME REALLY CLOSE A COUPLE OF TIMES.
OF COURSE, HE'S...
KEERUNCH!!
HARRELL
BOB AND WEAVE, BUDDY! BOB AND WEAVE!
THROW ANOTHER PIE!!
I GUESS WE'D BETTER CALL IN THE PROS TO MEDICATE HUMONGO'S TOE, HUH?
(OOF.)
PETE?
HARRELL
SWAT TEAM... NOW.
QUIT FOOLING AROUND. WE'VE GOT A CLOWN DOWN OVER HERE.
(MISERABLE GROAN.)

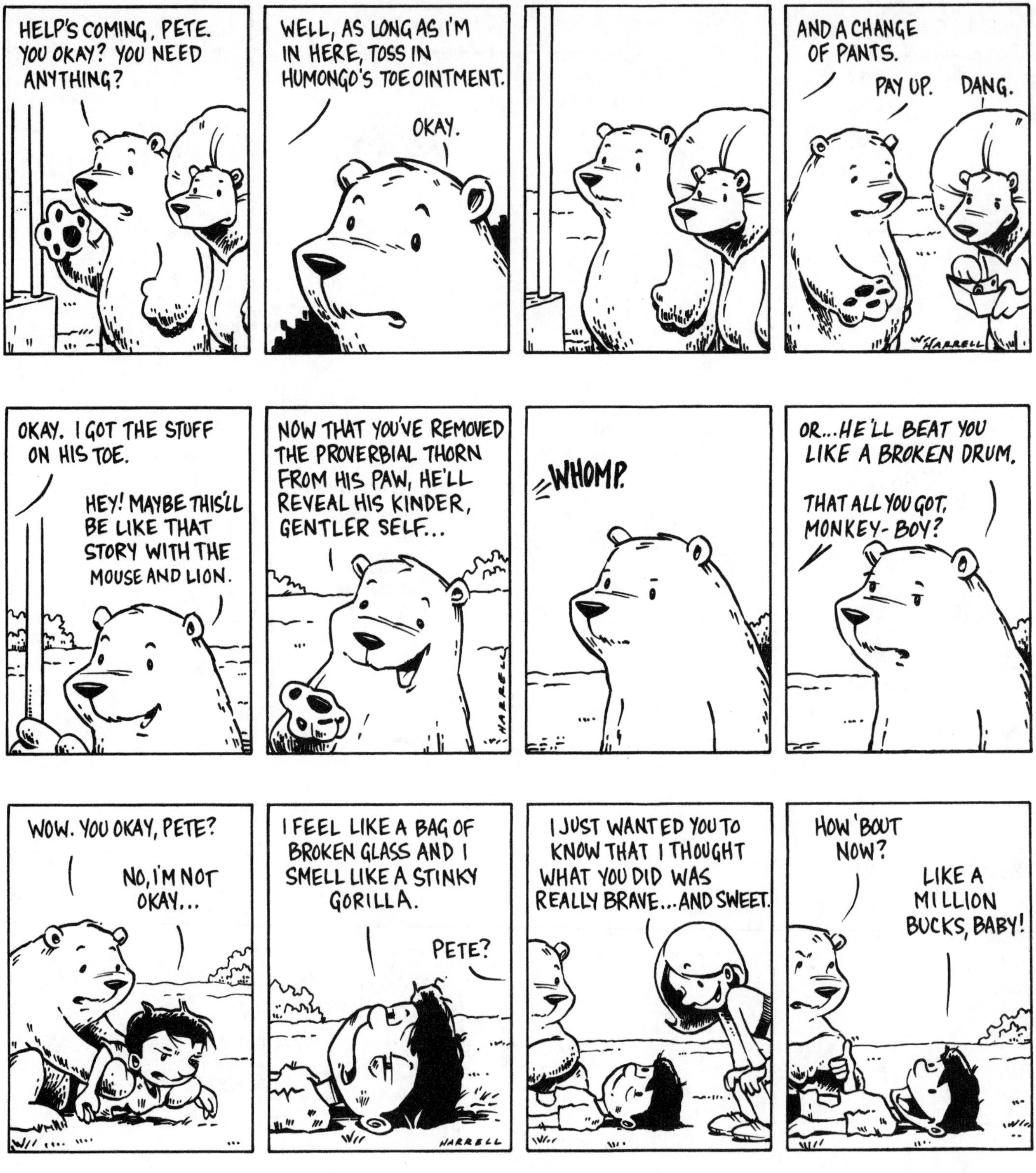

HELP'S COMING, PETE. YOU OKAY? YOU NEED ANYTHING?
WELL, AS LONG AS I'M IN HERE, TOSS IN HUMONGO'S TOE OINTMENT.
OKAY.
AND A CHANGE OF PANTS.
PAY UP.
DANG.
OKAY. I GOT THE STUFF ON HIS TOE.
HEY! MAYBE THIS'LL BE LIKE THAT STORY WITH THE MOUSE AND LION.
NOW THAT YOU'VE REMOVED THE PROVERBIAL THORN FROM HIS PAW, HE'LL REVEAL HIS KINDER, GENTLER SELF...
WHOMP.
OR...HE'LL BEAT YOU LIKE A BROKEN DRUM.
THAT ALL YOU GOT, MONKEY-BOY?
WOW. YOU OKAY, PETE?
NO, I'M NOT OKAY...
I FEEL LIKE A BAG OF BROKEN GLASS AND I SMELL LIKE A STINKY GORILLA.
PETE?
I JUST WANTED YOU TO KNOW THAT I THOUGHT WHAT YOU DID WAS REALLY BRAVE...AND SWEET.
HOW 'BOUT NOW?
LIKE A MILLION BUCKS, BABY!

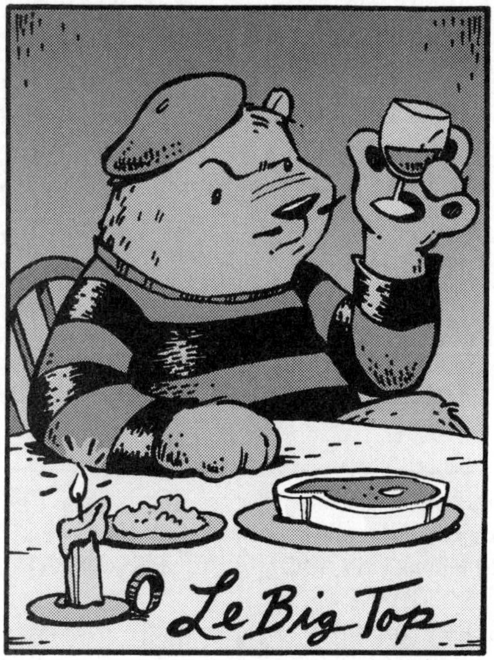
Le Big Top

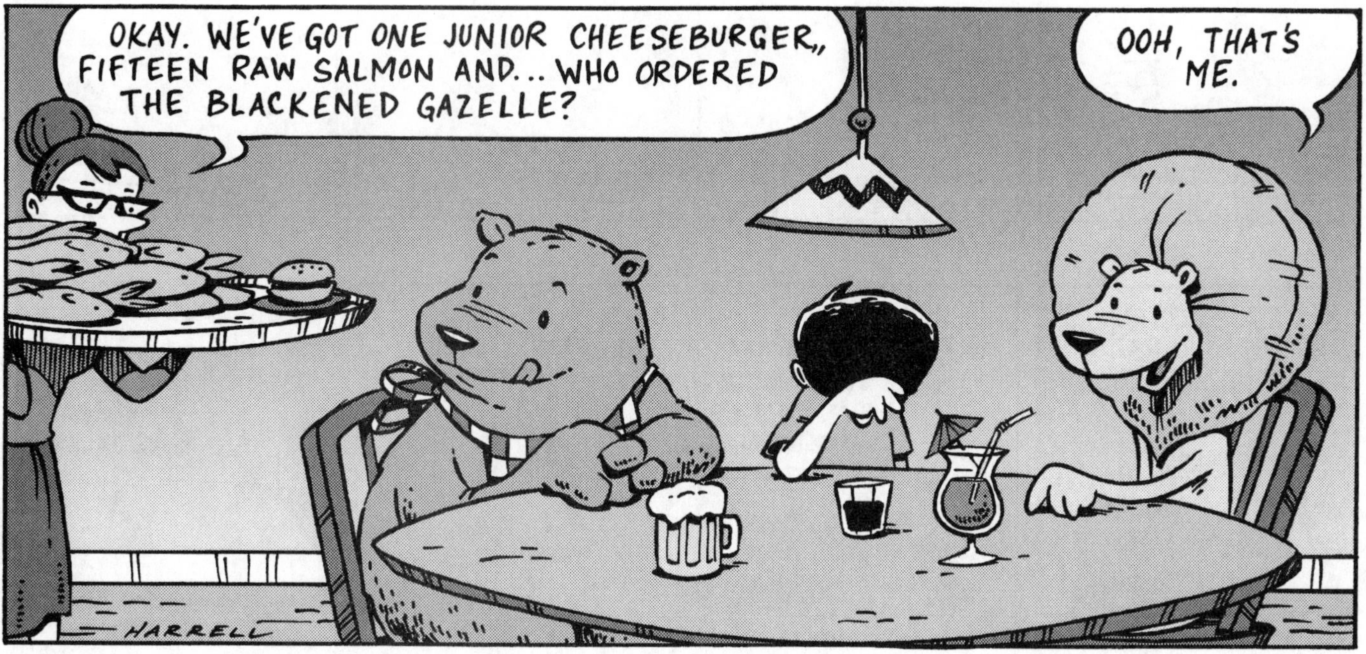
OKAY. WE'VE GOT ONE JUNIOR CHEESEBURGER, FIFTEEN RAW SALMON AND... WHO ORDERED THE BLACKENED GAZELLE?
OOH, THAT'S ME.
HARRELL

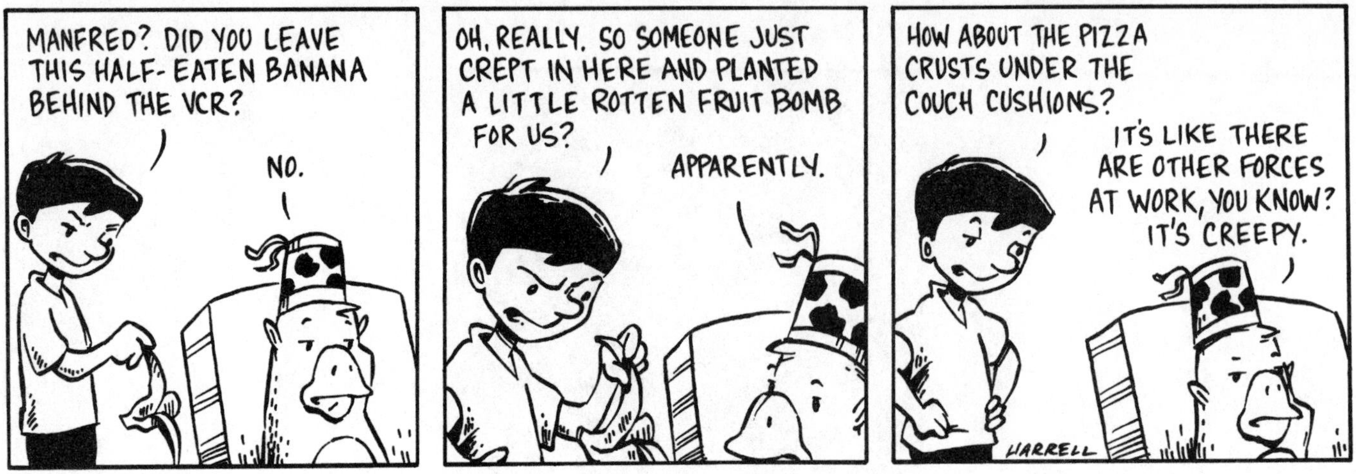
MANFRED? DID YOU LEAVE THIS HALF-EATEN BANANA BEHIND THE VCR?
NO.
OH, REALLY. SO SOMEONE JUST CREPT IN HERE AND PLANTED A LITTLE ROTTEN FRUIT BOMB FOR US?
APPARENTLY.
HOW ABOUT THE PIZZA CRUSTS UNDER THE COUCH CUSHIONS?
IT'S LIKE THERE ARE OTHER FORCES AT WORK, YOU KNOW? IT'S CREEPY.
HARRELL

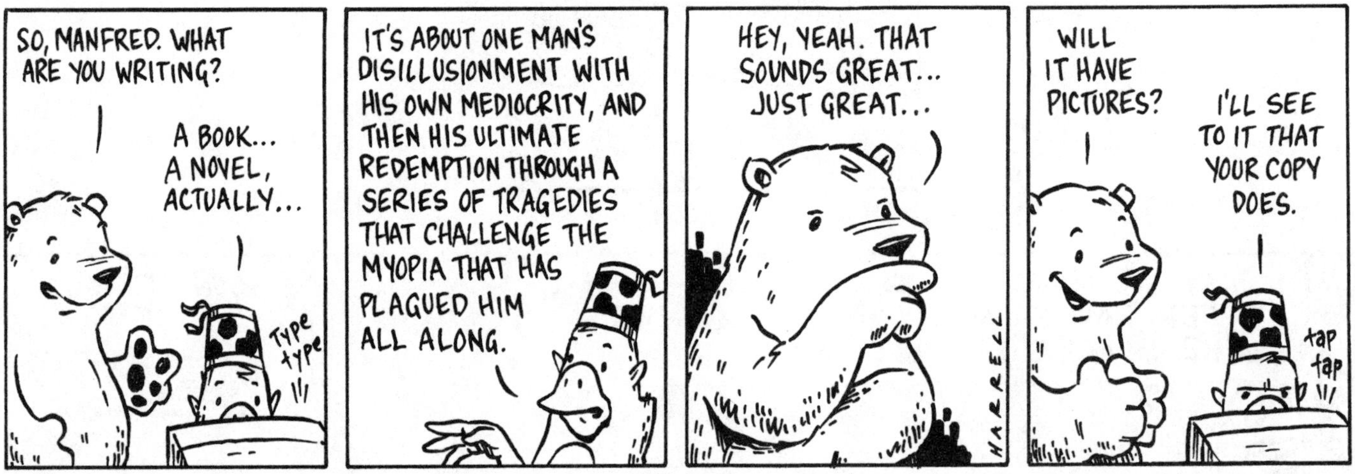
SO, MANFRED. WHAT ARE YOU WRITING?
A BOOK... A NOVEL, ACTUALLY...
type type
IT'S ABOUT ONE MAN'S DISILLUSIONMENT WITH HIS OWN MEDIOCRITY, AND THEN HIS ULTIMATE REDEMPTION THROUGH A SERIES OF TRAGEDIES THAT CHALLENGE THE MYOPIA THAT HAS PLAGUED HIM ALL ALONG.
HEY, YEAH. THAT SOUNDS GREAT... JUST GREAT...
HARRELL
WILL IT HAVE PICTURES?
I'LL SEE TO IT THAT YOUR COPY DOES.
tap tap

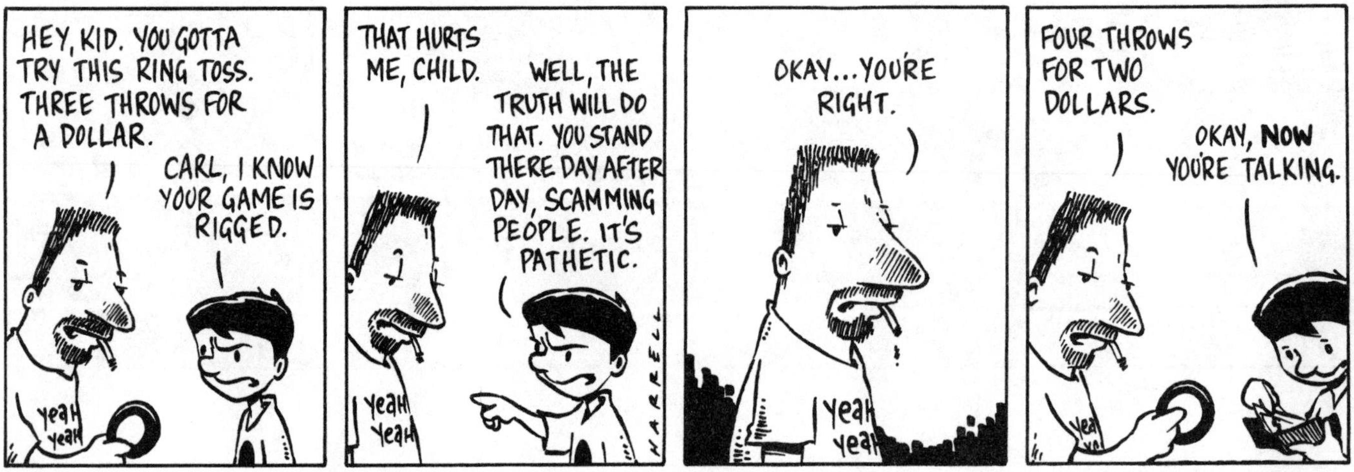
HEY, KID. YOU GOTTA TRY THIS RING TOSS. THREE THROWS FOR A DOLLAR.
CARL, I KNOW YOUR GAME IS RIGGED.
yeah yeah
THAT HURTS ME, CHILD.
WELL, THE TRUTH WILL DO THAT. YOU STAND THERE DAY AFTER DAY, SCAMMING PEOPLE. IT'S PATHETIC.
HARRELL
OKAY... YOU'RE RIGHT.
FOUR THROWS FOR TWO DOLLARS.
OKAY, **NOW** YOU'RE TALKING.

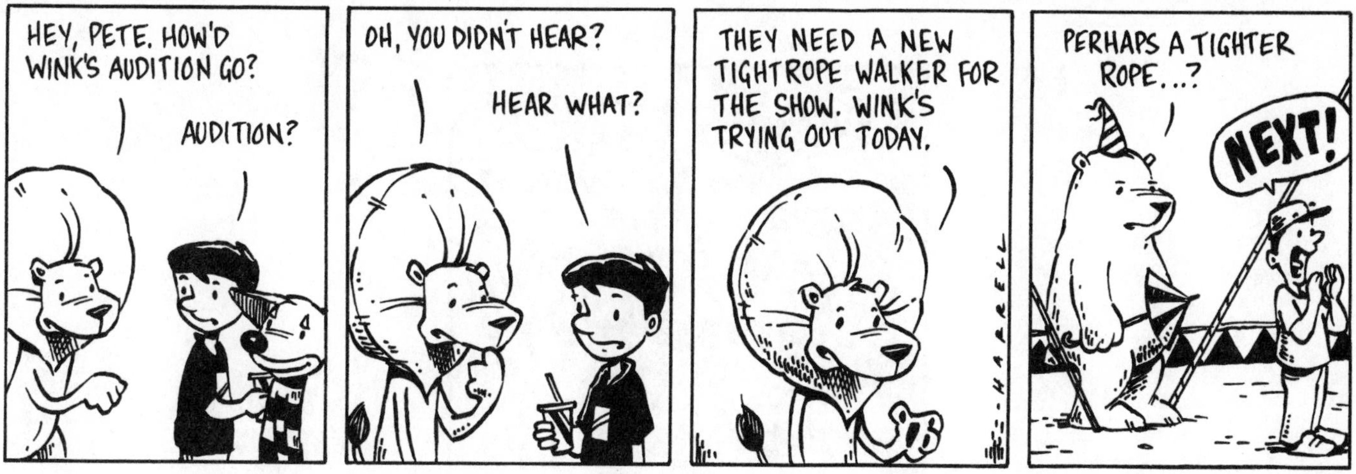
HEY, PETE. HOW'D WINK'S AUDITION GO?
AUDITION?
OH, YOU DIDN'T HEAR?
HEAR WHAT?
THEY NEED A NEW TIGHTROPE WALKER FOR THE SHOW. WINK'S TRYING OUT TODAY.
HARRELL
PERHAPS A TIGHTER ROPE...?
NEXT!

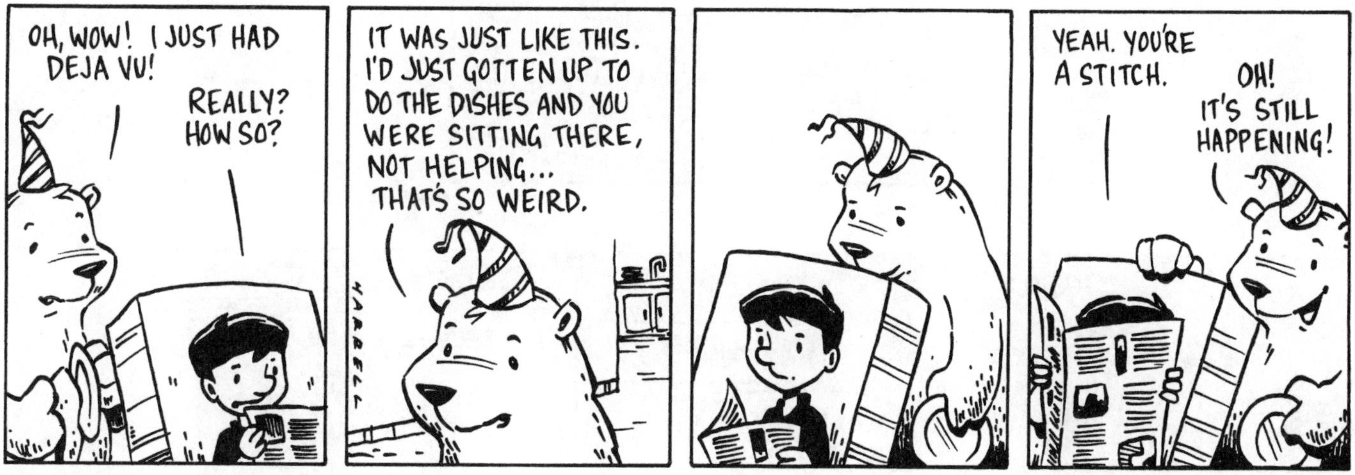
OH, WOW! I JUST HAD DEJA VU!
REALLY? HOW SO?
IT WAS JUST LIKE THIS. I'D JUST GOTTEN UP TO DO THE DISHES AND YOU WERE SITTING THERE, NOT HELPING... THAT'S SO WEIRD.
HARRELL
YEAH. YOU'RE A STITCH.
OH! IT'S STILL HAPPENING!

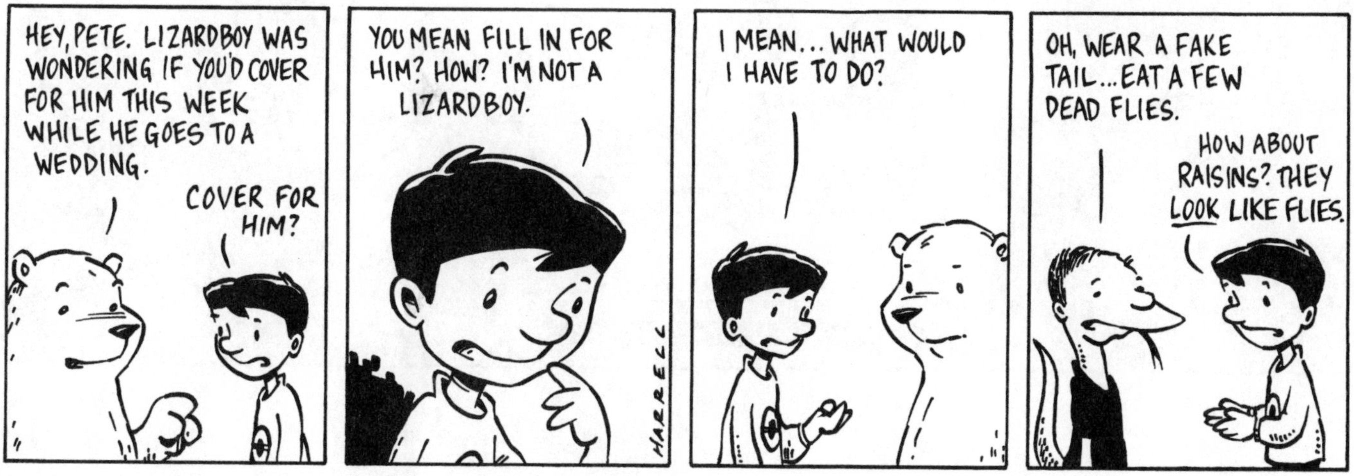
HEY, PETE. LIZARDBOY WAS WONDERING IF YOU'D COVER FOR HIM THIS WEEK WHILE HE GOES TO A WEDDING.
COVER FOR HIM?
YOU MEAN FILL IN FOR HIM? HOW? I'M NOT A LIZARDBOY.
HARRELL
I MEAN... WHAT WOULD I HAVE TO DO?
OH, WEAR A FAKE TAIL... EAT A FEW DEAD FLIES.
HOW ABOUT RAISINS? THEY LOOK LIKE FLIES.

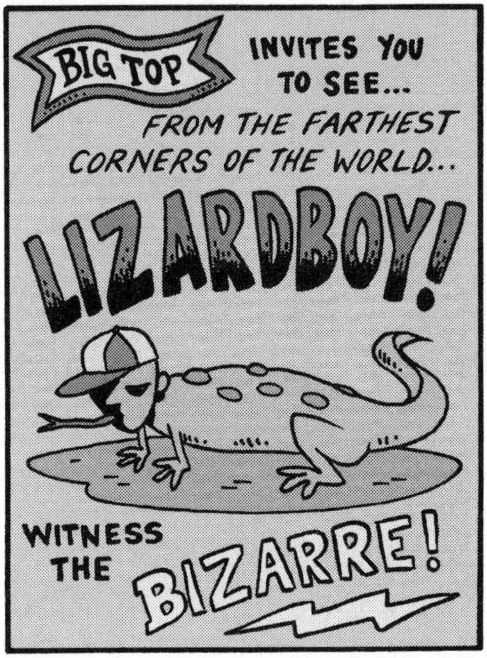
BIG TOP
INVITES YOU TO SEE...
FROM THE FARTHEST CORNERS OF THE WORLD...
LIZARDBOY!
WITNESS THE BIZARRE!

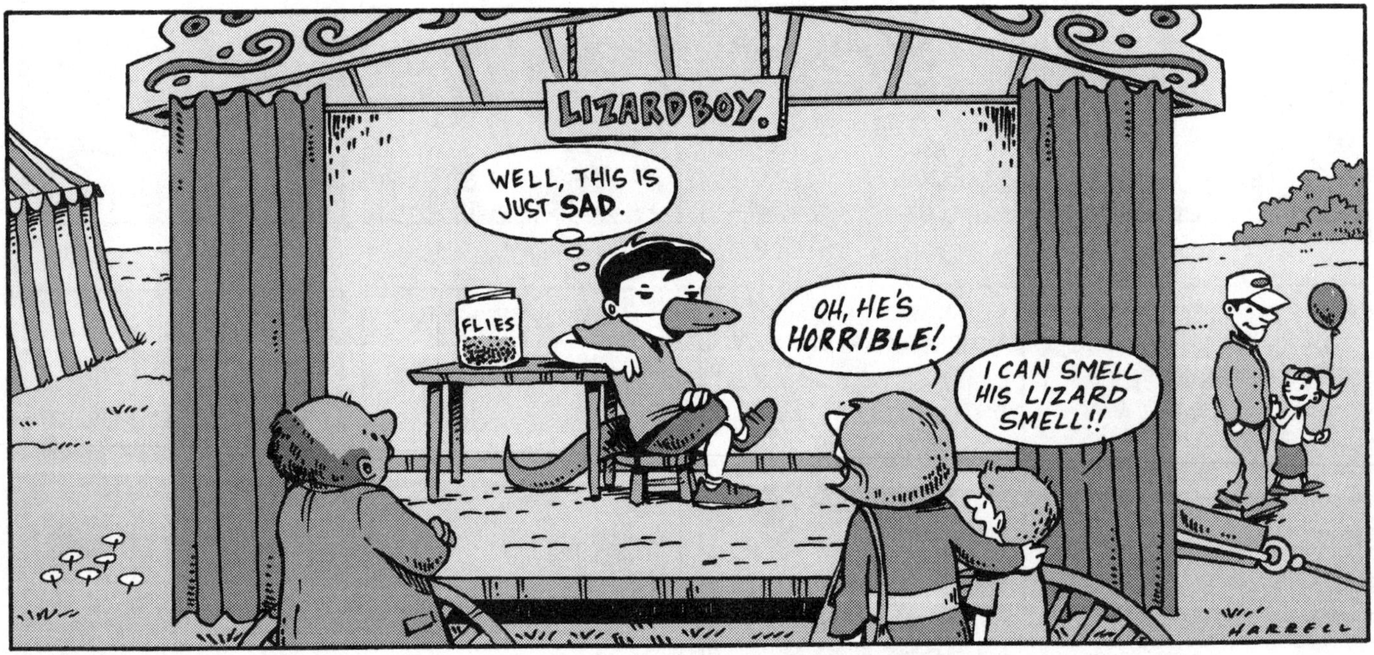
LIZARDBOY
WELL, THIS IS JUST SAD.
FLIES
OH, HE'S HORRIBLE!
I CAN SMELL HIS LIZARD SMELL!!
HARRELL

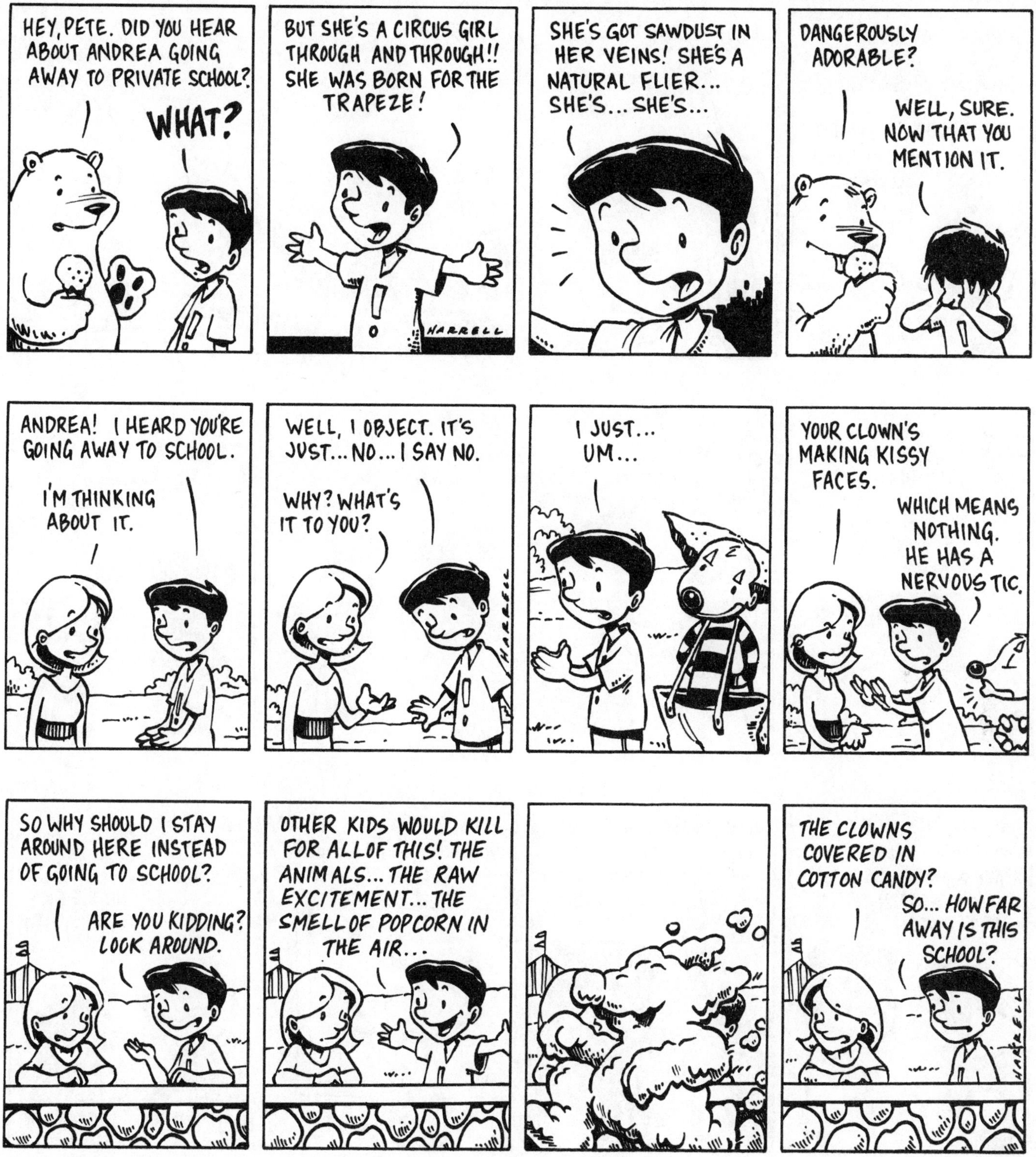
HEY, PETE. DID YOU HEAR ABOUT ANDREA GOING AWAY TO PRIVATE SCHOOL?
WHAT?
BUT SHE'S A CIRCUS GIRL THROUGH AND THROUGH!! SHE WAS BORN FOR THE TRAPEZE!
HARRELL
SHE'S GOT SAWDUST IN HER VEINS! SHE'S A NATURAL FLIER... SHE'S... SHE'S...
DANGEROUSLY ADORABLE?
WELL, SURE. NOW THAT YOU MENTION IT.
ANDREA! I HEARD YOU'RE GOING AWAY TO SCHOOL.
I'M THINKING ABOUT IT.
WELL, I OBJECT. IT'S JUST... NO... I SAY NO.
WHY? WHAT'S IT TO YOU?
HARRELL
I JUST... UM...
YOUR CLOWN'S MAKING KISSY FACES.
WHICH MEANS NOTHING. HE HAS A NERVOUS TIC.
SO WHY SHOULD I STAY AROUND HERE INSTEAD OF GOING TO SCHOOL?
ARE YOU KIDDING? LOOK AROUND.
OTHER KIDS WOULD KILL FOR ALL OF THIS! THE ANIMALS... THE RAW EXCITEMENT... THE SMELL OF POPCORN IN THE AIR...
THE CLOWNS COVERED IN COTTON CANDY?
SO... HOW FAR AWAY IS THIS SCHOOL?
HARRELL

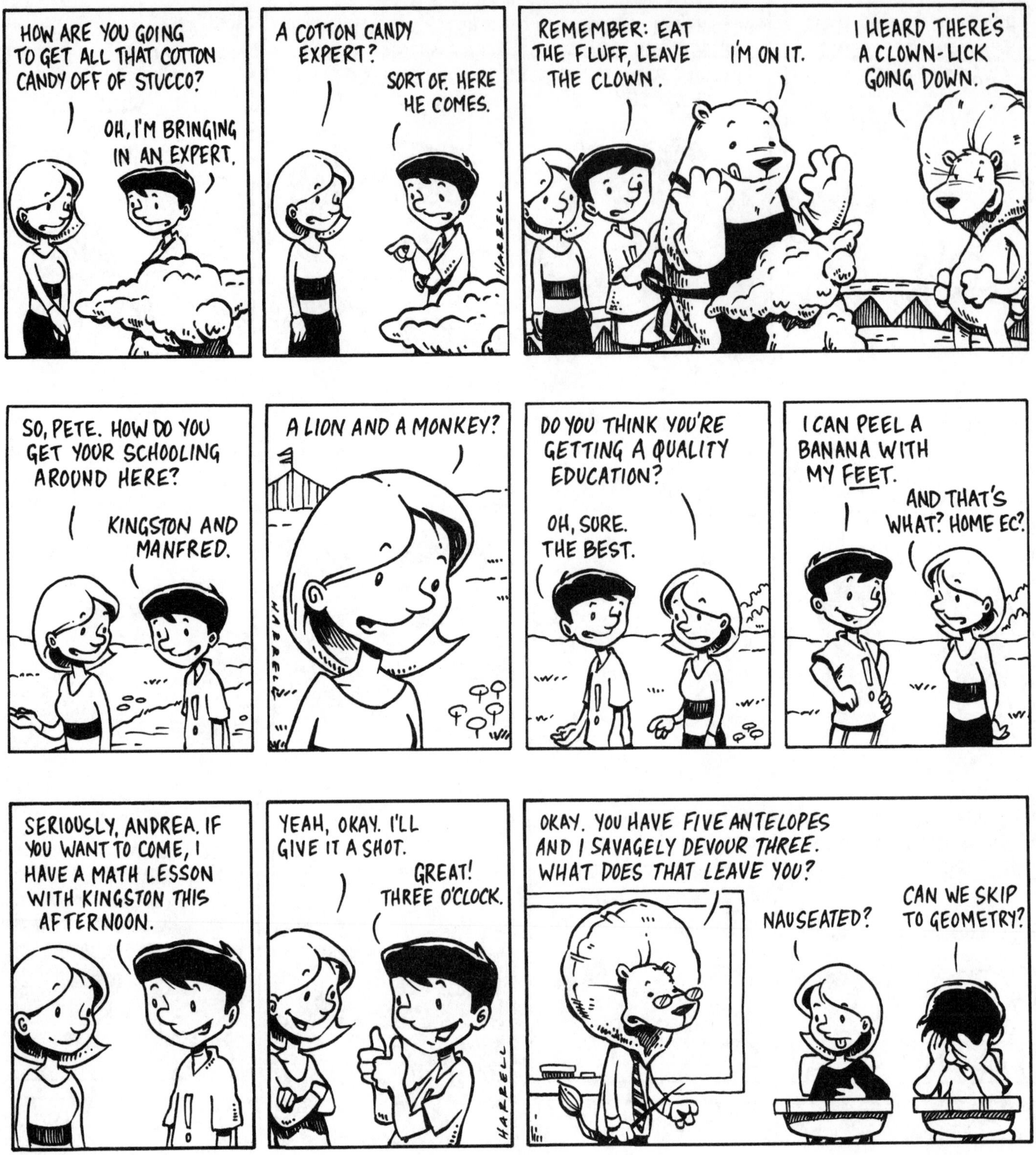
HOW ARE YOU GOING TO GET ALL THAT COTTON CANDY OFF OF STUCCO?
OH, I'M BRINGING IN AN EXPERT.
A COTTON CANDY EXPERT?
SORT OF. HERE HE COMES.
HARRELL
REMEMBER: EAT THE FLUFF, LEAVE THE CLOWN.
I'M ON IT.
I HEARD THERE'S A CLOWN-LICK GOING DOWN.
SO, PETE. HOW DO YOU GET YOUR SCHOOLING AROUND HERE?
KINGSTON AND MANFRED.
A LION AND A MONKEY?
HARRELL
DO YOU THINK YOU'RE GETTING A QUALITY EDUCATION?
OH, SURE. THE BEST.
I CAN PEEL A BANANA WITH MY FEET.
AND THAT'S WHAT? HOME EC?
SERIOUSLY, ANDREA. IF YOU WANT TO COME, I HAVE A MATH LESSON WITH KINGSTON THIS AFTERNOON.
YEAH, OKAY. I'LL GIVE IT A SHOT.
GREAT! THREE O'CLOCK.
HARRELL
OKAY. YOU HAVE FIVE ANTELOPES AND I SAVAGELY DEVOUR THREE. WHAT DOES THAT LEAVE YOU?
NAUSEATED?
CAN WE SKIP TO GEOMETRY?

BIG TOP

umblegrumblerrgrumblgrumblegr

PETER? ARE YOU OKAY? YOU SEEM TENSE.

I GUESS SO.

WELL, I'M GOING TO TELL YOU EXACTLY WHAT YOU NEED.

YOU GO RIGHT HOME AND MAKE YOURSELF SOME TEA WITH CHAMOMILE IN IT.

HARRELL

REALLY?

SURE! FIX YOU RIGHT UP.

WHATTA YOU THINK? SOOTHING?

I GUESS. IN A GRITTY KIND OF WAY.

CAMEL MEAL

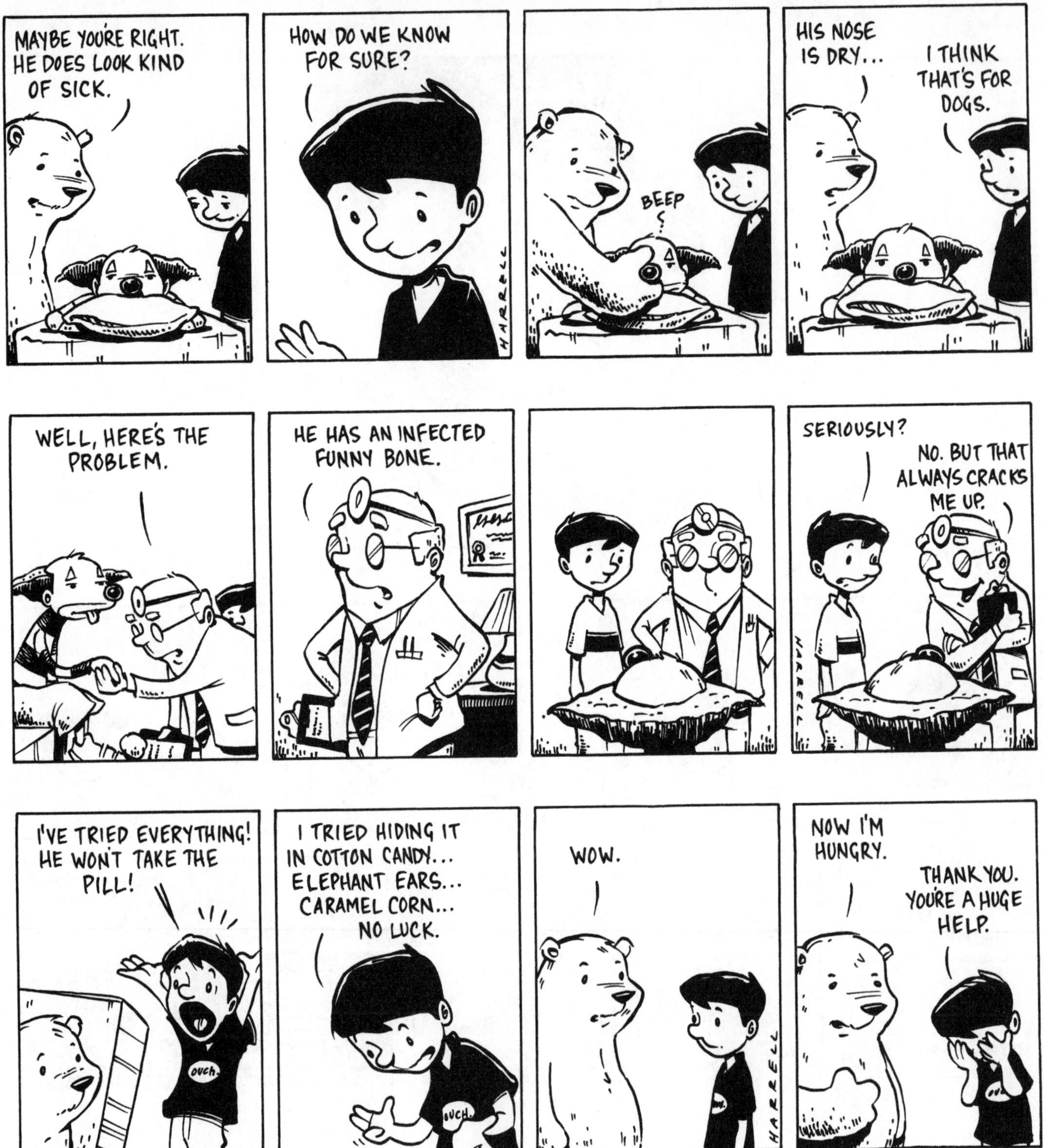
MAYBE YOU'RE RIGHT. HE DOES LOOK KIND OF SICK.
HOW DO WE KNOW FOR SURE?
BEEP
HIS NOSE IS DRY...
I THINK THAT'S FOR DOGS.
HARRELL
WELL, HERE'S THE PROBLEM.
HE HAS AN INFECTED FUNNY BONE.
SERIOUSLY?
NO. BUT THAT ALWAYS CRACKS ME UP.
HARRELL
I'VE TRIED EVERYTHING! HE WON'T TAKE THE PILL!
OUCH
I TRIED HIDING IT IN COTTON CANDY... ELEPHANT EARS... CARAMEL CORN... NO LUCK.
OUCH
WOW.
HARRELL
NOW I'M HUNGRY.
THANK YOU. YOU'RE A HUGE HELP.

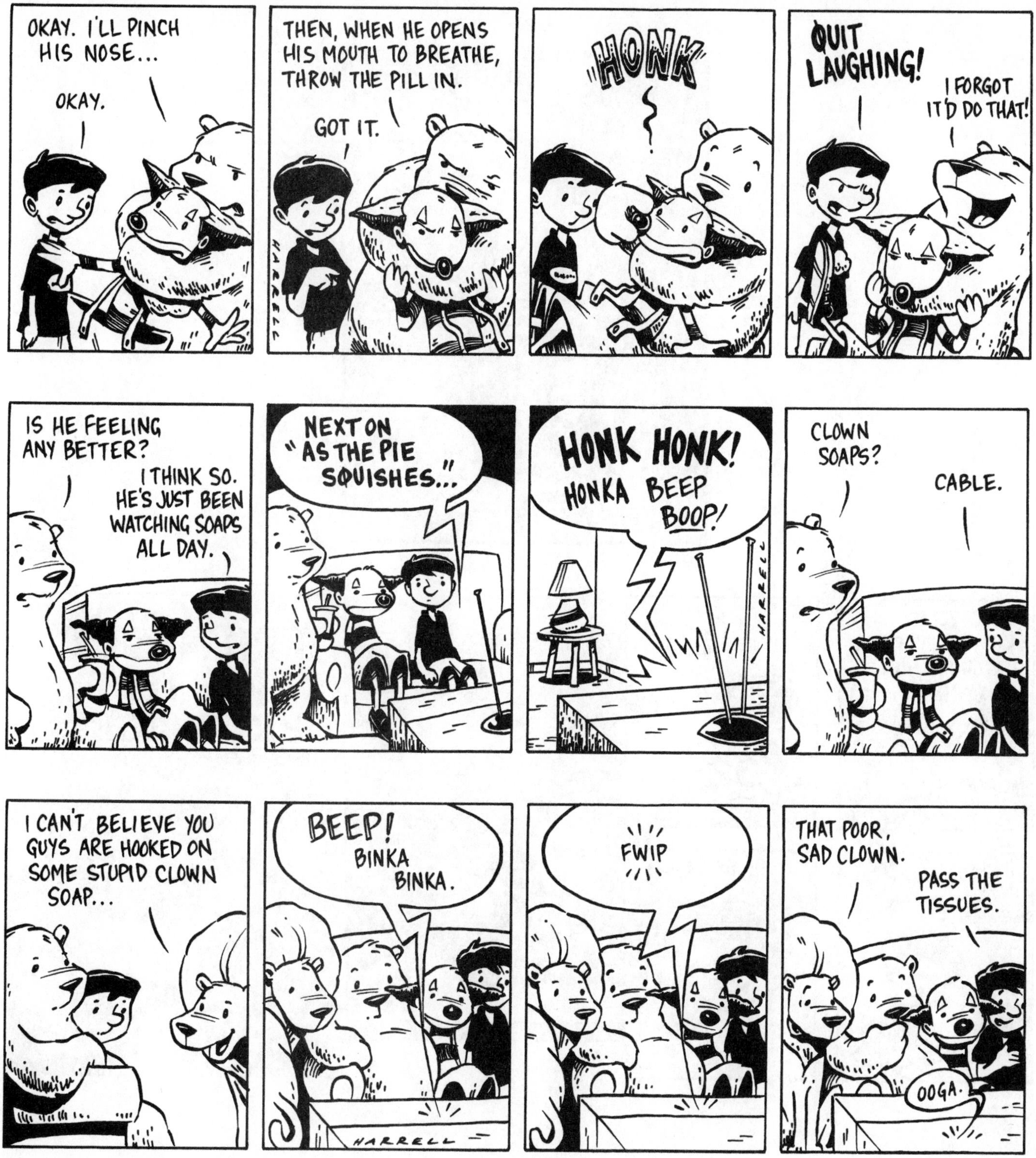
OKAY. I'LL PINCH HIS NOSE...
OKAY.
HARRELL
THEN, WHEN HE OPENS HIS MOUTH TO BREATHE, THROW THE PILL IN.
GOT IT.
HONK
QUIT LAUGHING!
I FORGOT IT'D DO THAT!
IS HE FEELING ANY BETTER?
I THINK SO. HE'S JUST BEEN WATCHING SOAPS ALL DAY.
"NEXT ON AS THE PIE SQUISHES..."
HONK HONK! HONKA BEEP BOOP!
HARRELL
CLOWN SOAPS?
CABLE.
I CAN'T BELIEVE YOU GUYS ARE HOOKED ON SOME STUPID CLOWN SOAP...
BEEP! BINKA BINKA.
HARRELL
FWIP
THAT POOR, SAD CLOWN.
PASS THE TISSUES.
OOGA.

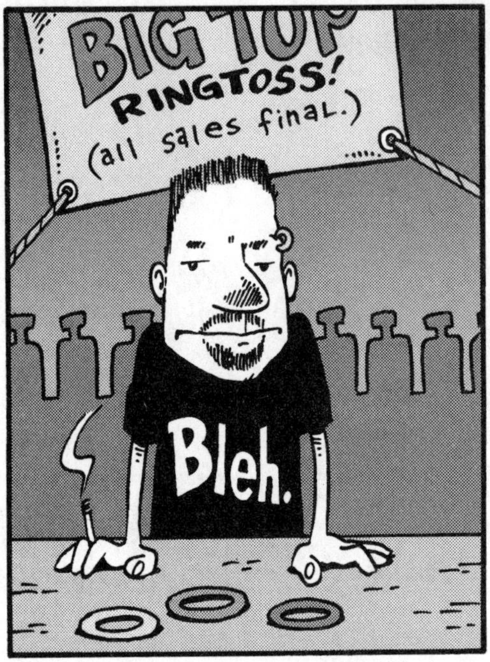
BIG TOP
RINGTOSS!
(all sales final.)
Bleh.

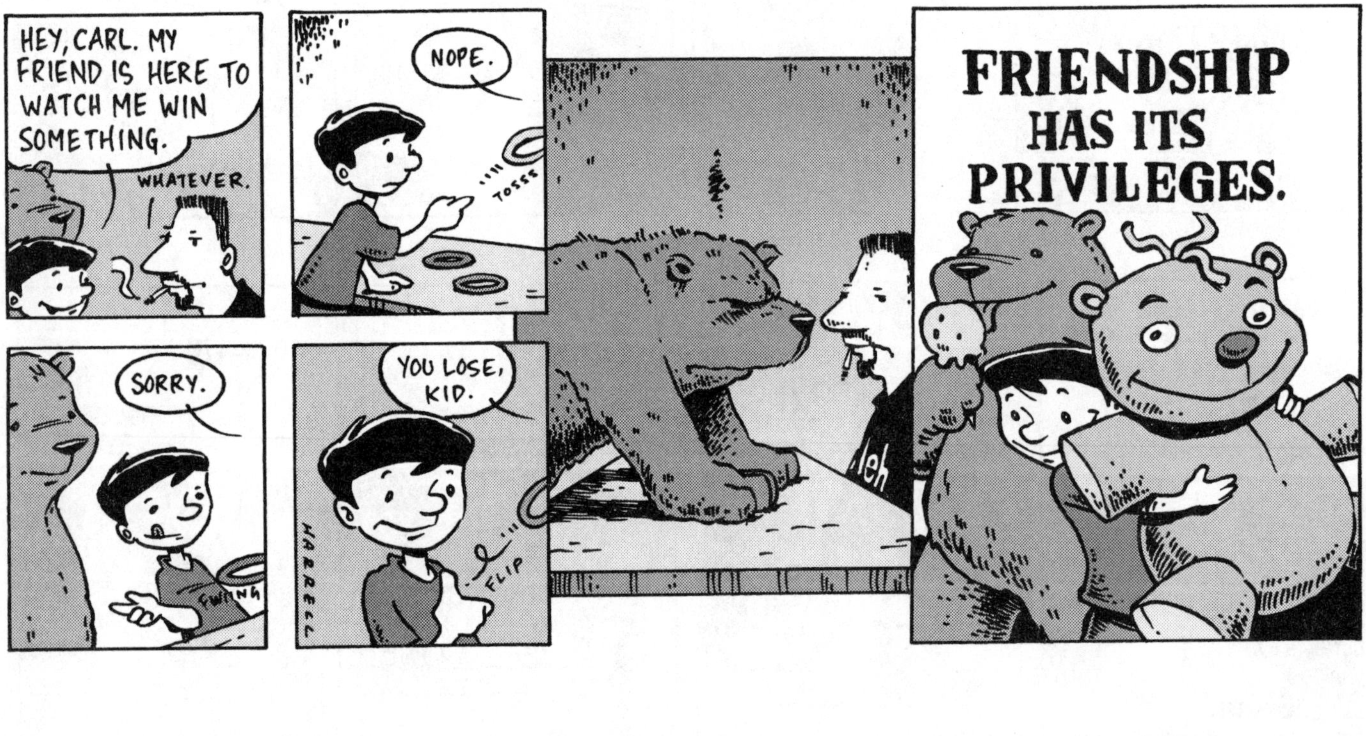
HEY, CARL. MY FRIEND IS HERE TO WATCH ME WIN SOMETHING.
WHATEVER.
NOPE.
TOSSS
SORRY.
SWING
YOU LOSE, KID.
FLIP
HARRELL
leh
FRIENDSHIP HAS ITS PRIVILEGES.

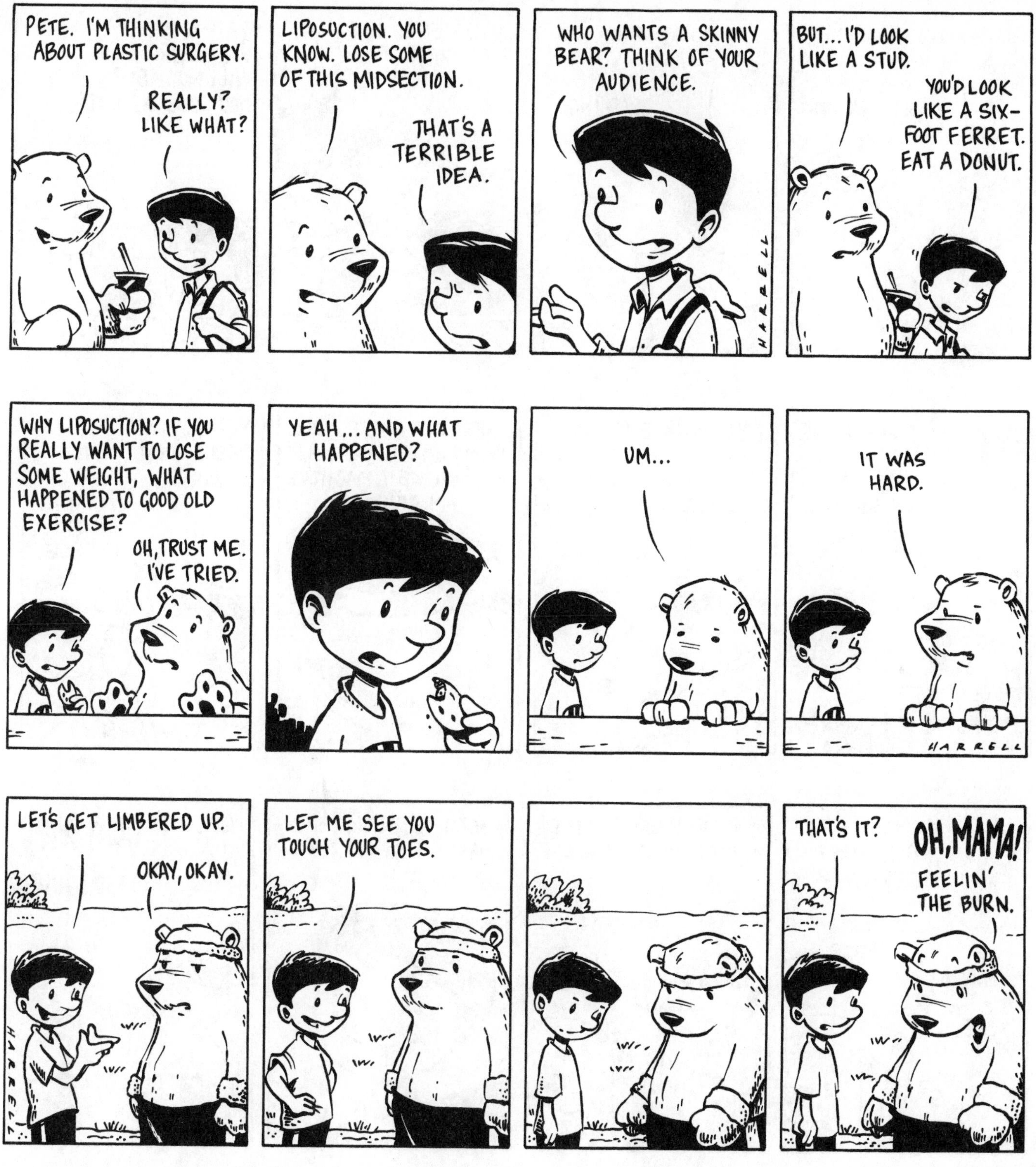
PETE. I'M THINKING ABOUT PLASTIC SURGERY.
REALLY? LIKE WHAT?
LIPOSUCTION. YOU KNOW. LOSE SOME OF THIS MIDSECTION.
THAT'S A TERRIBLE IDEA.
WHO WANTS A SKINNY BEAR? THINK OF YOUR AUDIENCE.
HARRELL
BUT... I'D LOOK LIKE A STUD.
YOU'D LOOK LIKE A SIX-FOOT FERRET. EAT A DONUT.
WHY LIPOSUCTION? IF YOU REALLY WANT TO LOSE SOME WEIGHT, WHAT HAPPENED TO GOOD OLD EXERCISE?
OH, TRUST ME. I'VE TRIED.
YEAH... AND WHAT HAPPENED?
UM...
IT WAS HARD.
HARRELL
LET'S GET LIMBERED UP.
OKAY, OKAY.
HARRELL
LET ME SEE YOU TOUCH YOUR TOES.
THAT'S IT?
OH, MAMA!
FEELIN' THE BURN.

THAT'S ENOUGH STRETCHING. YOU READY TO RUN?
SURE. WHY NOT?
WAIT. WHAT'S THAT IN YOUR BAG?
NOTHING.
A WRAPPER? HOW MANY OF THESE..?
HARRELL
EATING TWENTY-FIVE POWER BARS WILL NOT HELP YOU LOSE WEIGHT!
NO. BUT I'VE GOT A PRETTY GOOD BUZZ.
OKAY. HOW'S THAT FEELING?
WELL, MY KNEES HURT.
MY LUNGS ARE ACHING...
THERE'S A SHARP PAIN IN MY ANKLE AND WHAT FEELS LIKE A MACHETE IN MY SIDE.
HARRELL
YEAH, BUT IT FEELS GOOD, RIGHT?
OH. NOW I'M URKING UP MY COFFEE.
HEY, WINK. THAT WAS A PRETTY GOOD FIRST RUN YESTERDAY.
THANKS, PETE.
YOU FEELING A LITTLE BETTER ABOUT YOURSELF?
OH, YEAH. GREAT.
YEAH. RUNNING JUST MAKES YOU FEEL MORE ALIVE...
HARRELL
YOU SORE AT ALL?
DON'T TOUCH! DON'T TOUCH!

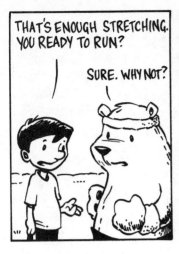

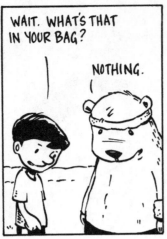

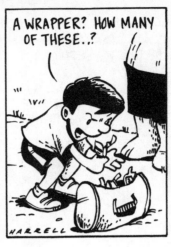

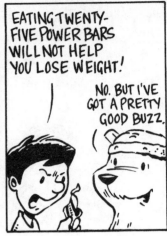

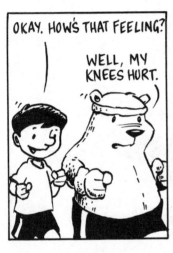

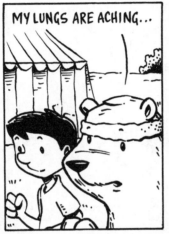

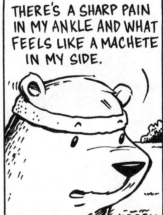

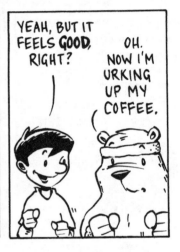

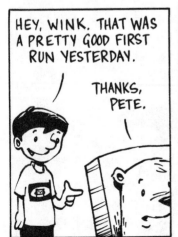

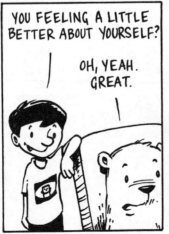

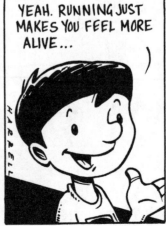

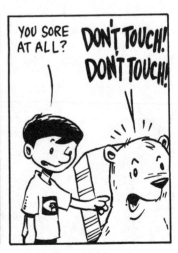

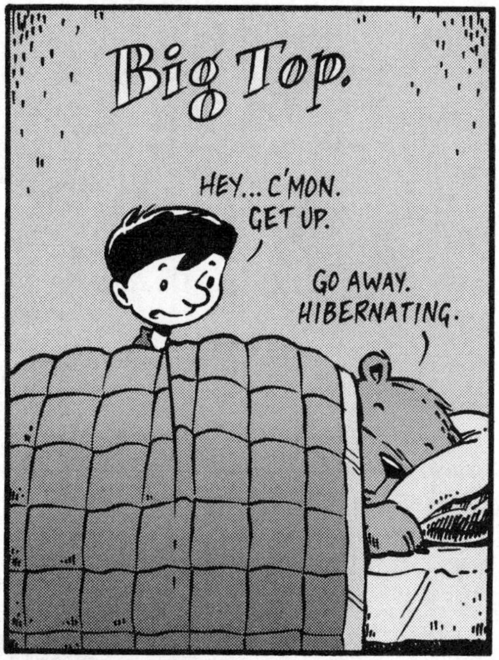
Big Top.
HEY... C'MON. GET UP.
GO AWAY. HIBERNATING.

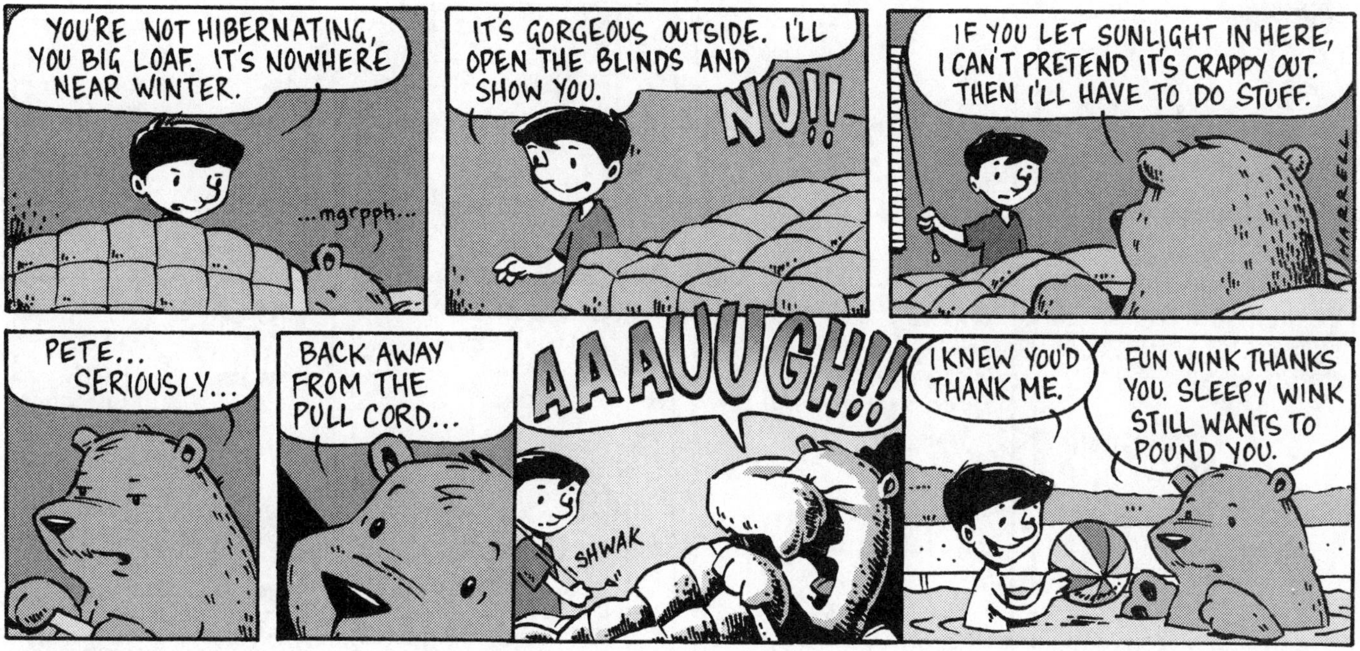
YOU'RE NOT HIBERNATING, YOU BIG LOAF. IT'S NOWHERE NEAR WINTER.
...mgrpph...
IT'S GORGEOUS OUTSIDE. I'LL OPEN THE BLINDS AND SHOW YOU.
NO!!
IF YOU LET SUNLIGHT IN HERE, I CAN'T PRETEND IT'S CRAPPY OUT. THEN I'LL HAVE TO DO STUFF.
HARRELL
PETE... SERIOUSLY...
BACK AWAY FROM THE PULL CORD...
AAAUUGH!!
SHWAK
I KNEW YOU'D THANK ME.
FUN WINK THANKS YOU. SLEEPY WINK STILL WANTS TO POUND YOU.

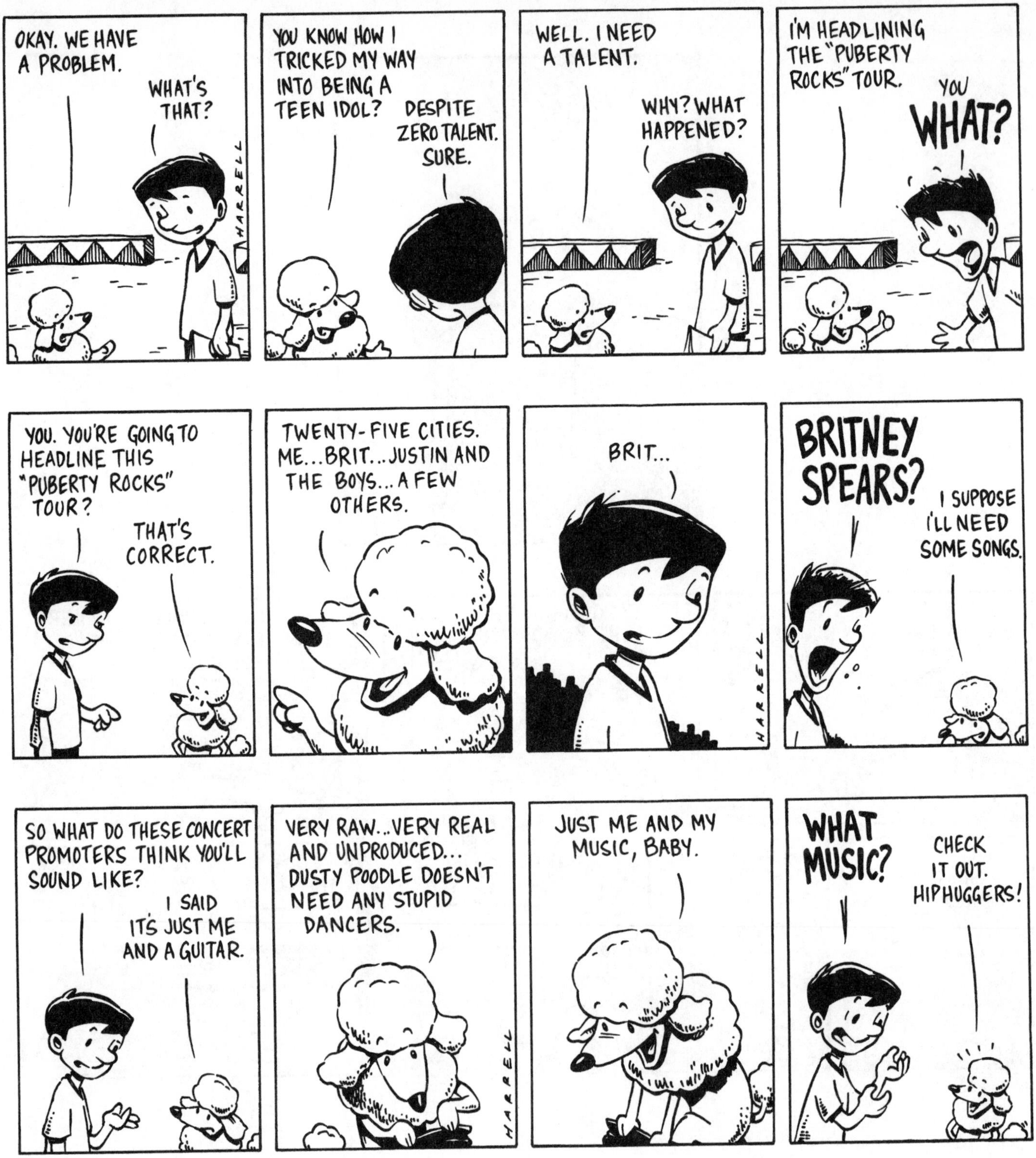
OKAY. WE HAVE A PROBLEM.
WHAT'S THAT?
HARRELL
YOU KNOW HOW I TRICKED MY WAY INTO BEING A TEEN IDOL?
DESPITE ZERO TALENT. SURE.
WELL. I NEED A TALENT.
WHY? WHAT HAPPENED?
I'M HEADLINING THE "PUBERTY ROCKS" TOUR.
YOU WHAT?
YOU. YOU'RE GOING TO HEADLINE THIS "PUBERTY ROCKS" TOUR?
THAT'S CORRECT.
TWENTY-FIVE CITIES. ME...BRIT...JUSTIN AND THE BOYS...A FEW OTHERS.
BRIT...
HARRELL
BRITNEY SPEARS?
I SUPPOSE I'LL NEED SOME SONGS.
SO WHAT DO THESE CONCERT PROMOTERS THINK YOU'LL SOUND LIKE?
I SAID IT'S JUST ME AND A GUITAR.
VERY RAW...VERY REAL AND UNPRODUCED... DUSTY POODLE DOESN'T NEED ANY STUPID DANCERS.
HARRELL
JUST ME AND MY MUSIC, BABY.
WHAT MUSIC?
CHECK IT OUT. HIPHUGGERS!

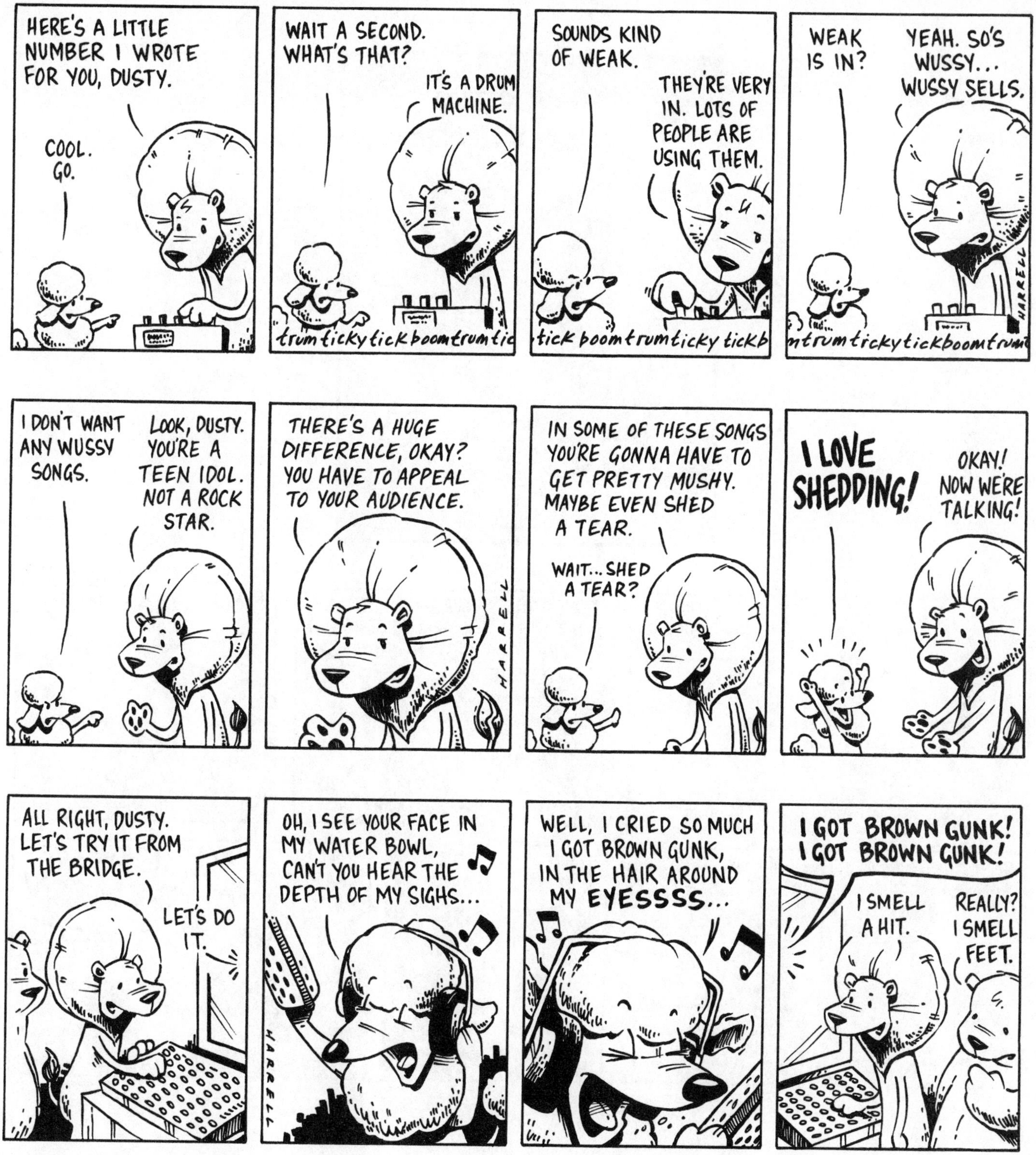
HERE'S A LITTLE NUMBER I WROTE FOR YOU, DUSTY.
COOL. GO.
trumtickytickboomtrumtic
WAIT A SECOND. WHAT'S THAT?
IT'S A DRUM MACHINE.
tickboomtrumtickytickb
SOUNDS KIND OF WEAK.
THEY'RE VERY IN. LOTS OF PEOPLE ARE USING THEM.
mtrumtickytickboomtrum
WEAK IS IN?
YEAH. SO'S WUSSY... WUSSY SELLS.
HARRELL
I DON'T WANT ANY WUSSY SONGS.
LOOK, DUSTY. YOU'RE A TEEN IDOL. NOT A ROCK STAR.
THERE'S A HUGE DIFFERENCE, OKAY? YOU HAVE TO APPEAL TO YOUR AUDIENCE.
HARRELL
IN SOME OF THESE SONGS YOU'RE GONNA HAVE TO GET PRETTY MUSHY. MAYBE EVEN SHED A TEAR.
WAIT... SHED A TEAR?
I LOVE SHEDDING!
OKAY! NOW WE'RE TALKING!
ALL RIGHT, DUSTY. LET'S TRY IT FROM THE BRIDGE.
LET'S DO IT.
OH, I SEE YOUR FACE IN MY WATER BOWL, CAN'T YOU HEAR THE DEPTH OF MY SIGHS...
HARRELL
WELL, I CRIED SO MUCH I GOT BROWN GUNK, IN THE HAIR AROUND MY EYESSSS...
I GOT BROWN GUNK! I GOT BROWN GUNK!
I SMELL A HIT.
REALLY? I SMELL FEET.

BIG TOP

JUST GRAB ON AND START CLIMBING. IT'S EASY...
BUT... I DON'T HAVE THUMBS.
THAT'S ALL PROPAGANDA. YOU DON'T NEED THUMBS TO CLIMB A TREE. YOU JUST NEED THE DESIRE.
OH, I WANT TO.
OKAY... SEE... THERE YOU GO.
HEY! YOU'RE DOING IT!
I'M DOING IT!
SCOOT SCOOT
WHO SAYS DOGS CAN'T CLIMB TREES?
HA HA!! LOOK AT ME GO!!
WOW! I COULD DO THIS ALL DAY!
SCOOT
HOPE YOU'RE NOT SCARED OF HEIGHTS.
I'M KING OF THE WORLD!!
HARRELL

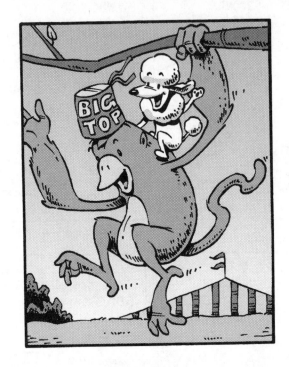

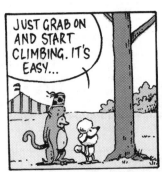

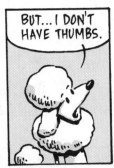

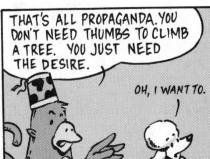

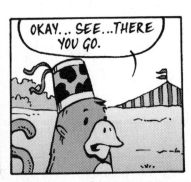

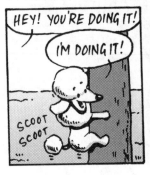

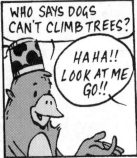

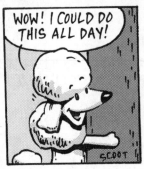

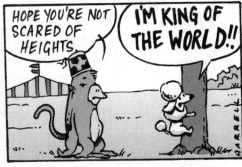

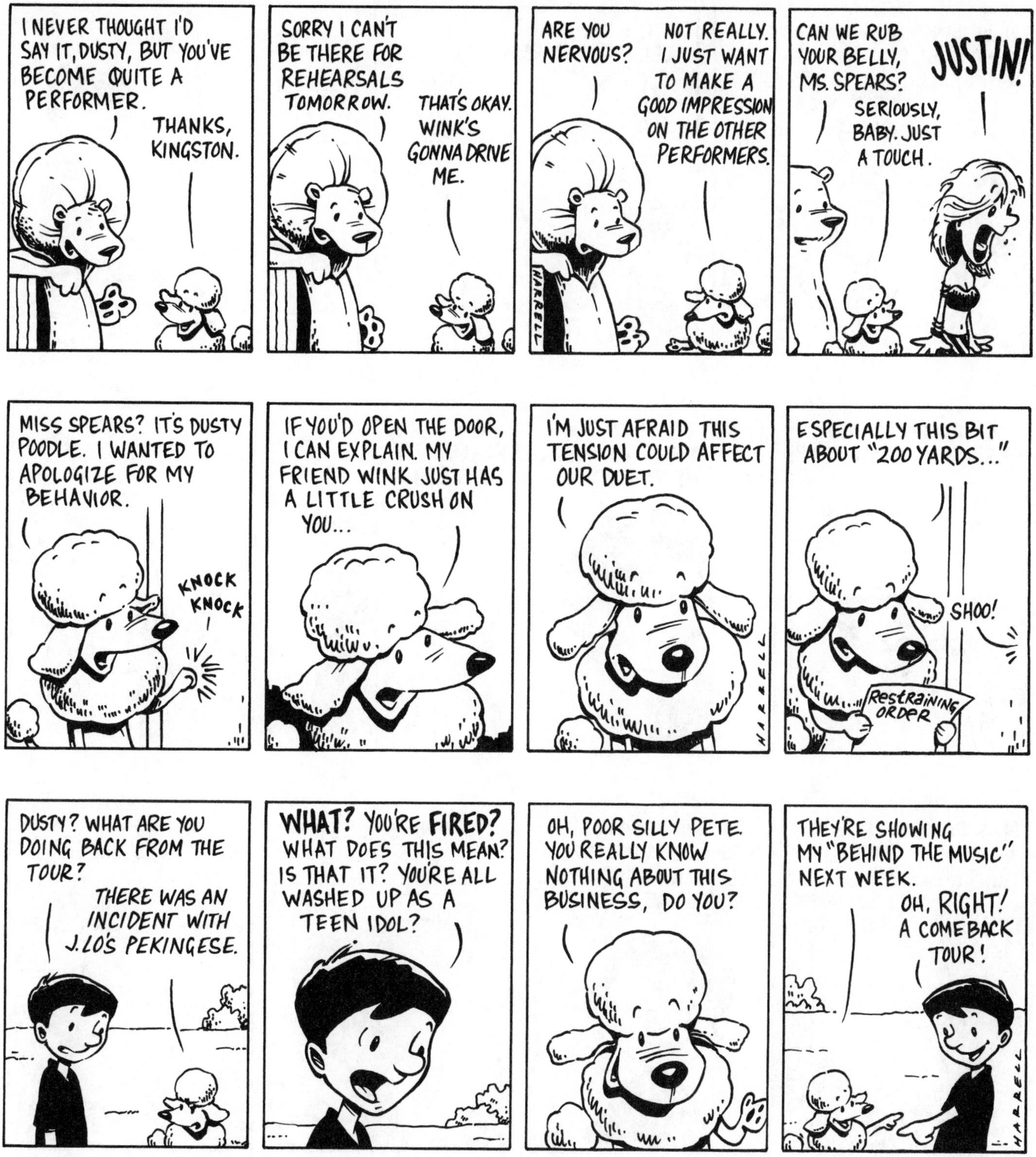
I NEVER THOUGHT I'D SAY IT, DUSTY, BUT YOU'VE BECOME QUITE A PERFORMER.
THANKS, KINGSTON.
SORRY I CAN'T BE THERE FOR REHEARSALS TOMORROW.
THAT'S OKAY. WINK'S GONNA DRIVE ME.
ARE YOU NERVOUS?
NOT REALLY. I JUST WANT TO MAKE A GOOD IMPRESSION ON THE OTHER PERFORMERS.
CAN WE RUB YOUR BELLY, MS. SPEARS?
SERIOUSLY, BABY. JUST A TOUCH.
JUSTIN!
HARRELL
MISS SPEARS? IT'S DUSTY POODLE. I WANTED TO APOLOGIZE FOR MY BEHAVIOR.
KNOCK KNOCK
IF YOU'D OPEN THE DOOR, I CAN EXPLAIN. MY FRIEND WINK JUST HAS A LITTLE CRUSH ON YOU...
I'M JUST AFRAID THIS TENSION COULD AFFECT OUR DUET.
ESPECIALLY THIS BIT ABOUT "200 YARDS..."
SHOO!
Restraining Order
HARRELL
DUSTY? WHAT ARE YOU DOING BACK FROM THE TOUR?
THERE WAS AN INCIDENT WITH J.LO'S PEKINGESE.
WHAT? YOU'RE FIRED? WHAT DOES THIS MEAN? IS THAT IT? YOU'RE ALL WASHED UP AS A TEEN IDOL?
OH, POOR SILLY PETE. YOU REALLY KNOW NOTHING ABOUT THIS BUSINESS, DO YOU?
THEY'RE SHOWING MY "BEHIND THE MUSIC" NEXT WEEK.
OH, RIGHT! A COMEBACK TOUR!
HARRELL

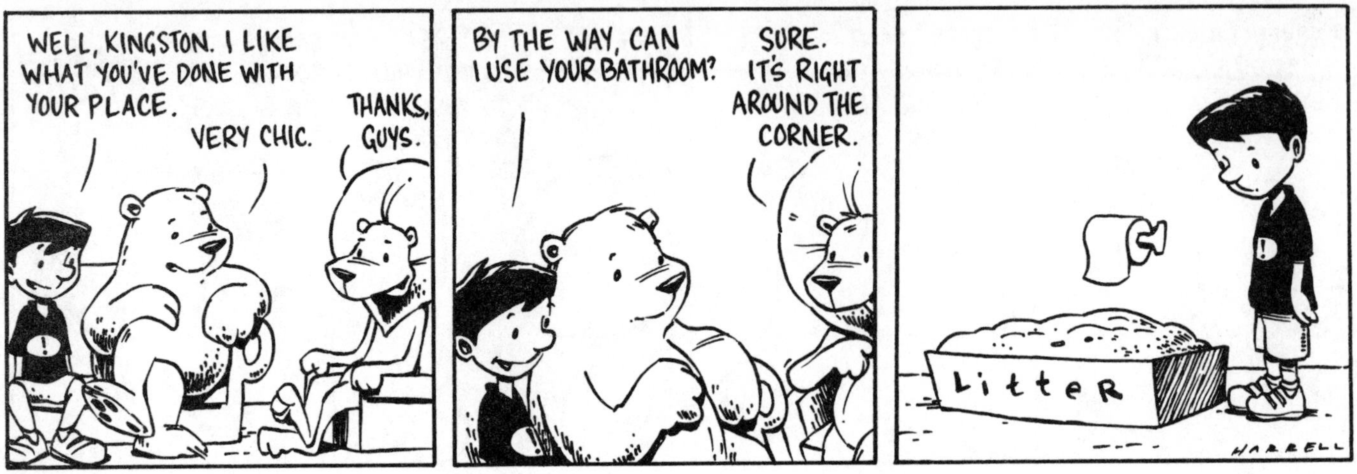
WELL, KINGSTON. I LIKE WHAT YOU'VE DONE WITH YOUR PLACE.
VERY CHIC.
THANKS, GUYS.
BY THE WAY, CAN I USE YOUR BATHROOM?
SURE. IT'S RIGHT AROUND THE CORNER.
LITTER
HARRELL

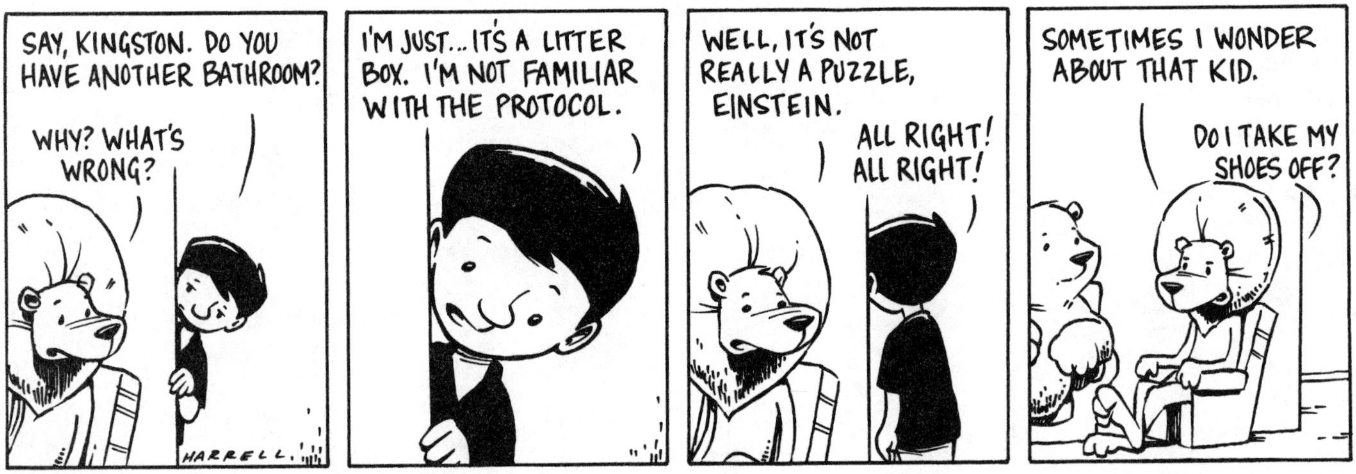
SAY, KINGSTON. DO YOU HAVE ANOTHER BATHROOM?
WHY? WHAT'S WRONG?
HARRELL
I'M JUST... IT'S A LITTER BOX. I'M NOT FAMILIAR WITH THE PROTOCOL.
WELL, IT'S NOT REALLY A PUZZLE, EINSTEIN.
ALL RIGHT! ALL RIGHT!
SOMETIMES I WONDER ABOUT THAT KID.
DO I TAKE MY SHOES OFF?

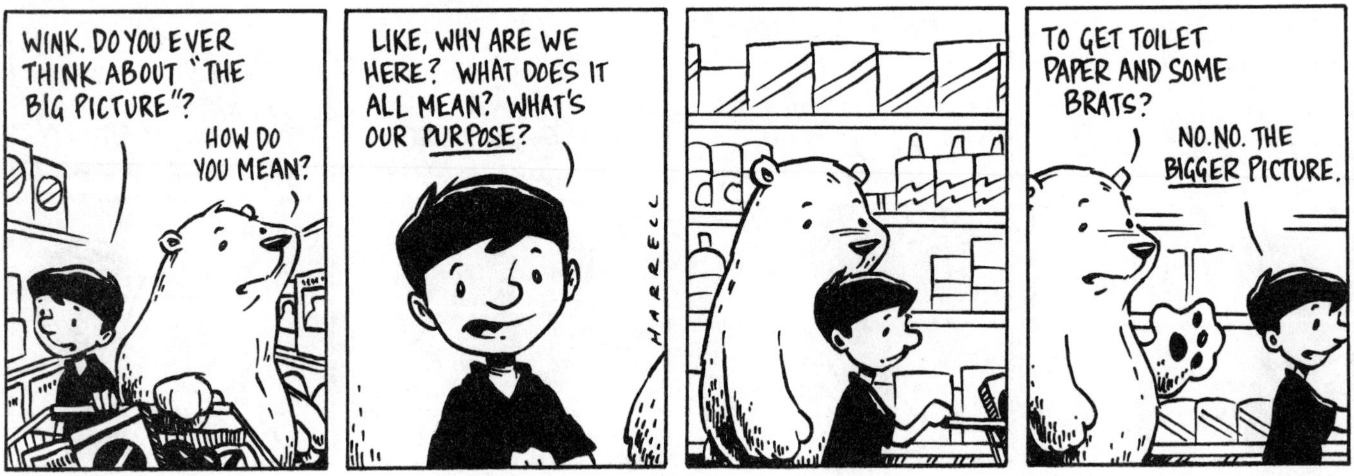
WINK. DO YOU EVER THINK ABOUT "THE BIG PICTURE"?
HOW DO YOU MEAN?
LIKE, WHY ARE WE HERE? WHAT DOES IT ALL MEAN? WHAT'S OUR PURPOSE?
HARRELL
TO GET TOILET PAPER AND SOME BRATS?
NO. NO. THE BIGGER PICTURE.

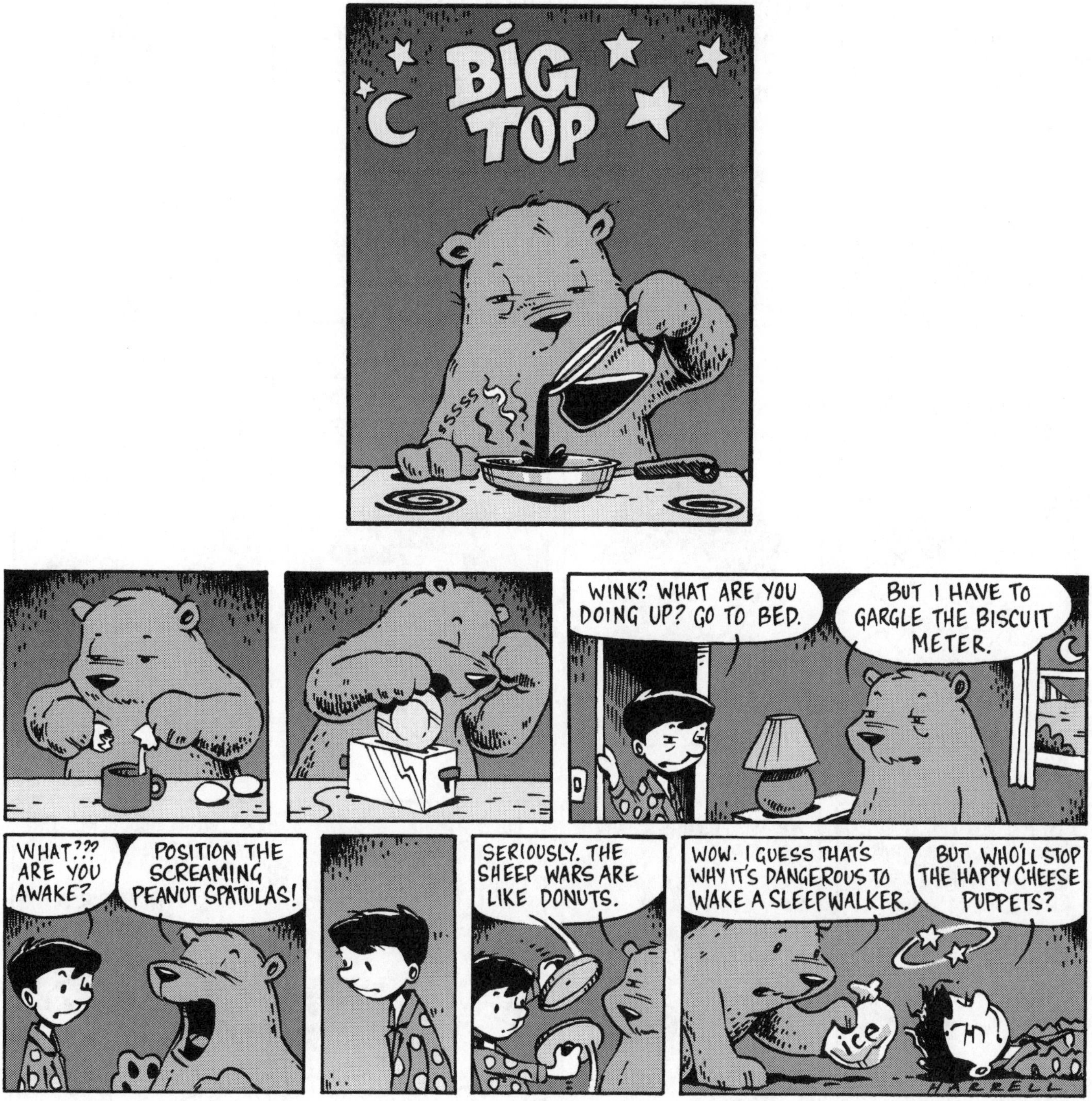
BIG TOP
SSSSS
WINK? WHAT ARE YOU DOING UP? GO TO BED.
BUT I HAVE TO GARGLE THE BISCUIT METER.
WHAT??? ARE YOU AWAKE?
POSITION THE SCREAMING PEANUT SPATULAS!
SERIOUSLY. THE SHEEP WARS ARE LIKE DONUTS.
WOW. I GUESS THAT'S WHY IT'S DANGEROUS TO WAKE A SLEEPWALKER.
BUT, WHO'LL STOP THE HAPPY CHEESE PUPPETS?
ice
HARRELL

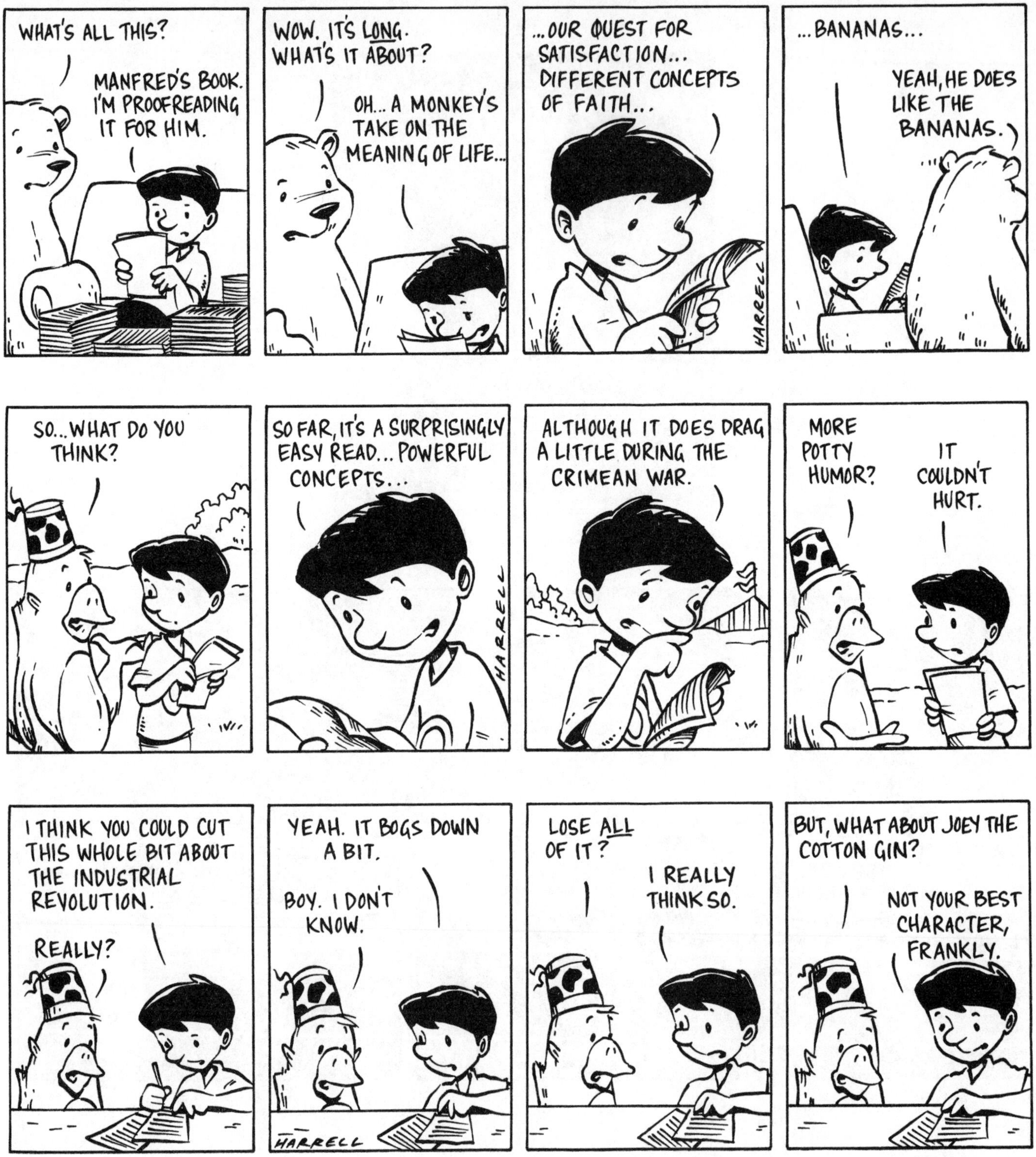
WHAT'S ALL THIS?
MANFRED'S BOOK. I'M PROOFREADING IT FOR HIM.
WOW. IT'S LONG. WHAT'S IT ABOUT?
OH... A MONKEY'S TAKE ON THE MEANING OF LIFE...
...OUR QUEST FOR SATISFACTION... DIFFERENT CONCEPTS OF FAITH...
...BANANAS...
YEAH, HE DOES LIKE THE BANANAS.
HARRELL
SO... WHAT DO YOU THINK?
SO FAR, IT'S A SURPRISINGLY EASY READ... POWERFUL CONCEPTS...
ALTHOUGH IT DOES DRAG A LITTLE DURING THE CRIMEAN WAR.
MORE POTTY HUMOR?
IT COULDN'T HURT.
HARRELL
I THINK YOU COULD CUT THIS WHOLE BIT ABOUT THE INDUSTRIAL REVOLUTION.
REALLY?
YEAH. IT BOGS DOWN A BIT.
BOY. I DON'T KNOW.
LOSE ALL OF IT?
I REALLY THINK SO.
BUT, WHAT ABOUT JOEY THE COTTON GIN?
NOT YOUR BEST CHARACTER, FRANKLY.
HARRELL

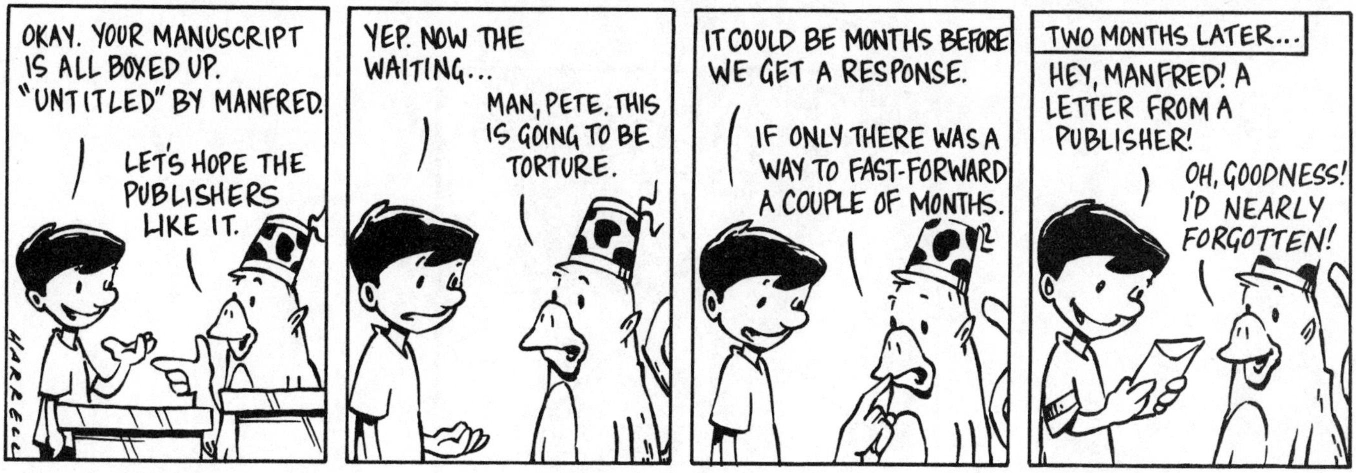
OKAY. YOUR MANUSCRIPT IS ALL BOXED UP. "UNTITLED" BY MANFRED.
LET'S HOPE THE PUBLISHERS LIKE IT.
HARRELL
YEP. NOW THE WAITING...
MAN, PETE. THIS IS GOING TO BE TORTURE.
IT COULD BE MONTHS BEFORE WE GET A RESPONSE.
IF ONLY THERE WAS A WAY TO FAST-FORWARD A COUPLE OF MONTHS.
TWO MONTHS LATER...
HEY, MANFRED! A LETTER FROM A PUBLISHER!
OH, GOODNESS! I'D NEARLY FORGOTTEN!

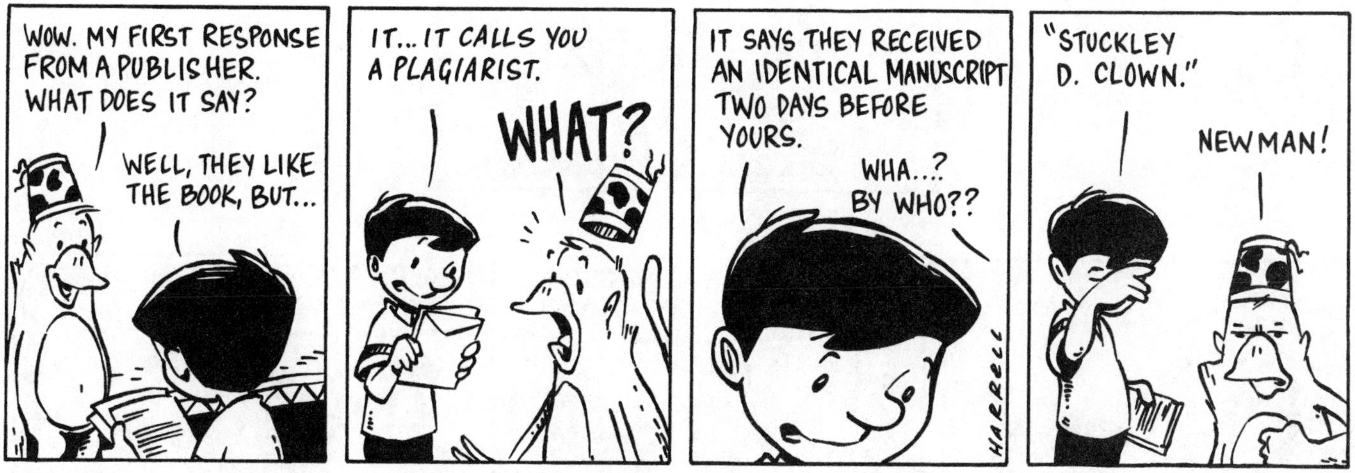
WOW. MY FIRST RESPONSE FROM A PUBLISHER. WHAT DOES IT SAY?
WELL, THEY LIKE THE BOOK, BUT...
IT... IT CALLS YOU A PLAGIARIST.
WHAT?
IT SAYS THEY RECEIVED AN IDENTICAL MANUSCRIPT TWO DAYS BEFORE YOURS.
WHA...? BY WHO??
HARRELL
"STUCKLEY D. CLOWN."
NEWMAN!

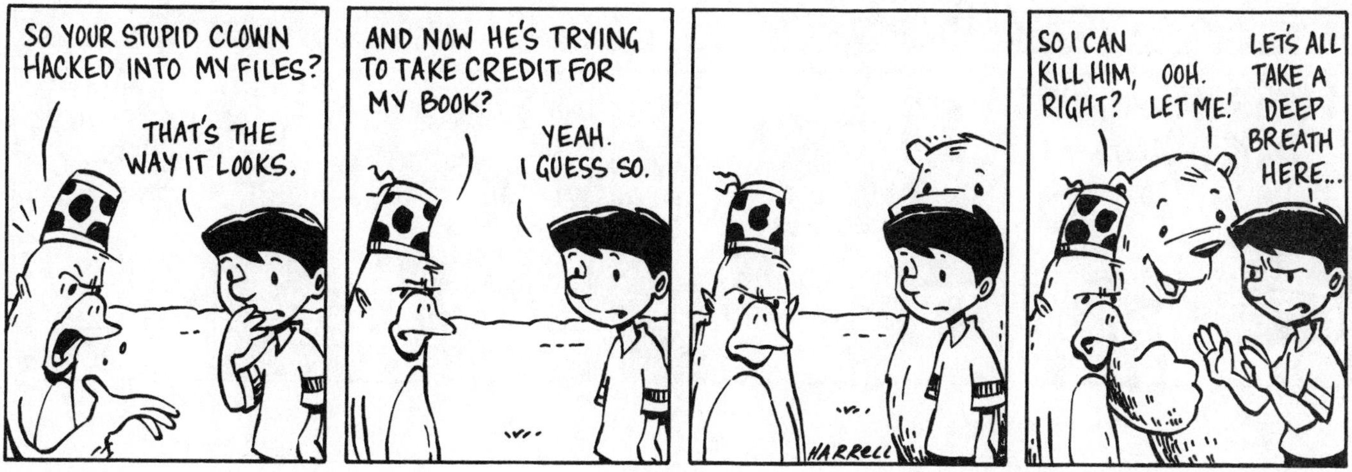
SO YOUR STUPID CLOWN HACKED INTO MY FILES?
THAT'S THE WAY IT LOOKS.
AND NOW HE'S TRYING TO TAKE CREDIT FOR MY BOOK?
YEAH. I GUESS SO.
HARRELL
SO I CAN KILL HIM, RIGHT?
OOH. LET ME!
LET'S ALL TAKE A DEEP BREATH HERE...

BIG TOP!
UH-OH.
TAP
TAP

BA DA
BUM BUM
WINK. CUT IT OUT.
YOU'RE DRIVING ME NUTS! QUIT DANCING AROUND!
SORRY, BUDDY. LISTEN TO THAT BEAT! NO WAY I CAN SIT STILL!
I GOTS THE DANCE IN MY PANTS!!
HMM
HMMM
HIP OR SHOULDER?
FIVE MORE MINUTES! I'VE GOT A FUNKY THING GOING ON HERE.
TRANQUIL DARTS
HARRELL

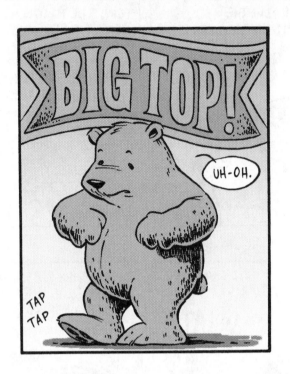

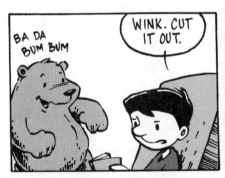

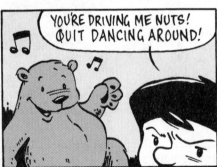

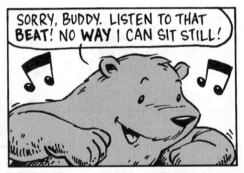

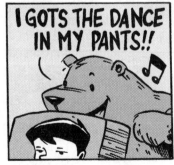

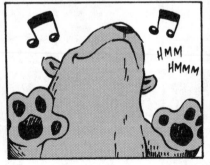

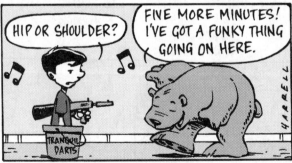

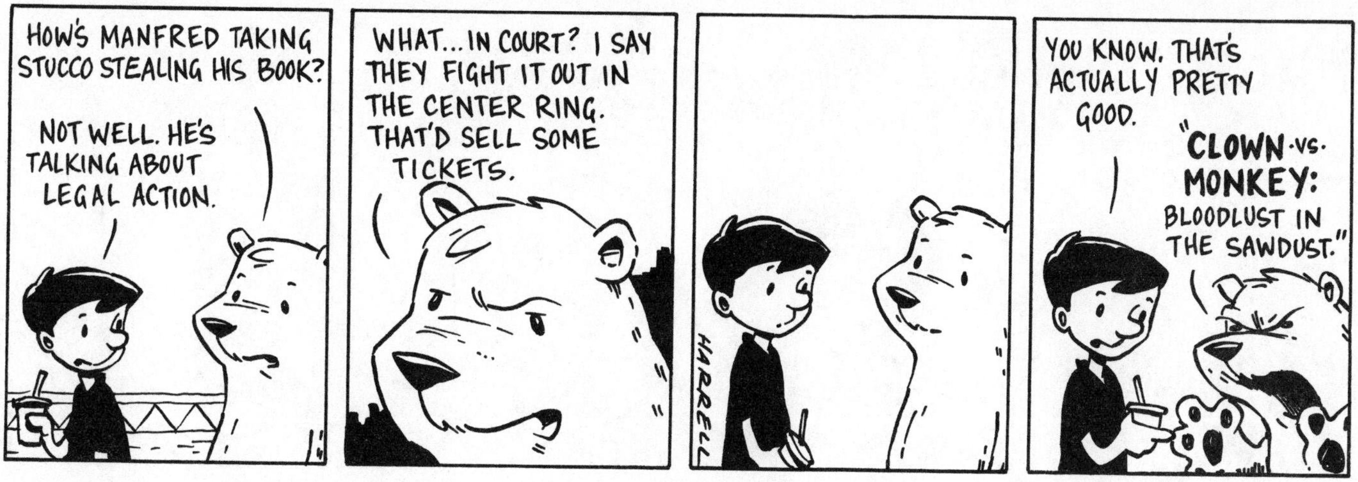
HOW'S MANFRED TAKING STUCCO STEALING HIS BOOK?
NOT WELL. HE'S TALKING ABOUT LEGAL ACTION.
WHAT... IN COURT? I SAY THEY FIGHT IT OUT IN THE CENTER RING. THAT'D SELL SOME TICKETS.
HARRELL
YOU KNOW, THAT'S ACTUALLY PRETTY GOOD.
"CLOWN ·VS· MONKEY: BLOODLUST IN THE SAWDUST."

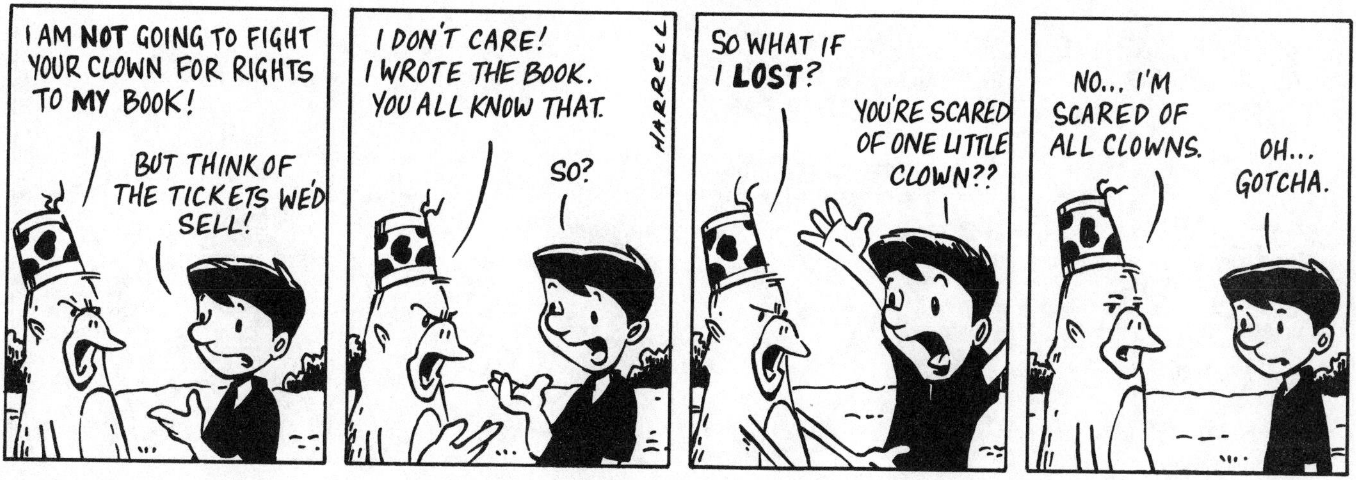
I AM NOT GOING TO FIGHT YOUR CLOWN FOR RIGHTS TO MY BOOK!
BUT THINK OF THE TICKETS WE'D SELL!
I DON'T CARE! I WROTE THE BOOK. YOU ALL KNOW THAT.
SO?
HARRELL
SO WHAT IF I LOST?
YOU'RE SCARED OF ONE LITTLE CLOWN??
NO... I'M SCARED OF ALL CLOWNS.
OH... GOTCHA.

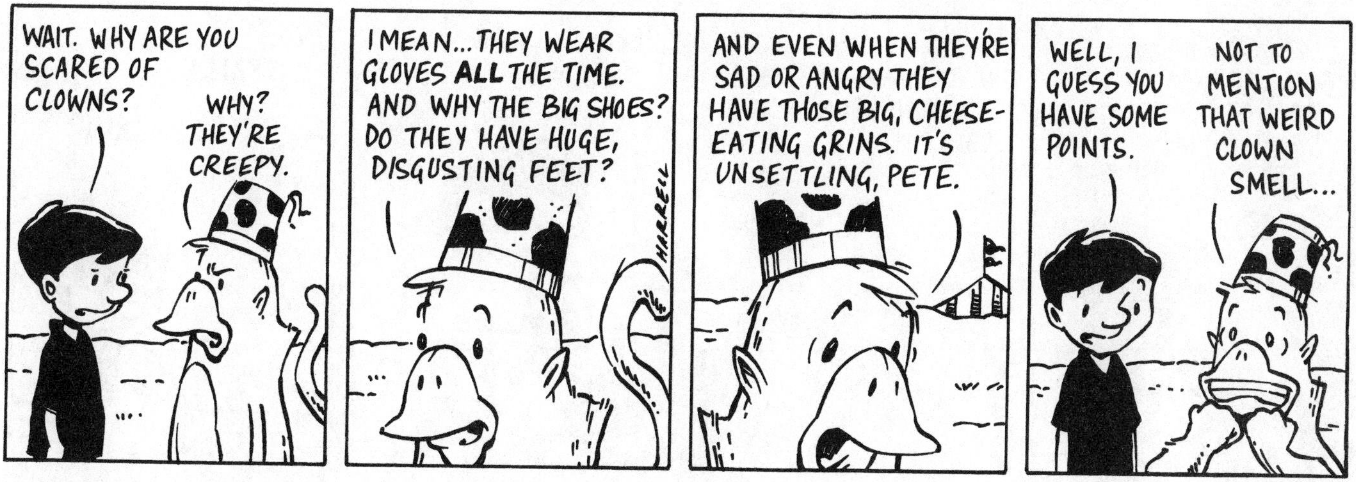
WAIT. WHY ARE YOU SCARED OF CLOWNS?
WHY? THEY'RE CREEPY.
I MEAN... THEY WEAR GLOVES ALL THE TIME. AND WHY THE BIG SHOES? DO THEY HAVE HUGE, DISGUSTING FEET?
HARRELL
AND EVEN WHEN THEY'RE SAD OR ANGRY THEY HAVE THOSE BIG, CHEESE-EATING GRINS. IT'S UNSETTLING, PETE.
WELL, I GUESS YOU HAVE SOME POINTS.
NOT TO MENTION THAT WEIRD CLOWN SMELL...

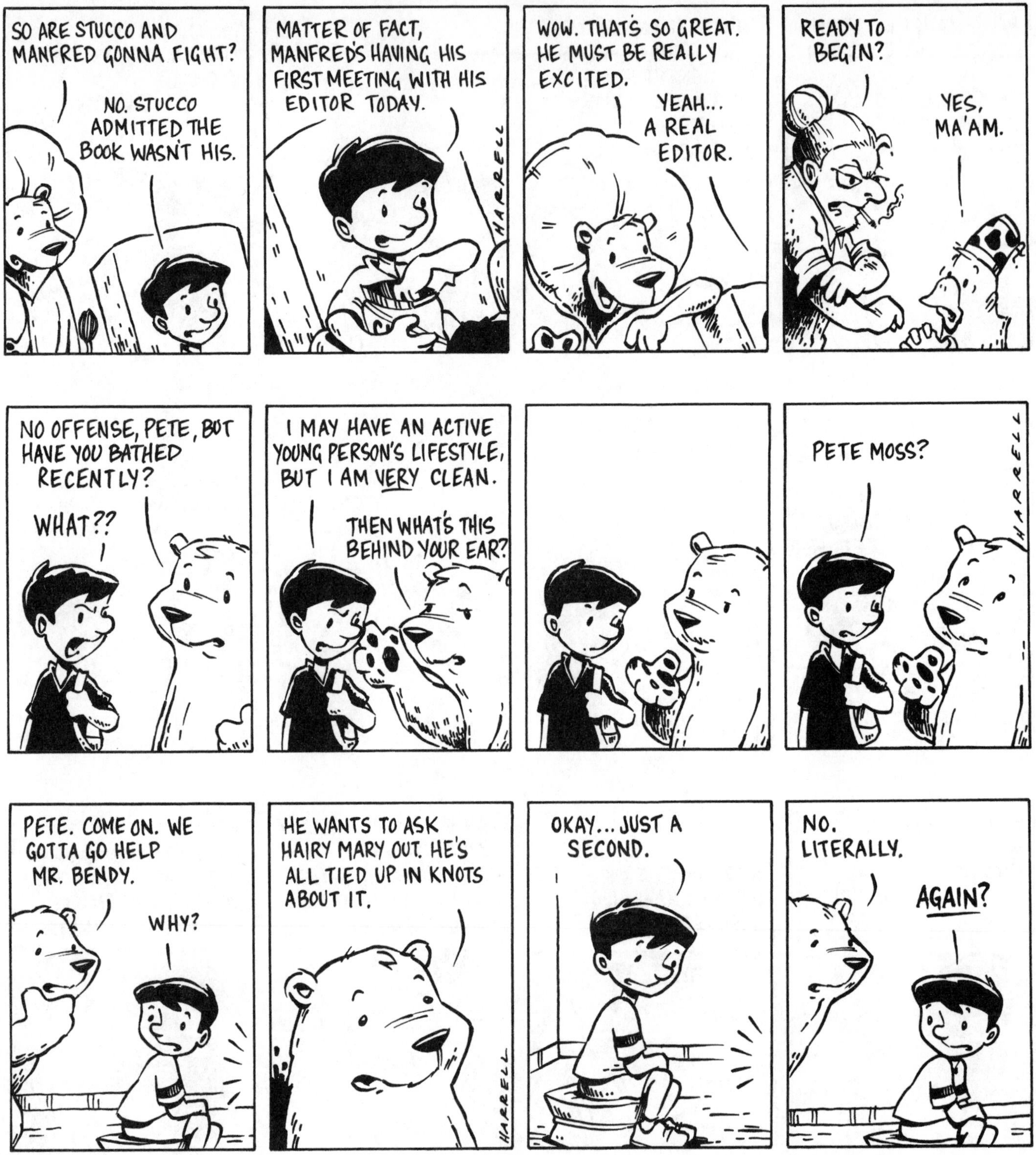
SO ARE STUCCO AND MANFRED GONNA FIGHT?
NO. STUCCO ADMITTED THE BOOK WASN'T HIS.
MATTER OF FACT, MANFRED'S HAVING HIS FIRST MEETING WITH HIS EDITOR TODAY.
HARRELL
WOW. THAT'S SO GREAT. HE MUST BE REALLY EXCITED.
YEAH... A REAL EDITOR.
READY TO BEGIN?
YES, MA'AM.
NO OFFENSE, PETE, BUT HAVE YOU BATHED RECENTLY?
WHAT??
I MAY HAVE AN ACTIVE YOUNG PERSON'S LIFESTYLE, BUT I AM VERY CLEAN.
THEN WHAT'S THIS BEHIND YOUR EAR?
HARRELL
PETE MOSS?
PETE. COME ON. WE GOTTA GO HELP MR. BENDY.
WHY?
HE WANTS TO ASK HAIRY MARY OUT. HE'S ALL TIED UP IN KNOTS ABOUT IT.
HARRELL
OKAY... JUST A SECOND.
NO. LITERALLY.
AGAIN?

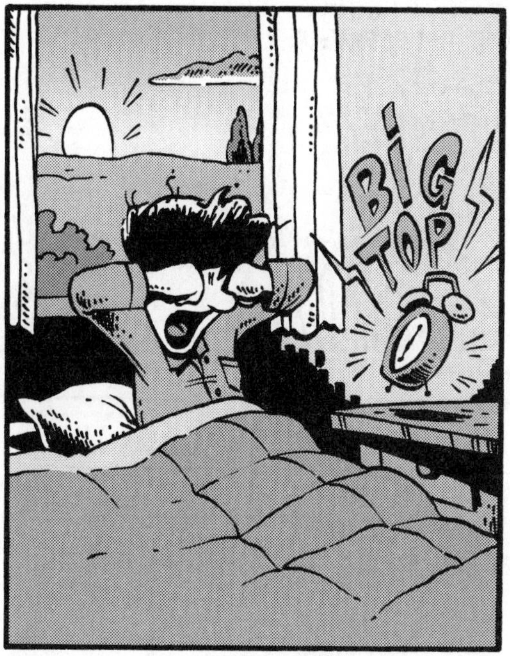
BIG TOP

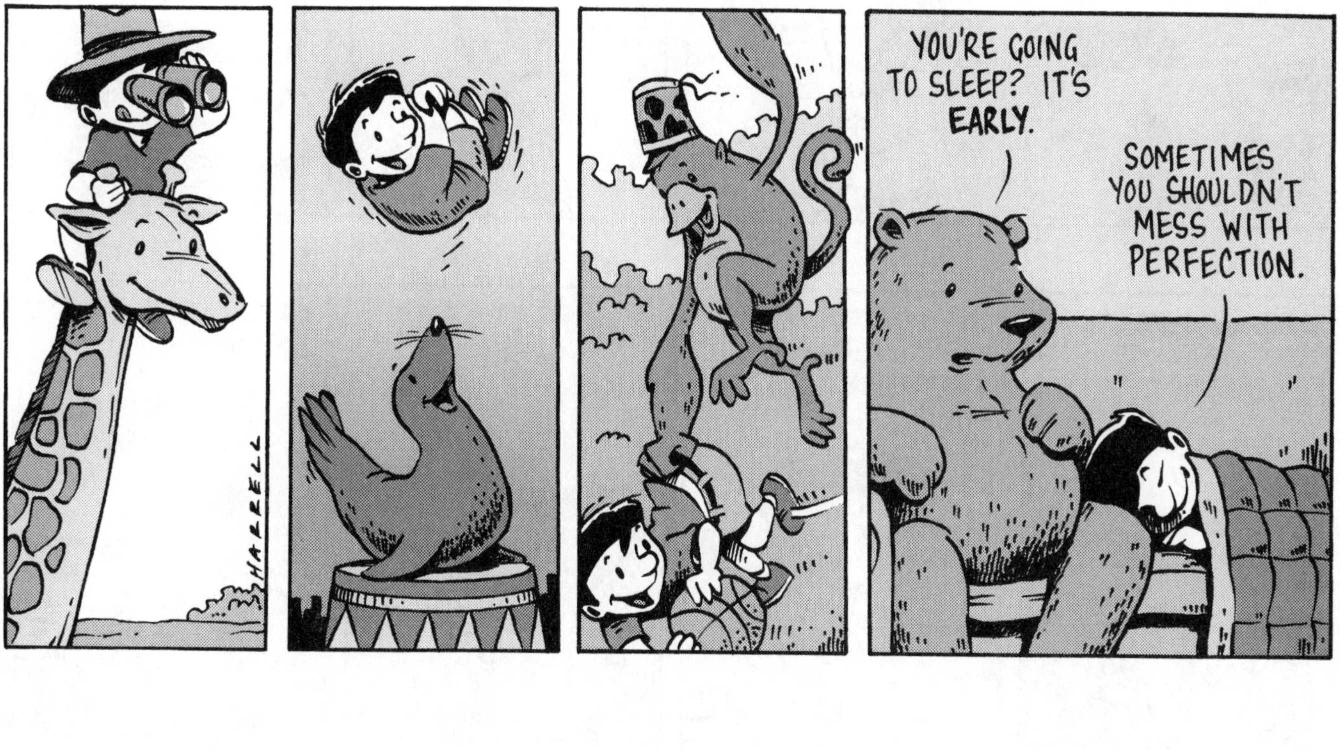
HARRELL
YOU'RE GOING TO SLEEP? IT'S **EARLY**.
SOMETIMES YOU SHOULDN'T MESS WITH PERFECTION.

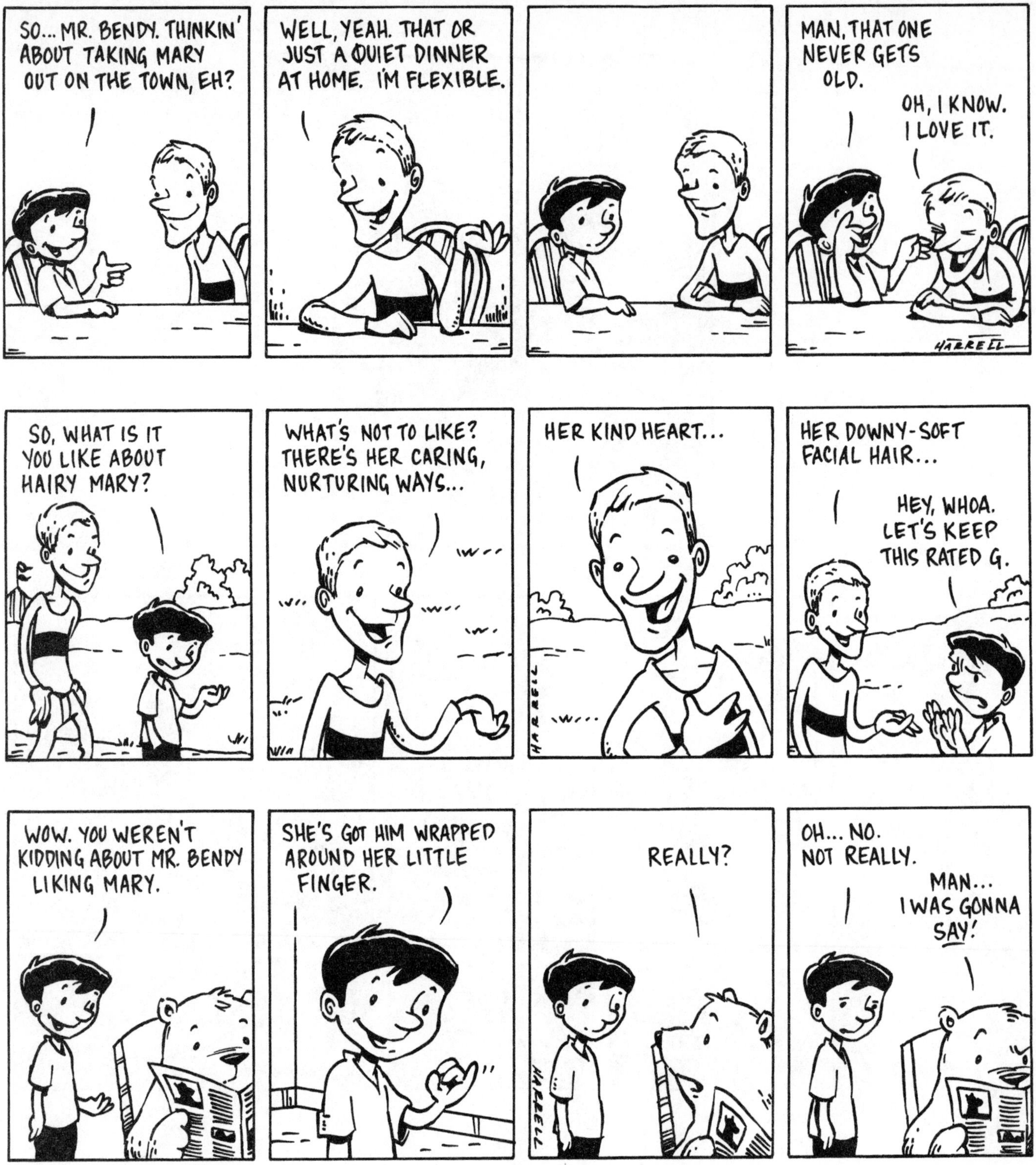
SO... MR. BENDY. THINKIN' ABOUT TAKING MARY OUT ON THE TOWN, EH?
WELL, YEAH. THAT OR JUST A QUIET DINNER AT HOME. I'M FLEXIBLE.
MAN, THAT ONE NEVER GETS OLD.
OH, I KNOW. I LOVE IT.
HARRELL
SO, WHAT IS IT YOU LIKE ABOUT HAIRY MARY?
WHAT'S NOT TO LIKE? THERE'S HER CARING, NURTURING WAYS...
HER KIND HEART...
HARRELL
HER DOWNY-SOFT FACIAL HAIR...
HEY, WHOA. LET'S KEEP THIS RATED G.
WOW. YOU WEREN'T KIDDING ABOUT MR. BENDY LIKING MARY.
SHE'S GOT HIM WRAPPED AROUND HER LITTLE FINGER.
REALLY?
HARRELL
OH... NO. NOT REALLY.
MAN... I WAS GONNA SAY!

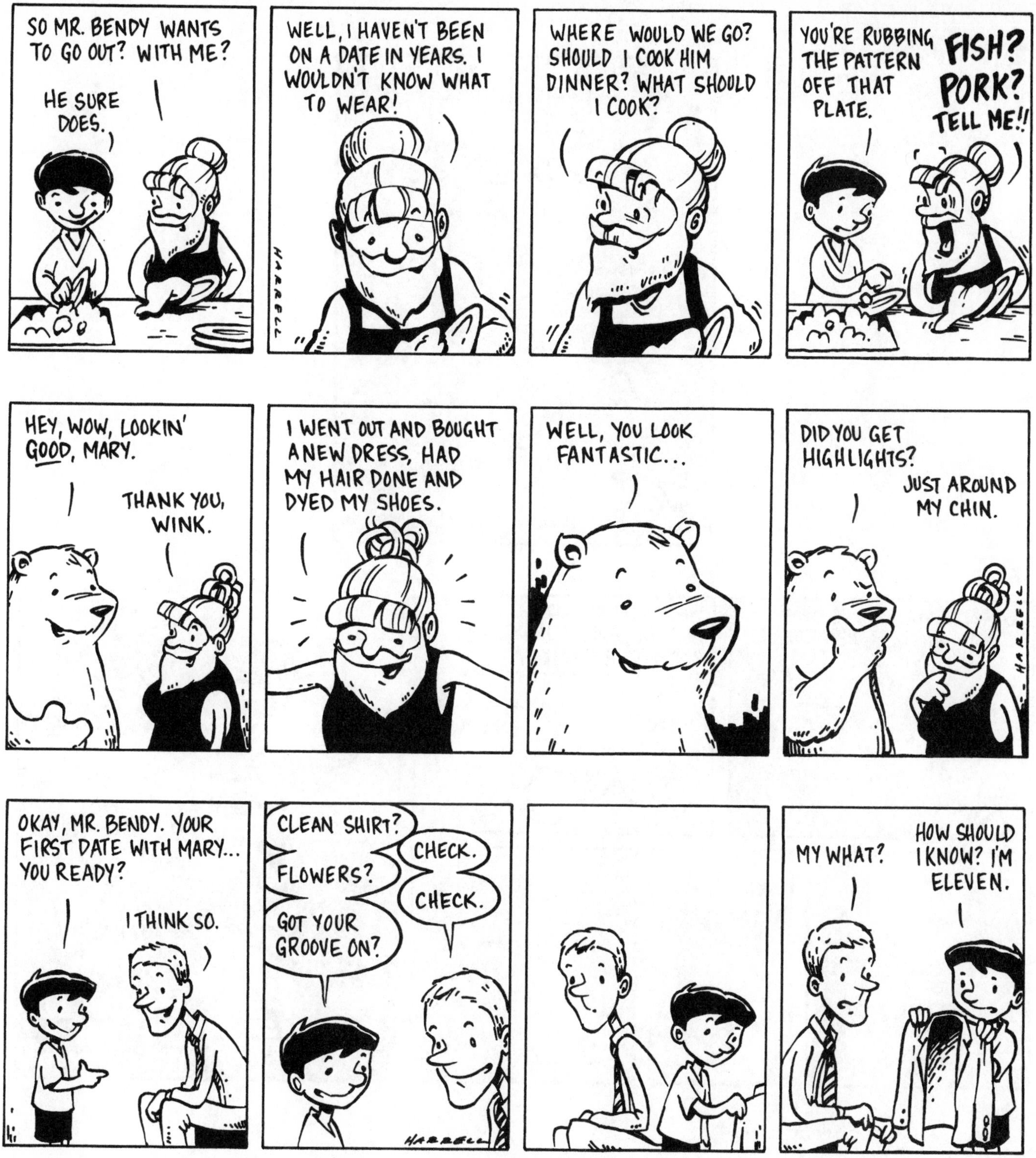
SO MR. BENDY WANTS TO GO OUT? WITH ME?
HE SURE DOES.
WELL, I HAVEN'T BEEN ON A DATE IN YEARS. I WOULDN'T KNOW WHAT TO WEAR!
HARRELL
WHERE WOULD WE GO? SHOULD I COOK HIM DINNER? WHAT SHOULD I COOK?
YOU'RE RUBBING THE PATTERN OFF THAT PLATE.
FISH? PORK? TELL ME!!
HEY, WOW, LOOKIN' GOOD, MARY.
THANK YOU, WINK.
I WENT OUT AND BOUGHT A NEW DRESS, HAD MY HAIR DONE AND DYED MY SHOES.
WELL, YOU LOOK FANTASTIC...
DID YOU GET HIGHLIGHTS?
JUST AROUND MY CHIN.
HARRELL
OKAY, MR. BENDY. YOUR FIRST DATE WITH MARY... YOU READY?
I THINK SO.
CLEAN SHIRT?
CHECK.
FLOWERS?
CHECK.
GOT YOUR GROOVE ON?
HARRELL
MY WHAT?
HOW SHOULD I KNOW? I'M ELEVEN.

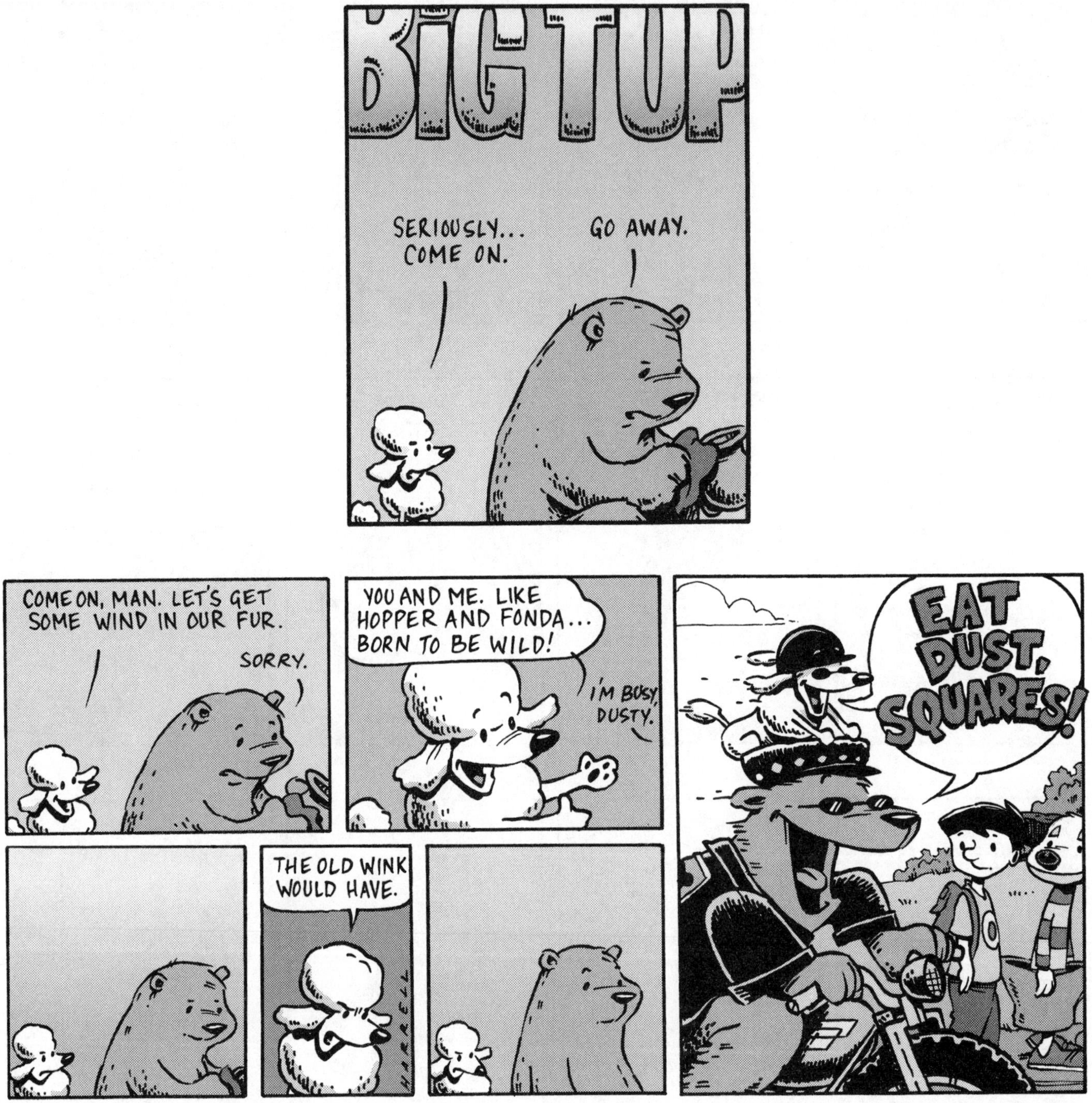
BIG TOP
SERIOUSLY... COME ON.
GO AWAY.
COME ON, MAN. LET'S GET SOME WIND IN OUR FUR.
SORRY.
YOU AND ME. LIKE HOPPER AND FONDA... BORN TO BE WILD!
I'M BUSY, DUSTY.
THE OLD WINK WOULD HAVE.
EAT DUST, SQUARES!

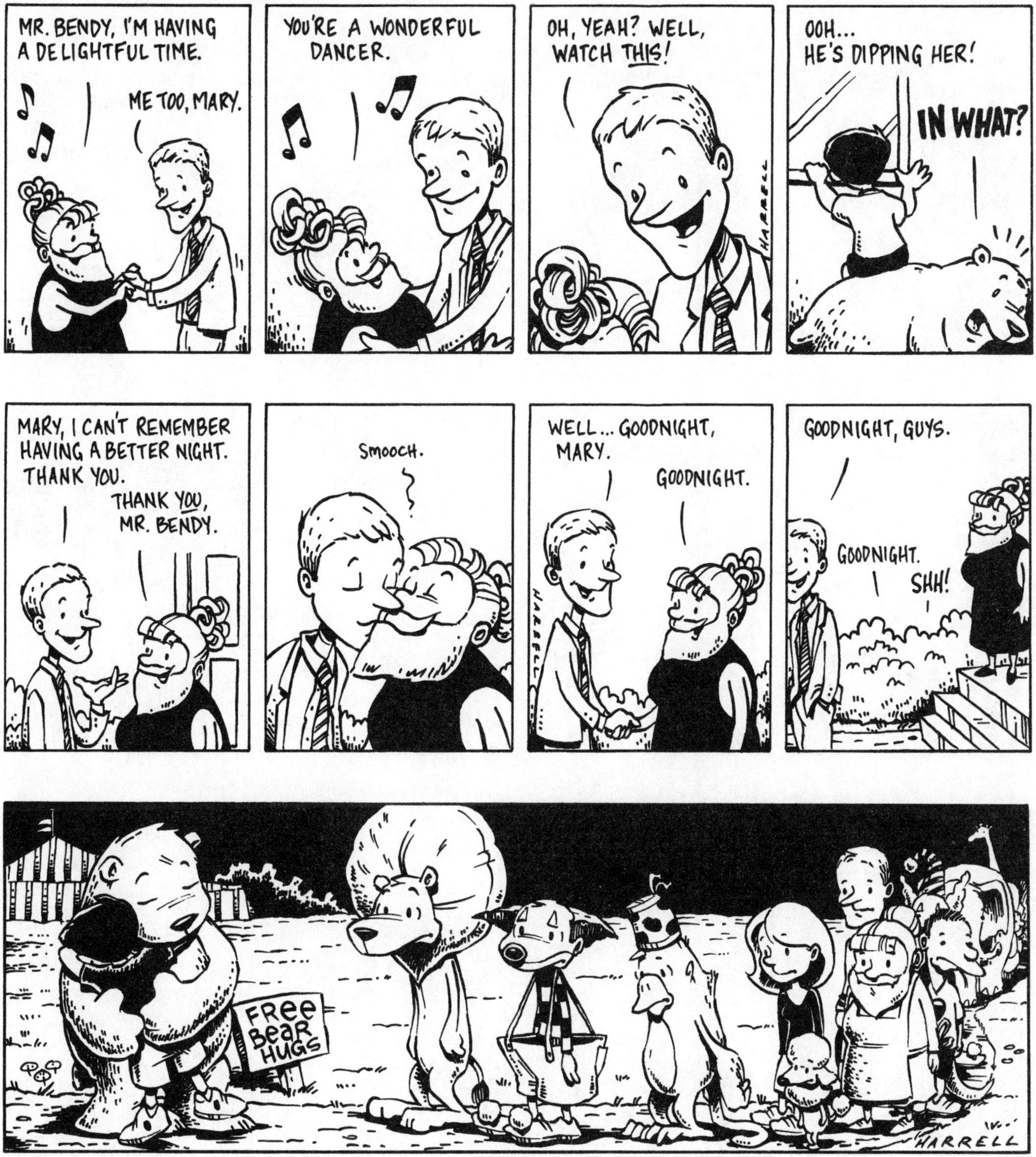
MR. BENDY, I'M HAVING A DELIGHTFUL TIME.
ME TOO, MARY.
YOU'RE A WONDERFUL DANCER.
OH, YEAH? WELL, WATCH THIS!
HARRELL
OOH... HE'S DIPPING HER!
IN WHAT?
MARY, I CAN'T REMEMBER HAVING A BETTER NIGHT. THANK YOU.
THANK YOU, MR. BENDY.
SMOOCH.
WELL... GOODNIGHT, MARY.
GOODNIGHT.
HARRELL
GOODNIGHT, GUYS.
GOODNIGHT.
SHH!
FREE BEAR HUGS
HARRELL

September 11, 2002

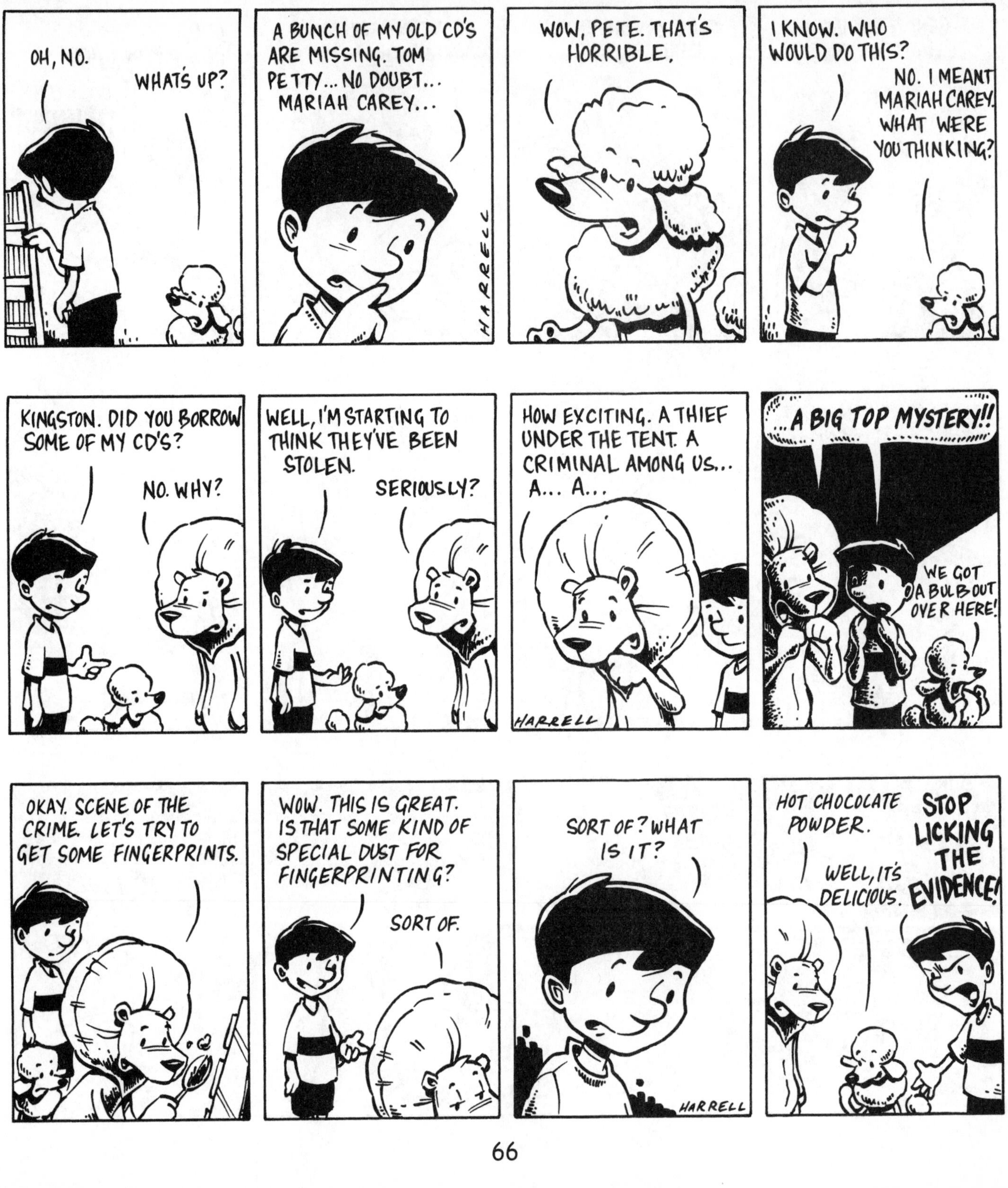
OH, NO.
WHAT'S UP?
A BUNCH OF MY OLD CD'S ARE MISSING. TOM PETTY... NO DOUBT... MARIAH CAREY...
HARRELL
WOW, PETE. THAT'S HORRIBLE.
I KNOW. WHO WOULD DO THIS?
NO. I MEANT MARIAH CAREY! WHAT WERE YOU THINKING?
KINGSTON. DID YOU BORROW SOME OF MY CD'S?
NO. WHY?
WELL, I'M STARTING TO THINK THEY'VE BEEN STOLEN.
SERIOUSLY?
HOW EXCITING. A THIEF UNDER THE TENT. A CRIMINAL AMONG US... A... A...
HARRELL
...A BIG TOP MYSTERY!!
WE GOT A BULB OUT OVER HERE!
OKAY. SCENE OF THE CRIME. LET'S TRY TO GET SOME FINGERPRINTS.
WOW. THIS IS GREAT. IS THAT SOME KIND OF SPECIAL DUST FOR FINGERPRINTING?
SORT OF.
SORT OF? WHAT IS IT?
HARRELL
HOT CHOCOLATE POWDER.
WELL, IT'S DELICIOUS.
STOP LICKING THE EVIDENCE!

BIG TOP!
OOH. SCORE!

WHAT'S THIS?
A POTTER'S WHEEL. I GOT IT OFF E-BAY.
THOUGHT I'D TEACH MYSELF TO THROW POTS.
HOW'S IT WORK?
WELL, I THINK YOU WORK THE BUBBLES OUT OF THE CLAY.
WOW. THIS IS MESSY.
THEN YOU KIND OF JAM THE STUFF DOWN ON THE WHEEL LIKE THIS.
HOW DO I GET IT TO SPIN?
PUSH DOWN ON THAT FOOT PEDAL.
OKAY...
HARRELL
I AM SO NEVER TEACHING YOU TO DRIVE.
MEDIC.

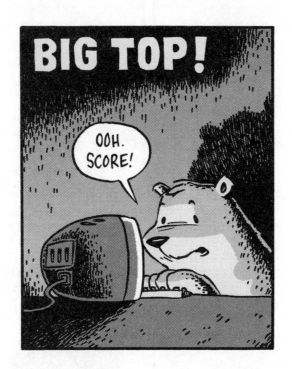

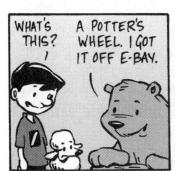

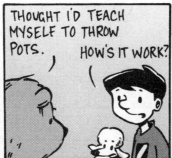

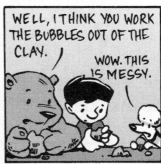

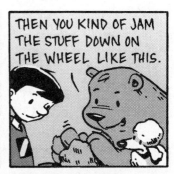

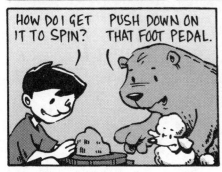

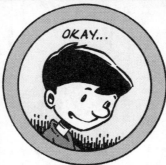

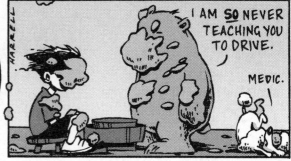

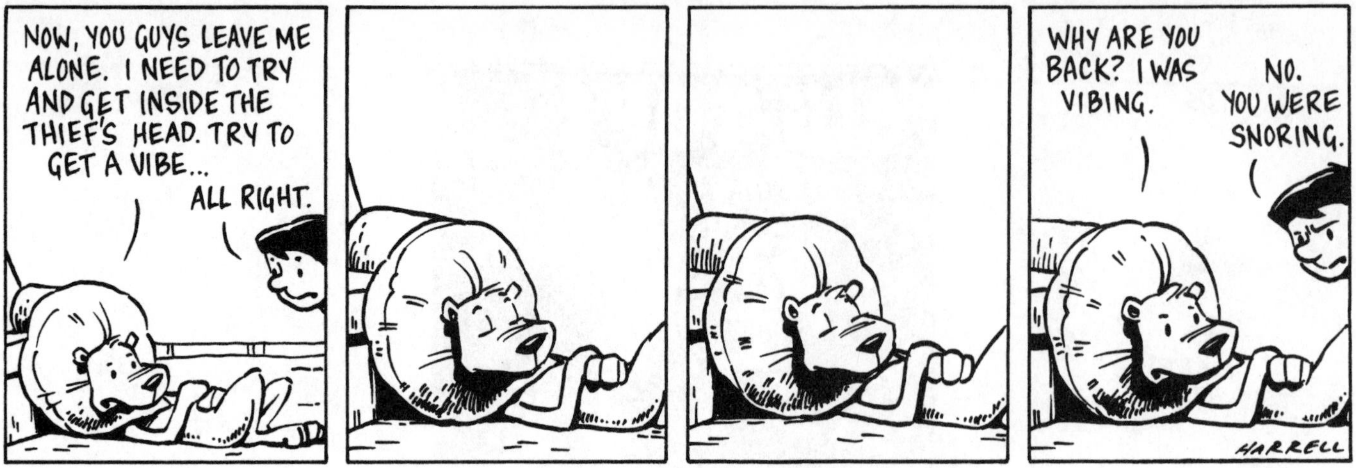
NOW, YOU GUYS LEAVE ME ALONE. I NEED TO TRY AND GET INSIDE THE THIEF'S HEAD. TRY TO GET A VIBE...
ALL RIGHT.
WHY ARE YOU BACK? I WAS VIBING.
NO. YOU WERE SNORING.
HARRELL

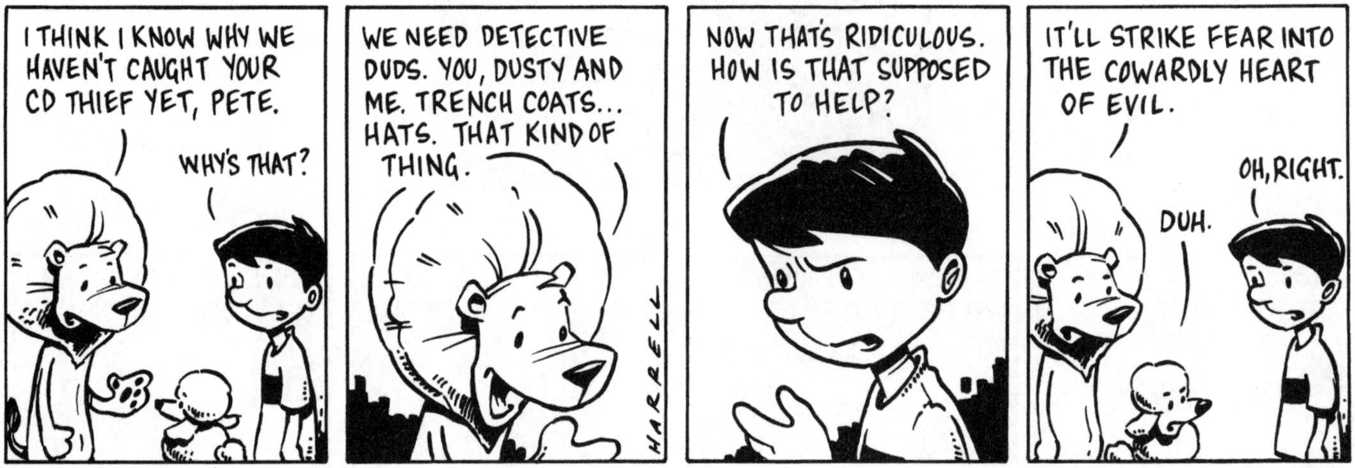
I THINK I KNOW WHY WE HAVEN'T CAUGHT YOUR CD THIEF YET, PETE.
WHY'S THAT?
WE NEED DETECTIVE DUDS. YOU, DUSTY AND ME. TRENCH COATS... HATS. THAT KIND OF THING.
HARRELL
NOW THAT'S RIDICULOUS. HOW IS THAT SUPPOSED TO HELP?
IT'LL STRIKE FEAR INTO THE COWARDLY HEART OF EVIL.
DUH.
OH, RIGHT.

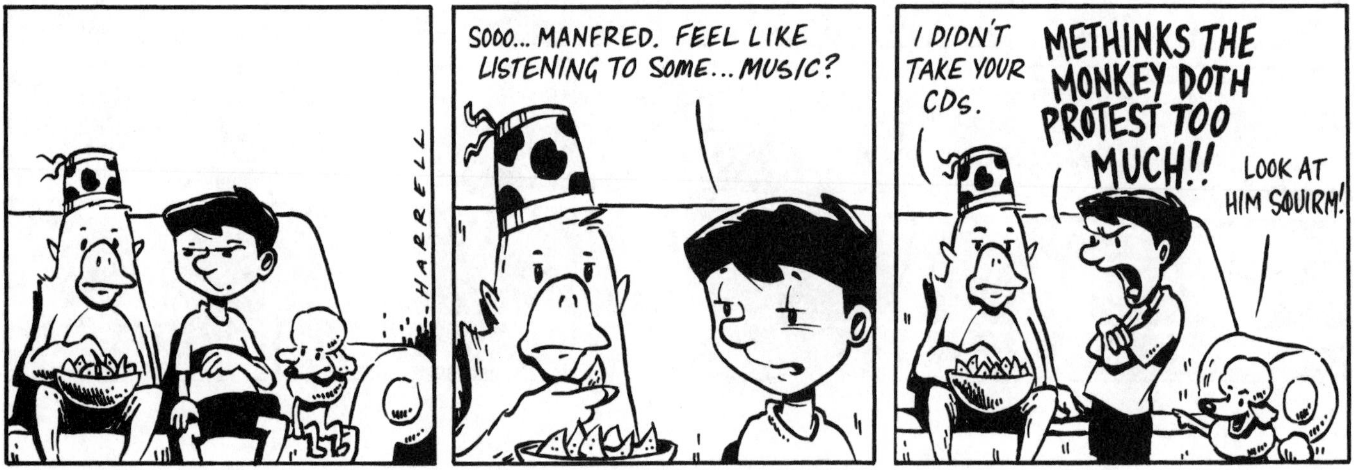
HARRELL
SOOO... MANFRED. FEEL LIKE LISTENING TO SOME... MUSIC?
I DIDN'T TAKE YOUR CDs.
METHINKS THE MONKEY DOTH PROTEST TOO MUCH!!
LOOK AT HIM SQUIRM!

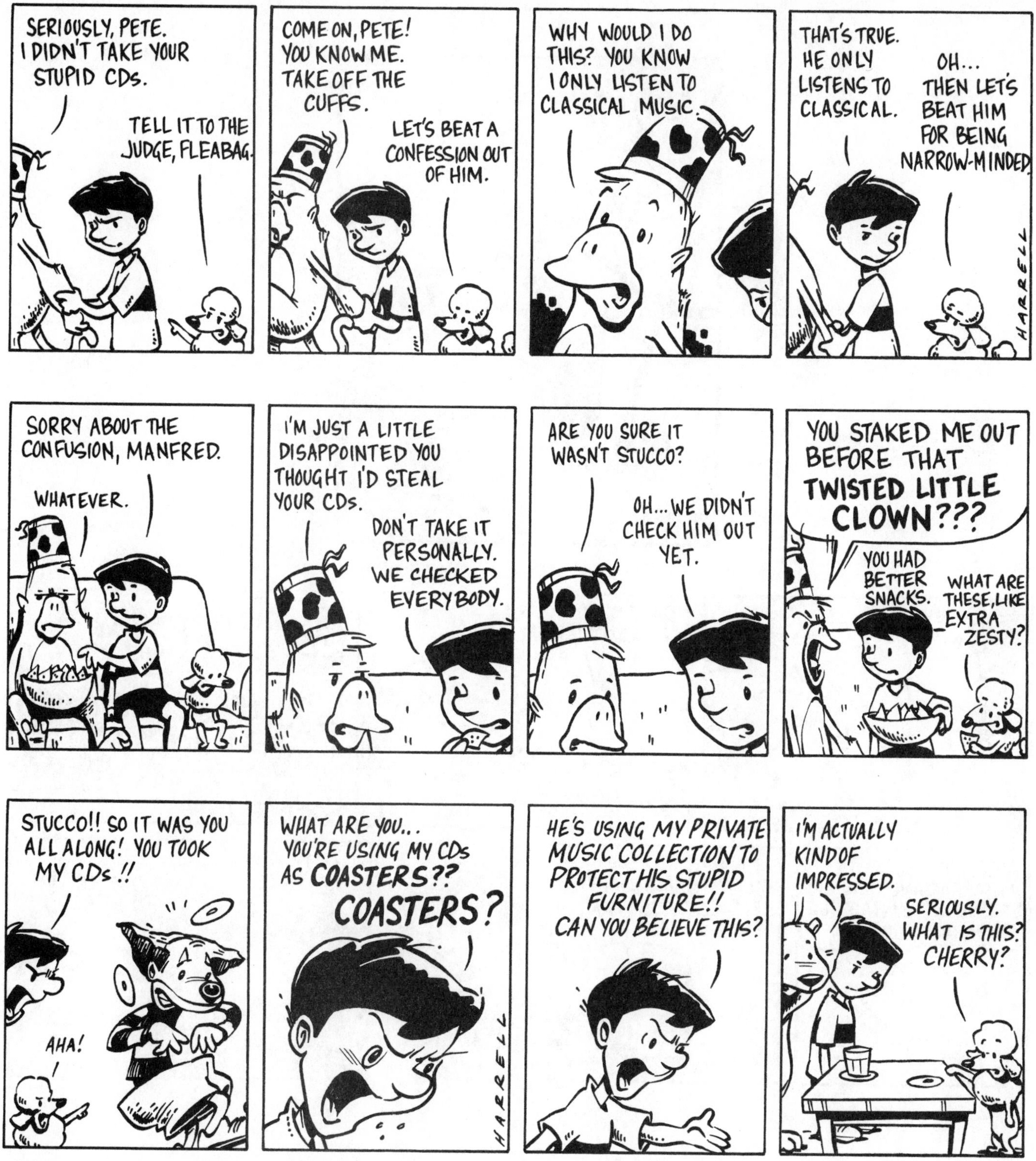
SERIOUSLY, PETE. I DIDN'T TAKE YOUR STUPID CDs.
TELL IT TO THE JUDGE, FLEABAG.
COME ON, PETE! YOU KNOW ME. TAKE OFF THE CUFFS.
LET'S BEAT A CONFESSION OUT OF HIM.
WHY WOULD I DO THIS? YOU KNOW I ONLY LISTEN TO CLASSICAL MUSIC.
THAT'S TRUE. HE ONLY LISTENS TO CLASSICAL.
OH... THEN LET'S BEAT HIM FOR BEING NARROW-MINDED.
HARRELL
SORRY ABOUT THE CONFUSION, MANFRED.
WHATEVER.
I'M JUST A LITTLE DISAPPOINTED YOU THOUGHT I'D STEAL YOUR CDs.
DON'T TAKE IT PERSONALLY. WE CHECKED EVERYBODY.
ARE YOU SURE IT WASN'T STUCCO?
OH... WE DIDN'T CHECK HIM OUT YET.
YOU STAKED ME OUT BEFORE THAT **TWISTED LITTLE CLOWN???**
YOU HAD BETTER SNACKS.
WHAT ARE THESE, LIKE EXTRA ZESTY?
STUCCO!! SO IT WAS YOU ALL ALONG! YOU TOOK MY CDs!!
AHA!
WHAT ARE YOU... YOU'RE USING MY CDs AS **COASTERS??**
COASTERS?
HARRELL
HE'S USING MY PRIVATE MUSIC COLLECTION TO PROTECT HIS STUPID FURNITURE!! CAN YOU BELIEVE THIS?
I'M ACTUALLY KIND OF IMPRESSED.
SERIOUSLY. WHAT IS THIS? CHERRY?

Big Top

HEY, PAL. WHAT'S UP?

SHUT YOUR YAP, MAN. YOU'RE CATCHING FLIES.

PANT DROOL

HELLOOOOO?

LEAVE HIM ALONE, DUSTY. HE'S JUST HOT.

SURE, BUT IT'S PRETTY EMBARRASSING. YOU DON'T SEE ME WITH MY TONGUE ALL HANGIN' OUT.

IT MAKES YOU LOOK STUPID. SHOW SOME SELF-CONTROL, FOR PETE'S SAKE.

WAIT... FOR MY SAKE?

(WOW. IT IS HOT IN HERE.)

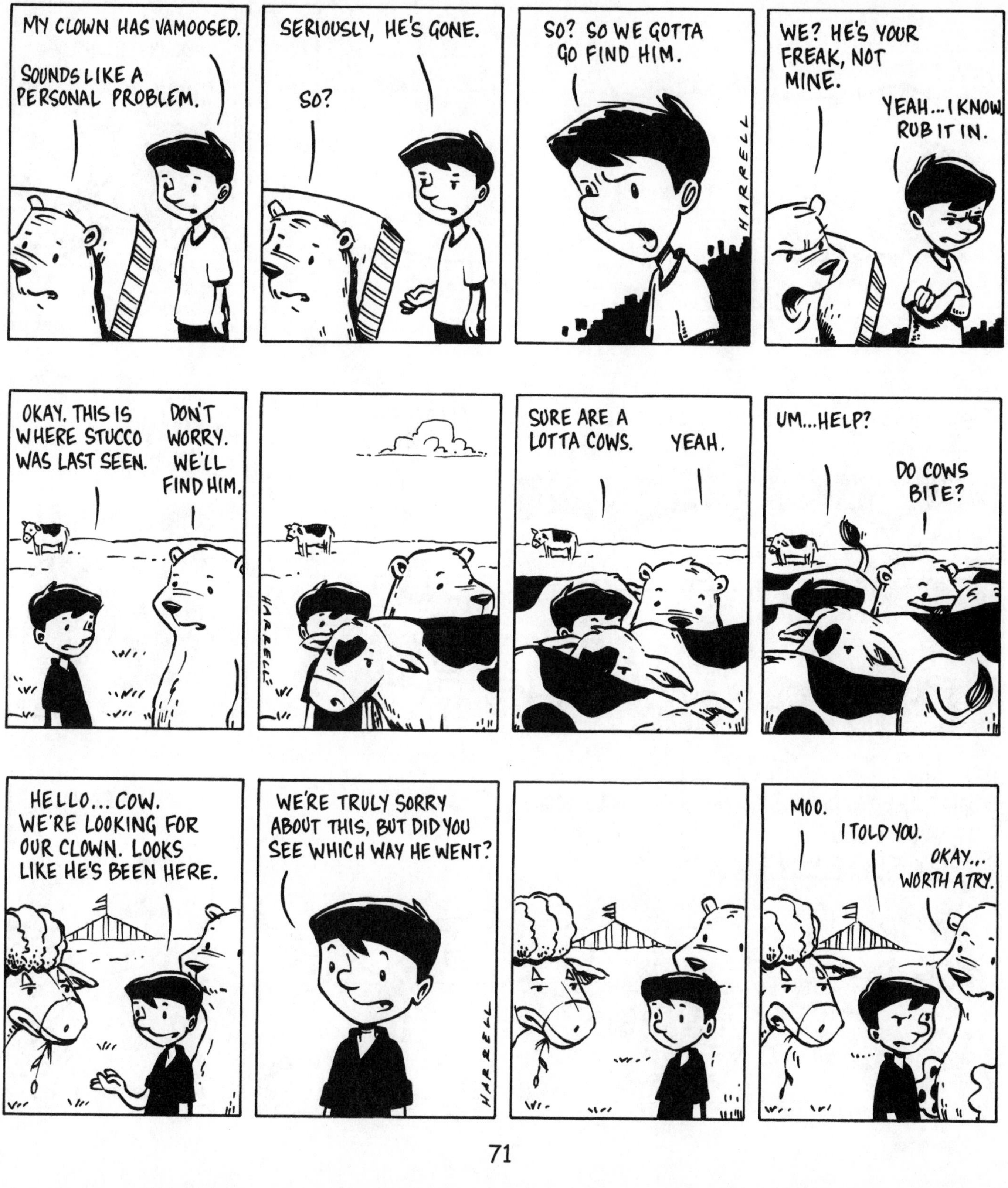
MY CLOWN HAS VAMOOSED.
SOUNDS LIKE A PERSONAL PROBLEM.
SERIOUSLY, HE'S GONE.
SO?
SO? SO WE GOTTA GO FIND HIM.
HARRELL
WE? HE'S YOUR FREAK, NOT MINE.
YEAH...I KNOW. RUB IT IN.
OKAY. THIS IS WHERE STUCCO WAS LAST SEEN.
DON'T WORRY. WE'LL FIND HIM.
HARRELL
SURE ARE A LOTTA COWS.
YEAH.
UM...HELP?
DO COWS BITE?
HELLO... COW. WE'RE LOOKING FOR OUR CLOWN. LOOKS LIKE HE'S BEEN HERE.
WE'RE TRULY SORRY ABOUT THIS, BUT DID YOU SEE WHICH WAY HE WENT?
HARRELL
MOO.
I TOLD YOU.
OKAY... WORTH A TRY.

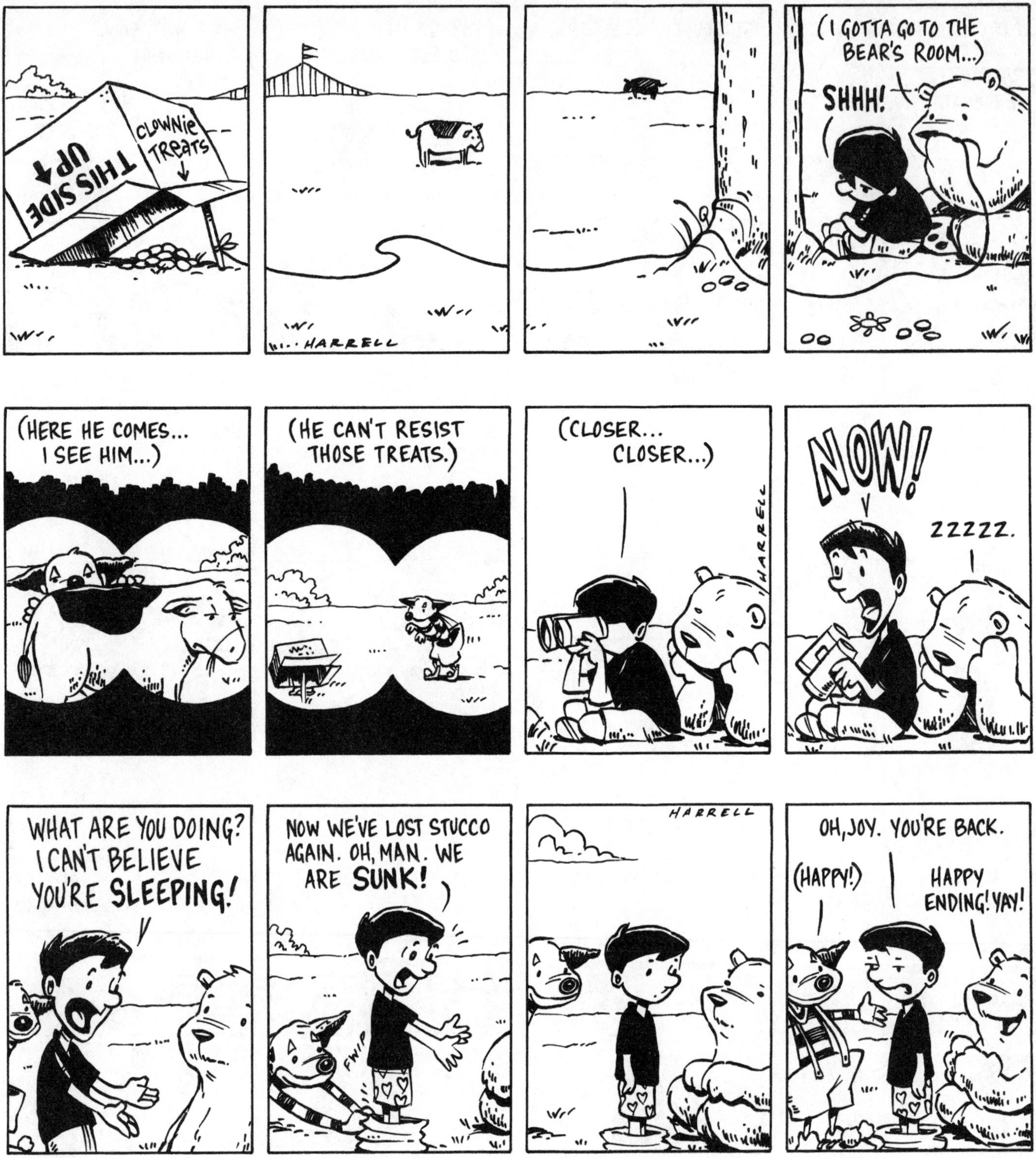
THIS SIDE UP
CLOWNIE TREATS
HARRELL
(I GOTTA GO TO THE BEAR'S ROOM...)
SHHH!
(HERE HE COMES... I SEE HIM...)
(HE CAN'T RESIST THOSE TREATS.)
(CLOSER... CLOSER...)
HARRELL
NOW!
ZZZZZ.
WHAT ARE YOU DOING? I CAN'T BELIEVE YOU'RE SLEEPING!
NOW WE'VE LOST STUCCO AGAIN. OH, MAN. WE ARE SUNK!
FWIP
HARRELL
OH, JOY. YOU'RE BACK.
(HAPPY!)
HAPPY ENDING! YAY!

BIG TOP

BE COOL, MANFRED. BE COOL.
I'M OKAY.
YOU ALRIGHT?
UM...NO.
BANANAS
HARRELL
I'M NOT BAILING YOU OUT, AGAIN. THAT WAS OUR DEAL.
OH, BUT IT WAS **SO** WORTH IT.

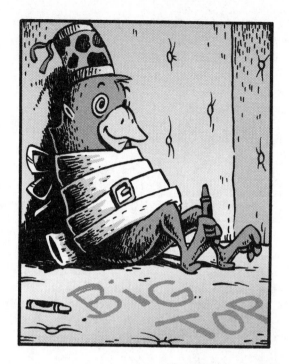

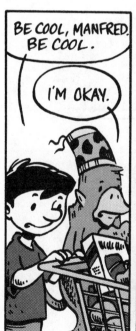

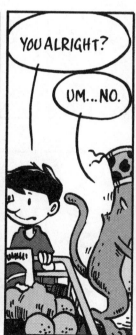

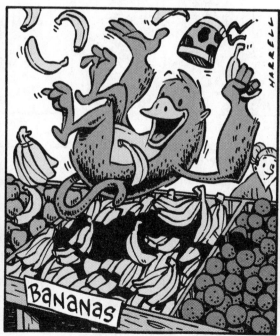

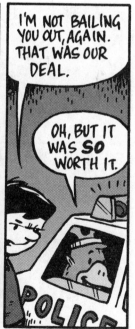

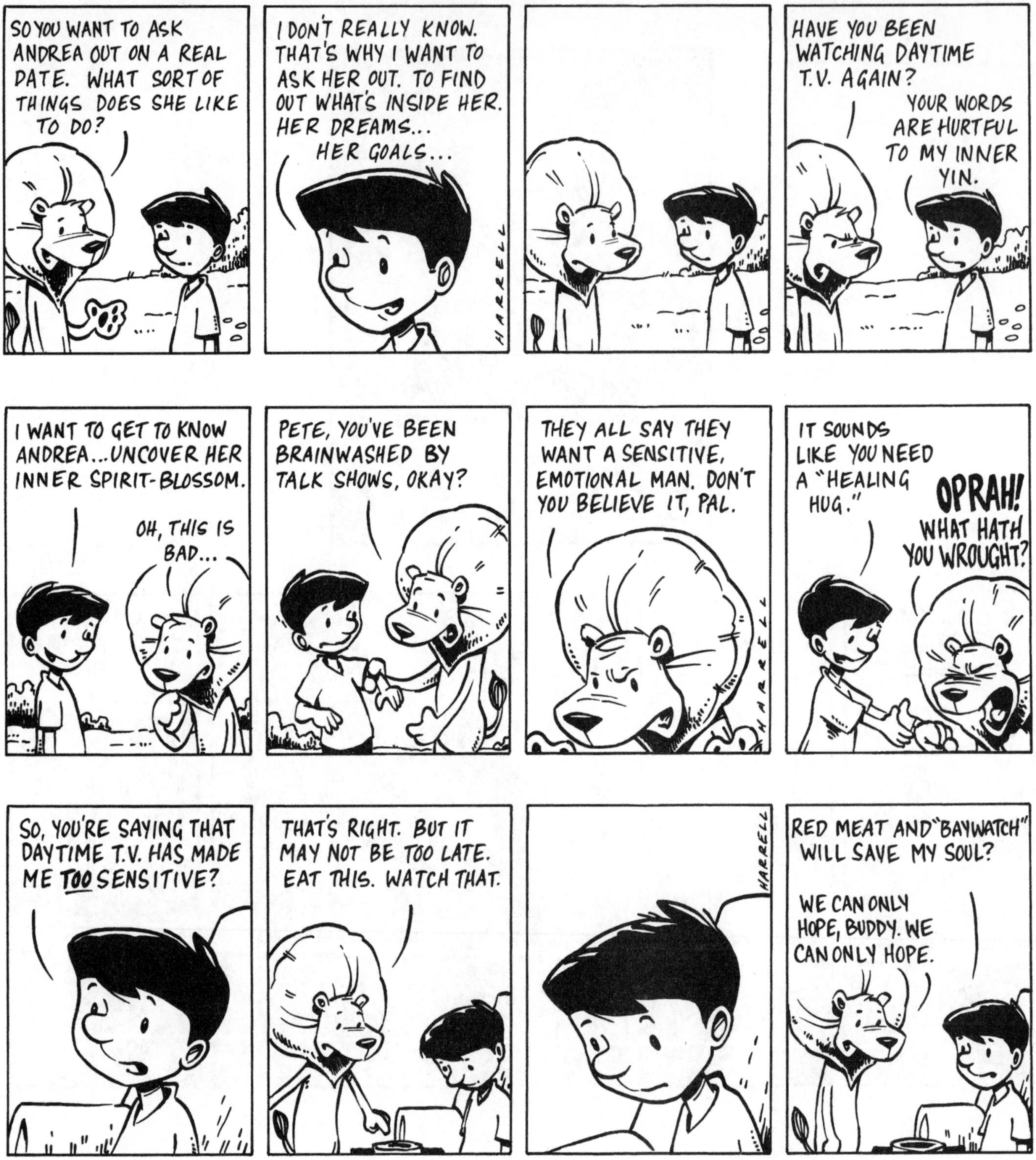
SO YOU WANT TO ASK ANDREA OUT ON A REAL DATE. WHAT SORT OF THINGS DOES SHE LIKE TO DO?
I DON'T REALLY KNOW. THAT'S WHY I WANT TO ASK HER OUT. TO FIND OUT WHAT'S INSIDE HER. HER DREAMS... HER GOALS...
HARRELL
HAVE YOU BEEN WATCHING DAYTIME T.V. AGAIN?
YOUR WORDS ARE HURTFUL TO MY INNER YIN.
I WANT TO GET TO KNOW ANDREA...UNCOVER HER INNER SPIRIT-BLOSSOM.
OH, THIS IS BAD...
PETE, YOU'VE BEEN BRAINWASHED BY TALK SHOWS, OKAY?
THEY ALL SAY THEY WANT A SENSITIVE, EMOTIONAL MAN. DON'T YOU BELIEVE IT, PAL.
HARRELL
IT SOUNDS LIKE YOU NEED A "HEALING HUG."
OPRAH! WHAT HATH YOU WROUGHT?
SO, YOU'RE SAYING THAT DAYTIME T.V. HAS MADE ME TOO SENSITIVE?
THAT'S RIGHT. BUT IT MAY NOT BE TOO LATE. EAT THIS. WATCH THAT.
HARRELL
RED MEAT AND "BAYWATCH" WILL SAVE MY SOUL?
WE CAN ONLY HOPE, BUDDY. WE CAN ONLY HOPE.

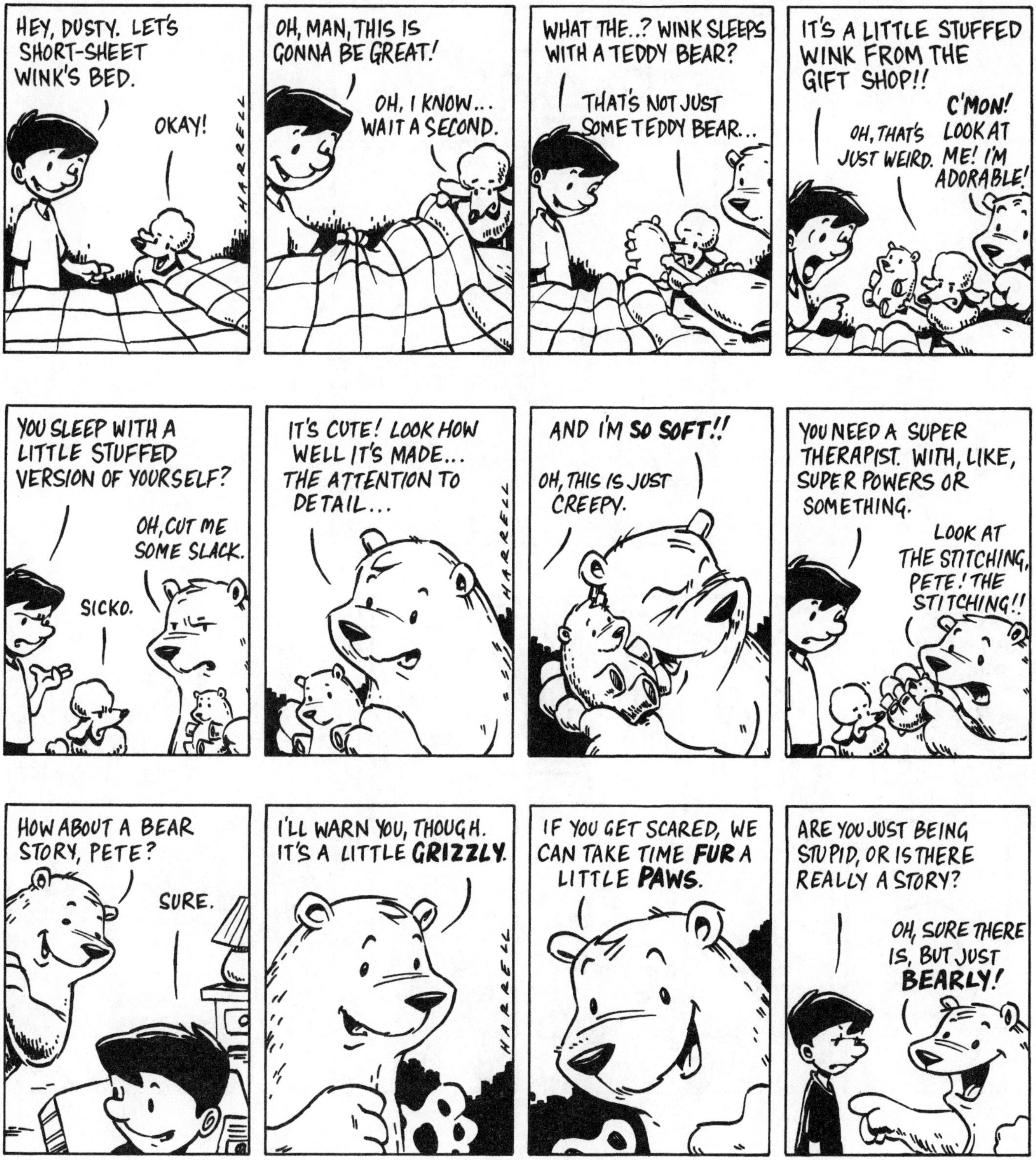
HEY, DUSTY. LET'S SHORT-SHEET WINK'S BED.
OKAY!
HARRELL
OH, MAN, THIS IS GONNA BE GREAT!
OH, I KNOW... WAIT A SECOND.
WHAT THE..? WINK SLEEPS WITH A TEDDY BEAR?
THAT'S NOT JUST SOME TEDDY BEAR...
IT'S A LITTLE STUFFED WINK FROM THE GIFT SHOP!!
OH, THAT'S JUST WEIRD.
C'MON! LOOK AT ME! I'M ADORABLE!
YOU SLEEP WITH A LITTLE STUFFED VERSION OF YOURSELF?
OH, CUT ME SOME SLACK.
SICKO.
IT'S CUTE! LOOK HOW WELL IT'S MADE... THE ATTENTION TO DETAIL...
HARRELL
AND I'M SO SOFT!!
OH, THIS IS JUST CREEPY.
YOU NEED A SUPER THERAPIST. WITH, LIKE, SUPER POWERS OR SOMETHING.
LOOK AT THE STITCHING, PETE! THE STITCHING!!
HOW ABOUT A BEAR STORY, PETE?
SURE.
I'LL WARN YOU, THOUGH. IT'S A LITTLE GRIZZLY.
HARRELL
IF YOU GET SCARED, WE CAN TAKE TIME FUR A LITTLE PAWS.
ARE YOU JUST BEING STUPID, OR IS THERE REALLY A STORY?
OH, SURE THERE IS, BUT JUST BEARLY!

BIG TOP
POLICE
IT'S A PRIMAL THING.

HEAR THAT SIREN? WATCH THIS.
HARRELL
OWOOOOOOOOOO
WHAT THE HECK WAS THAT?
THAT WAS LIKE A PARTY IN MY EARS, BABY!

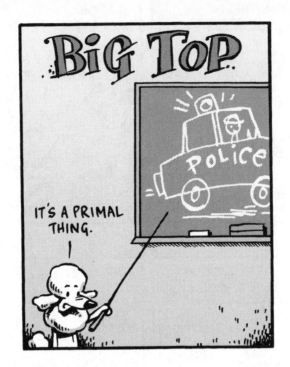

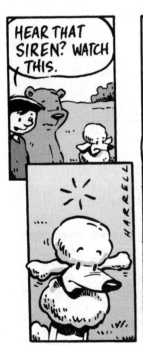

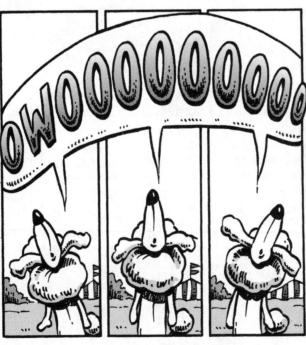

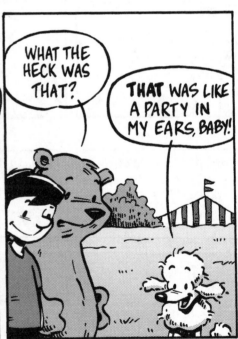

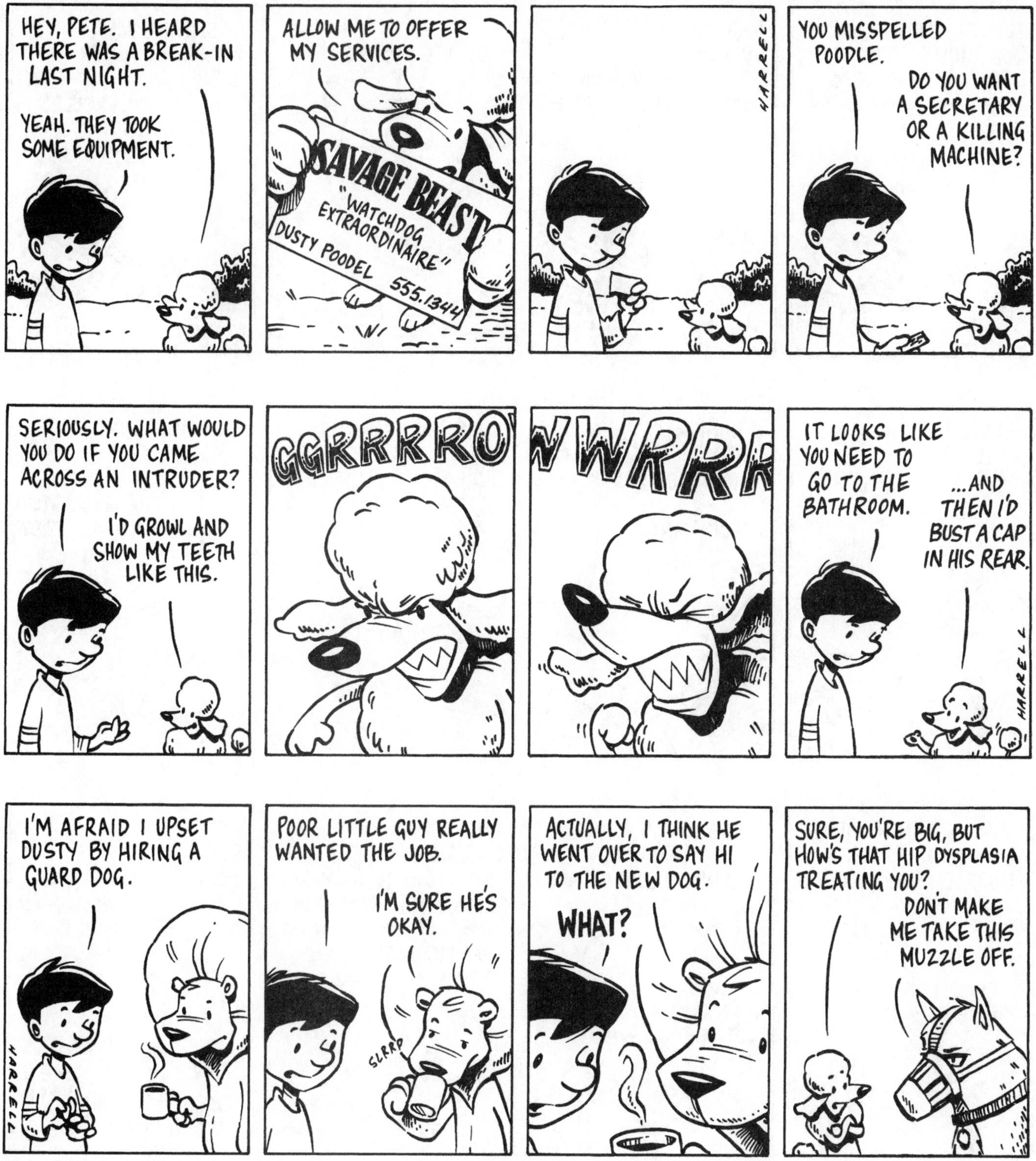
HEY, PETE. I HEARD THERE WAS A BREAK-IN LAST NIGHT.
YEAH. THEY TOOK SOME EQUIPMENT.
ALLOW ME TO OFFER MY SERVICES.
SAVAGE BEAST "WATCHDOG EXTRAORDINAIRE" DUSTY POODEL 555.1344
HARRELL
YOU MISSPELLED POODLE.
DO YOU WANT A SECRETARY OR A KILLING MACHINE?
SERIOUSLY. WHAT WOULD YOU DO IF YOU CAME ACROSS AN INTRUDER?
I'D GROWL AND SHOW MY TEETH LIKE THIS.
GGRRRRROWWRRRR
IT LOOKS LIKE YOU NEED TO GO TO THE BATHROOM.
...AND THEN I'D BUST A CAP IN HIS REAR.
HARRELL
I'M AFRAID I UPSET DUSTY BY HIRING A GUARD DOG.
HARRELL
POOR LITTLE GUY REALLY WANTED THE JOB.
I'M SURE HE'S OKAY.
SLRRP
ACTUALLY, I THINK HE WENT OVER TO SAY HI TO THE NEW DOG.
WHAT?
SURE, YOU'RE BIG, BUT HOW'S THAT HIP DYSPLASIA TREATING YOU?
DON'T MAKE ME TAKE THIS MUZZLE OFF.

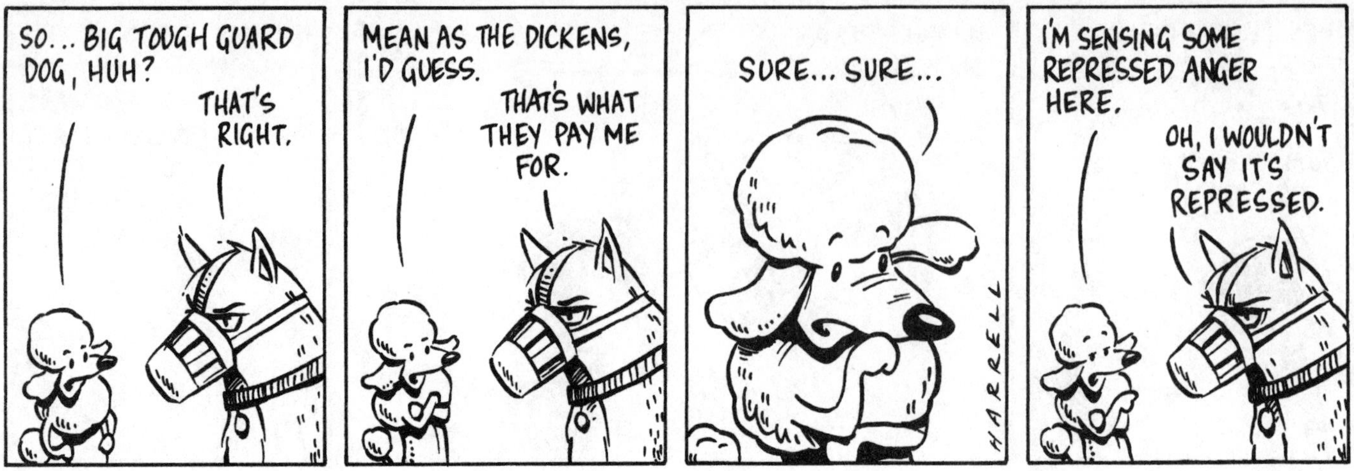
SO... BIG TOUGH GUARD DOG, HUH?
THAT'S RIGHT.
MEAN AS THE DICKENS, I'D GUESS.
THAT'S WHAT THEY PAY ME FOR.
SURE... SURE...
I'M SENSING SOME REPRESSED ANGER HERE.
OH, I WOULDN'T SAY IT'S REPRESSED.
HARRELL

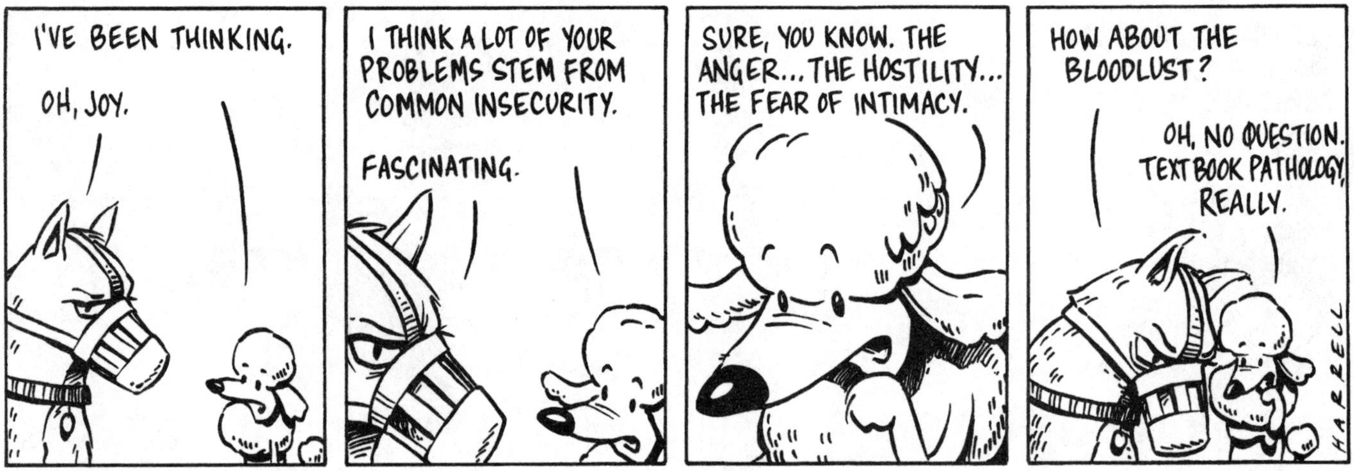
I'VE BEEN THINKING.
OH, JOY.
I THINK A LOT OF YOUR PROBLEMS STEM FROM COMMON INSECURITY.
FASCINATING.
SURE, YOU KNOW. THE ANGER... THE HOSTILITY... THE FEAR OF INTIMACY.
HOW ABOUT THE BLOODLUST?
OH, NO QUESTION. TEXTBOOK PATHOLOGY, REALLY.
HARRELL

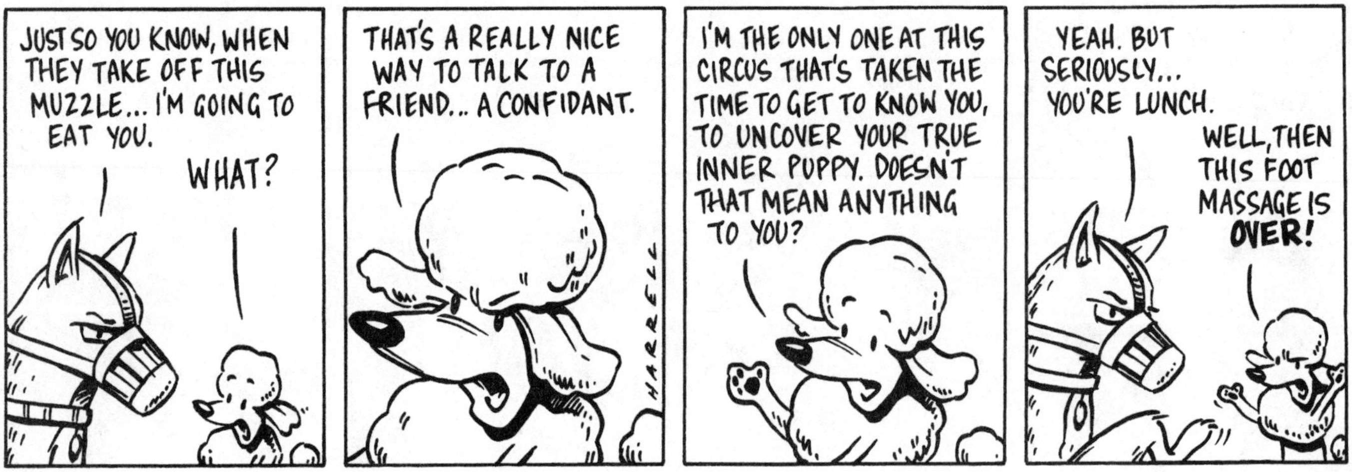
JUST SO YOU KNOW, WHEN THEY TAKE OFF THIS MUZZLE... I'M GOING TO EAT YOU.
WHAT?
THAT'S A REALLY NICE WAY TO TALK TO A FRIEND... A CONFIDANT.
HARRELL
I'M THE ONLY ONE AT THIS CIRCUS THAT'S TAKEN THE TIME TO GET TO KNOW YOU, TO UNCOVER YOUR TRUE INNER PUPPY. DOESN'T THAT MEAN ANYTHING TO YOU?
YEAH. BUT SERIOUSLY... YOU'RE LUNCH.
WELL, THEN THIS FOOT MASSAGE IS **OVER!**

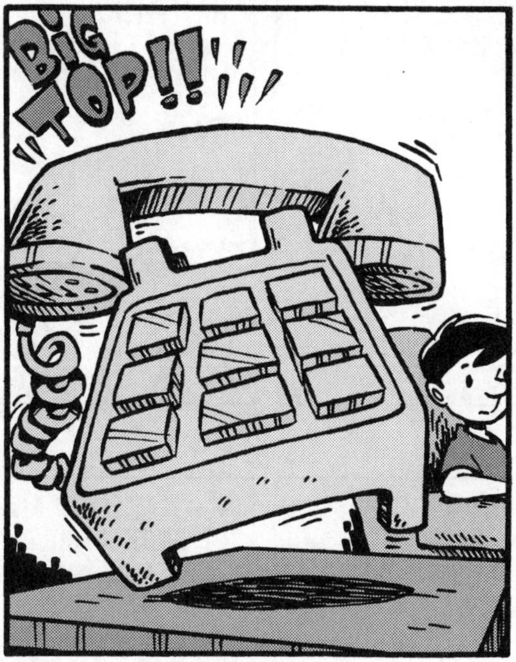
BIG TOP!!

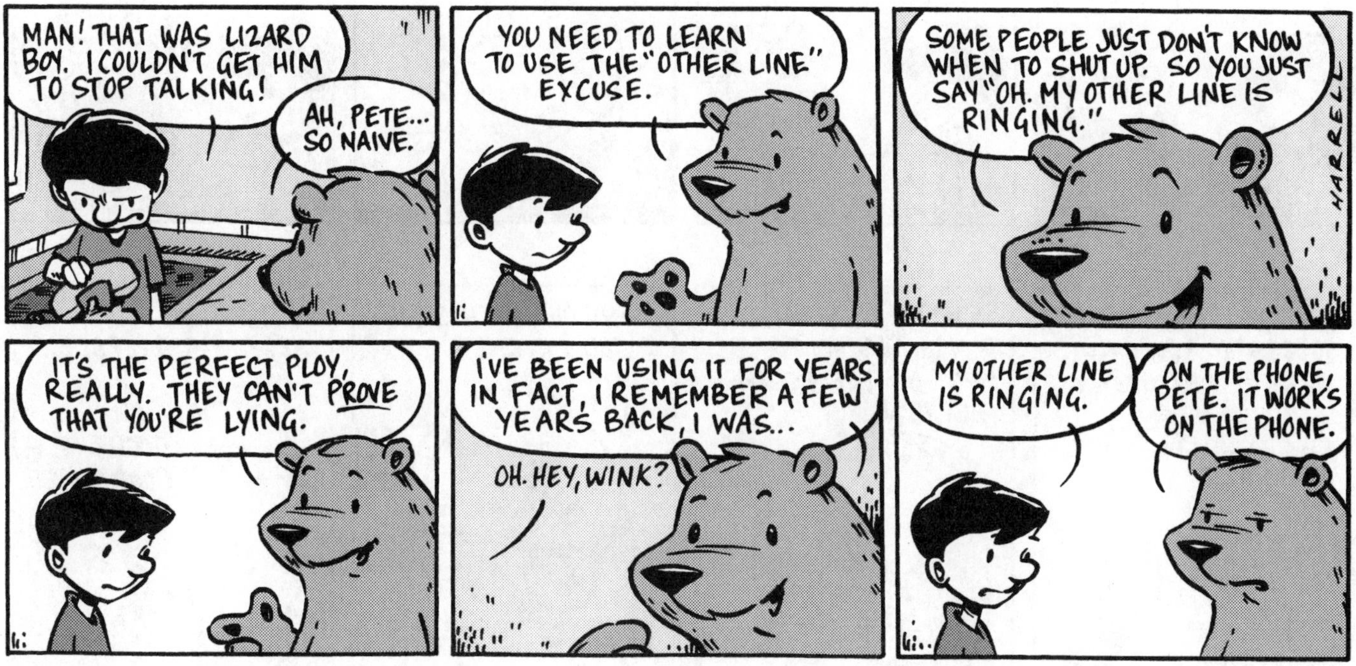
MAN! THAT WAS LIZARD BOY. I COULDN'T GET HIM TO STOP TALKING!
AH, PETE... SO NAIVE.
YOU NEED TO LEARN TO USE THE "OTHER LINE" EXCUSE.
SOME PEOPLE JUST DON'T KNOW WHEN TO SHUT UP. SO YOU JUST SAY "OH. MY OTHER LINE IS RINGING."
-HARRELL
IT'S THE PERFECT PLOY, REALLY. THEY CAN'T PROVE THAT YOU'RE LYING.
I'VE BEEN USING IT FOR YEARS. IN FACT, I REMEMBER A FEW YEARS BACK, I WAS...
OH. HEY, WINK?
MY OTHER LINE IS RINGING.
ON THE PHONE, PETE. IT WORKS ON THE PHONE.

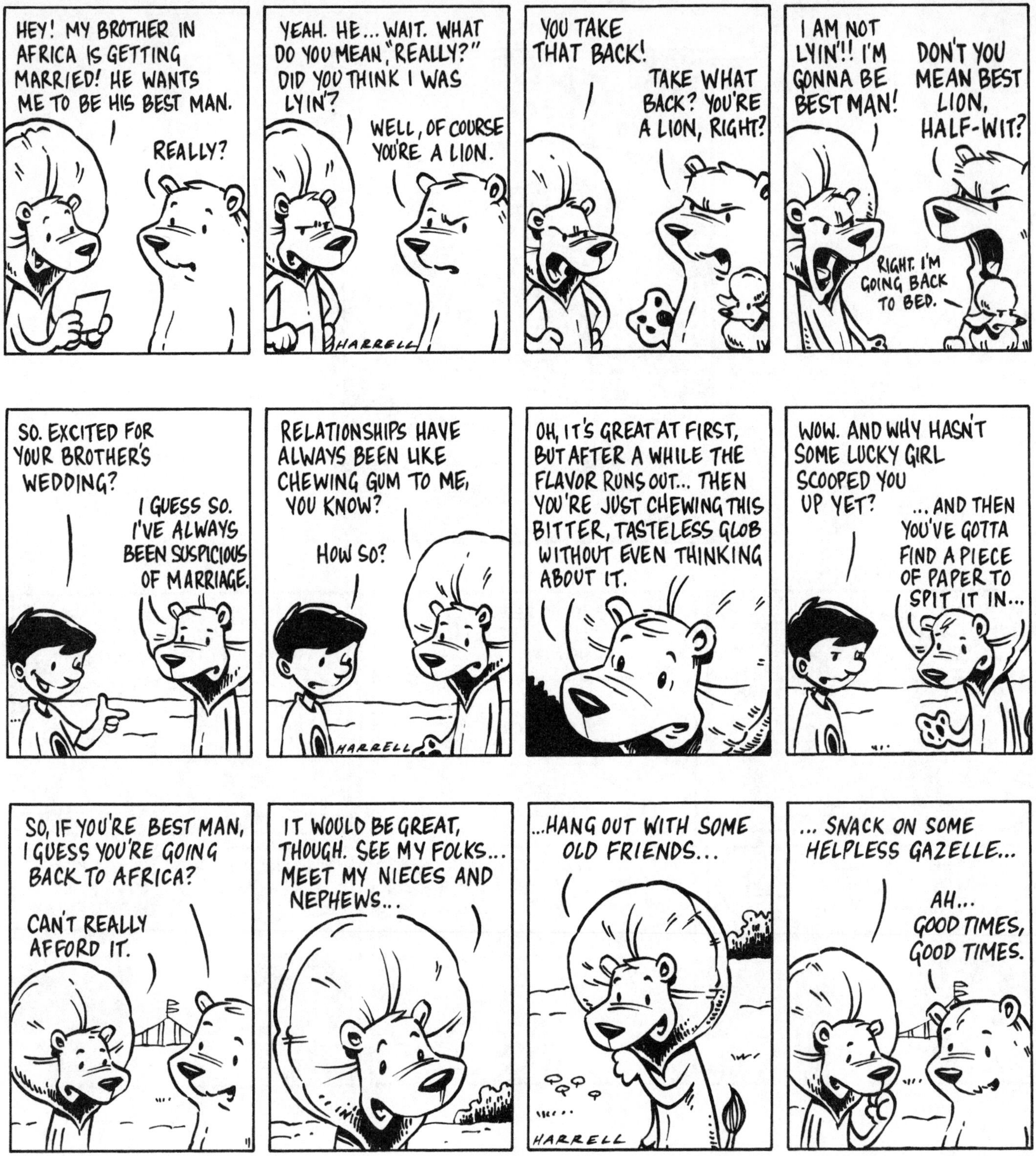
HEY! MY BROTHER IN AFRICA IS GETTING MARRIED! HE WANTS ME TO BE HIS BEST MAN.
REALLY?
YEAH. HE... WAIT. WHAT DO YOU MEAN, "REALLY?" DID YOU THINK I WAS LYIN'?
WELL, OF COURSE YOU'RE A LION.
HARRELL
YOU TAKE THAT BACK!
TAKE WHAT BACK? YOU'RE A LION, RIGHT?
I AM NOT LYIN'!! I'M GONNA BE BEST MAN!
DON'T YOU MEAN BEST LION, HALF-WIT?
RIGHT. I'M GOING BACK TO BED.
SO. EXCITED FOR YOUR BROTHER'S WEDDING?
I GUESS SO. I'VE ALWAYS BEEN SUSPICIOUS OF MARRIAGE.
RELATIONSHIPS HAVE ALWAYS BEEN LIKE CHEWING GUM TO ME, YOU KNOW?
HOW SO?
HARRELL
OH, IT'S GREAT AT FIRST, BUT AFTER A WHILE THE FLAVOR RUNS OUT... THEN YOU'RE JUST CHEWING THIS BITTER, TASTELESS GLOB WITHOUT EVEN THINKING ABOUT IT.
WOW. AND WHY HASN'T SOME LUCKY GIRL SCOOPED YOU UP YET?
...AND THEN YOU'VE GOTTA FIND A PIECE OF PAPER TO SPIT IT IN...
SO, IF YOU'RE BEST MAN, I GUESS YOU'RE GOING BACK TO AFRICA?
CAN'T REALLY AFFORD IT.
IT WOULD BE GREAT, THOUGH. SEE MY FOLKS... MEET MY NIECES AND NEPHEWS...
...HANG OUT WITH SOME OLD FRIENDS...
HARRELL
... SNACK ON SOME HELPLESS GAZELLE...
AH... GOOD TIMES, GOOD TIMES.

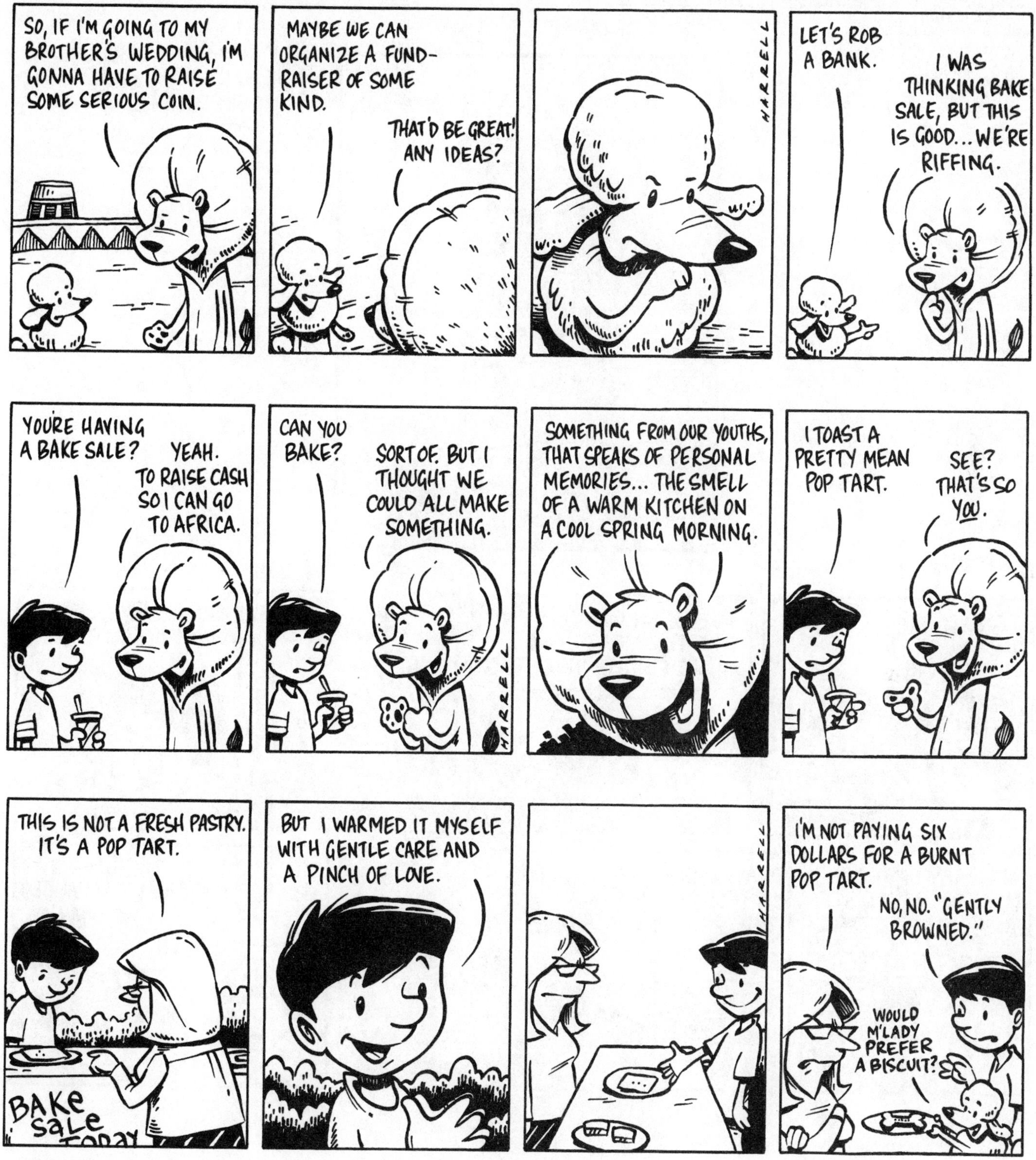
SO, IF I'M GOING TO MY BROTHER'S WEDDING, I'M GONNA HAVE TO RAISE SOME SERIOUS COIN.
MAYBE WE CAN ORGANIZE A FUND-RAISER OF SOME KIND.
THAT'D BE GREAT! ANY IDEAS?
HARRELL
LET'S ROB A BANK.
I WAS THINKING BAKE SALE, BUT THIS IS GOOD... WE'RE RIFFING.
YOU'RE HAVING A BAKE SALE?
YEAH. TO RAISE CASH SO I CAN GO TO AFRICA.
CAN YOU BAKE?
SORT OF. BUT I THOUGHT WE COULD ALL MAKE SOMETHING.
HARRELL
SOMETHING FROM OUR YOUTHS, THAT SPEAKS OF PERSONAL MEMORIES... THE SMELL OF A WARM KITCHEN ON A COOL SPRING MORNING.
I TOAST A PRETTY MEAN POP TART.
SEE? THAT'S SO YOU.
THIS IS NOT A FRESH PASTRY. IT'S A POP TART.
BAKE SALE TODAY
BUT I WARMED IT MYSELF WITH GENTLE CARE AND A PINCH OF LOVE.
HARRELL
I'M NOT PAYING SIX DOLLARS FOR A BURNT POP TART.
NO, NO. "GENTLY BROWNED."
WOULD M'LADY PREFER A BISCUIT?

PETE, I'D LIKE YOU TO BE THE FIRST TO SEE SOMETHING.

WHAT'S THAT?

I'VE BEEN WORKING ON THIS FOR YEARS AND I HAVE FINALLY INVENTED...

...A ROBOT!!

NO WAY!

THIS IS SO COOL!! WHAT DOES IT DO?

IF I MAY SAY SO MYSELF, IT'S QUITE AMAZING.

HARRELL

OKAY. WHEN YOU PULL ON THIS ARM...

...THE LIGHT ON HIS HEAD COMES ON!!

THAT'S NOT A ROBOT. IT'S A LAMP.

SHHH! HE'S VERY ADVANCED. HE MAY UNDERSTAND YOU!

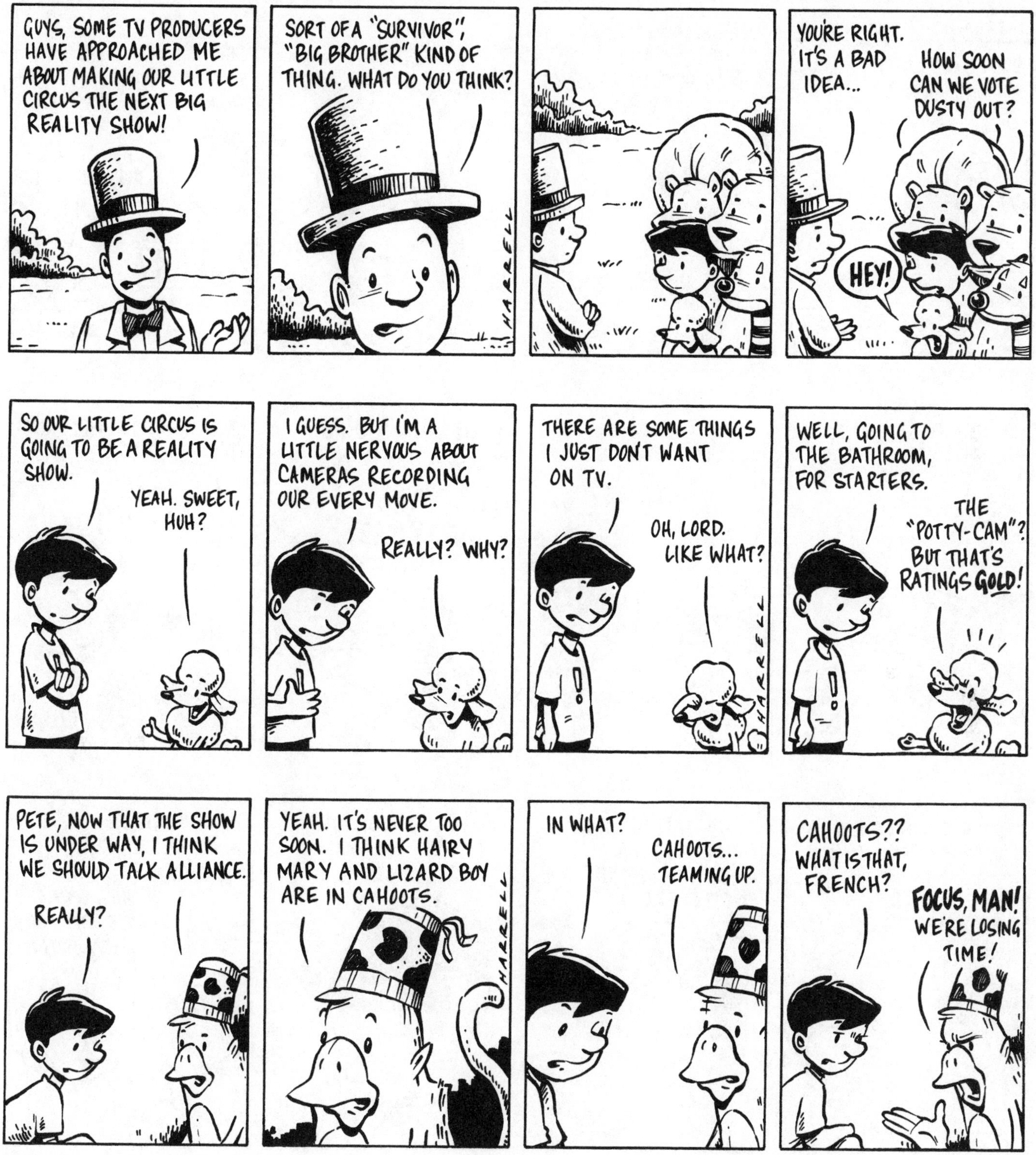
GUYS, SOME TV PRODUCERS HAVE APPROACHED ME ABOUT MAKING OUR LITTLE CIRCUS THE NEXT BIG REALITY SHOW!
SORT OF A "SURVIVOR", "BIG BROTHER" KIND OF THING. WHAT DO YOU THINK?
HARRELL
YOU'RE RIGHT. IT'S A BAD IDEA...
HOW SOON CAN WE VOTE DUSTY OUT?
HEY!
SO OUR LITTLE CIRCUS IS GOING TO BE A REALITY SHOW.
YEAH. SWEET, HUH?
I GUESS. BUT I'M A LITTLE NERVOUS ABOUT CAMERAS RECORDING OUR EVERY MOVE.
REALLY? WHY?
THERE ARE SOME THINGS I JUST DON'T WANT ON TV.
OH, LORD. LIKE WHAT?
HARRELL
WELL, GOING TO THE BATHROOM, FOR STARTERS.
THE "POTTY-CAM"? BUT THAT'S RATINGS GOLD!
PETE, NOW THAT THE SHOW IS UNDER WAY, I THINK WE SHOULD TALK ALLIANCE.
REALLY?
YEAH. IT'S NEVER TOO SOON. I THINK HAIRY MARY AND LIZARD BOY ARE IN CAHOOTS.
HARRELL
IN WHAT?
CAHOOTS... TEAMING UP.
CAHOOTS?? WHAT IS THAT, FRENCH?
FOCUS, MAN! WE'RE LOSING TIME!

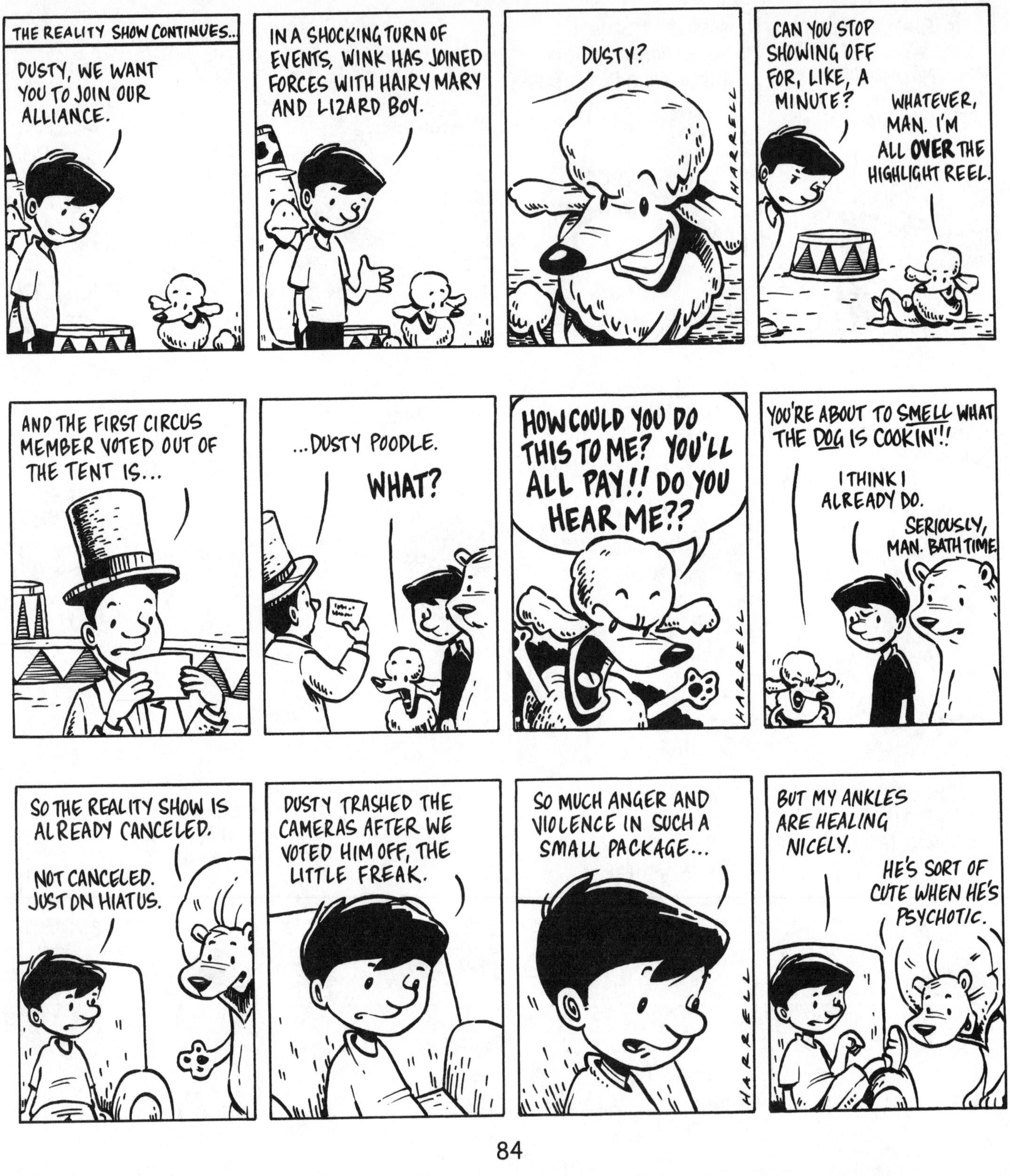
THE REALITY SHOW CONTINUES...
DUSTY, WE WANT YOU TO JOIN OUR ALLIANCE.
IN A SHOCKING TURN OF EVENTS, WINK HAS JOINED FORCES WITH HAIRY MARY AND LIZARD BOY.
DUSTY?
HARRELL
CAN YOU STOP SHOWING OFF FOR, LIKE, A MINUTE?
WHATEVER, MAN. I'M ALL OVER THE HIGHLIGHT REEL.
AND THE FIRST CIRCUS MEMBER VOTED OUT OF THE TENT IS...
...DUSTY POODLE.
WHAT?
HOW COULD YOU DO THIS TO ME? YOU'LL ALL PAY!! DO YOU HEAR ME??
HARRELL
YOU'RE ABOUT TO SMELL WHAT THE DOG IS COOKIN'!!
I THINK I ALREADY DO.
SERIOUSLY, MAN. BATH TIME.
SO THE REALITY SHOW IS ALREADY CANCELED.
NOT CANCELED. JUST ON HIATUS.
DUSTY TRASHED THE CAMERAS AFTER WE VOTED HIM OFF, THE LITTLE FREAK.
SO MUCH ANGER AND VIOLENCE IN SUCH A SMALL PACKAGE...
HARRELL
BUT MY ANKLES ARE HEALING NICELY.
HE'S SORT OF CUTE WHEN HE'S PSYCHOTIC.

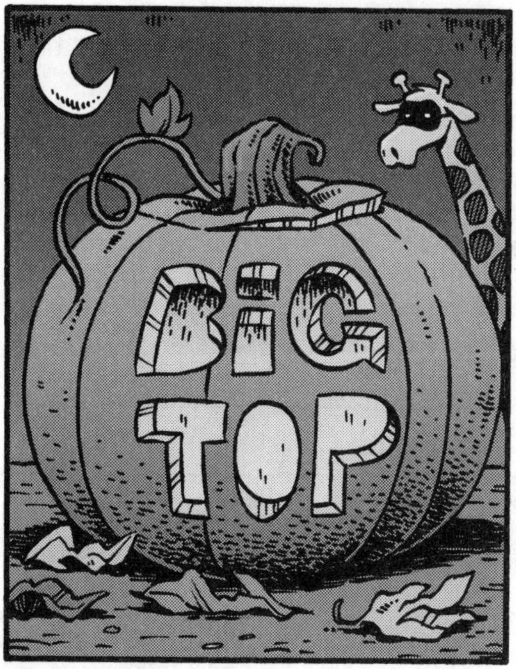
BIG TOP

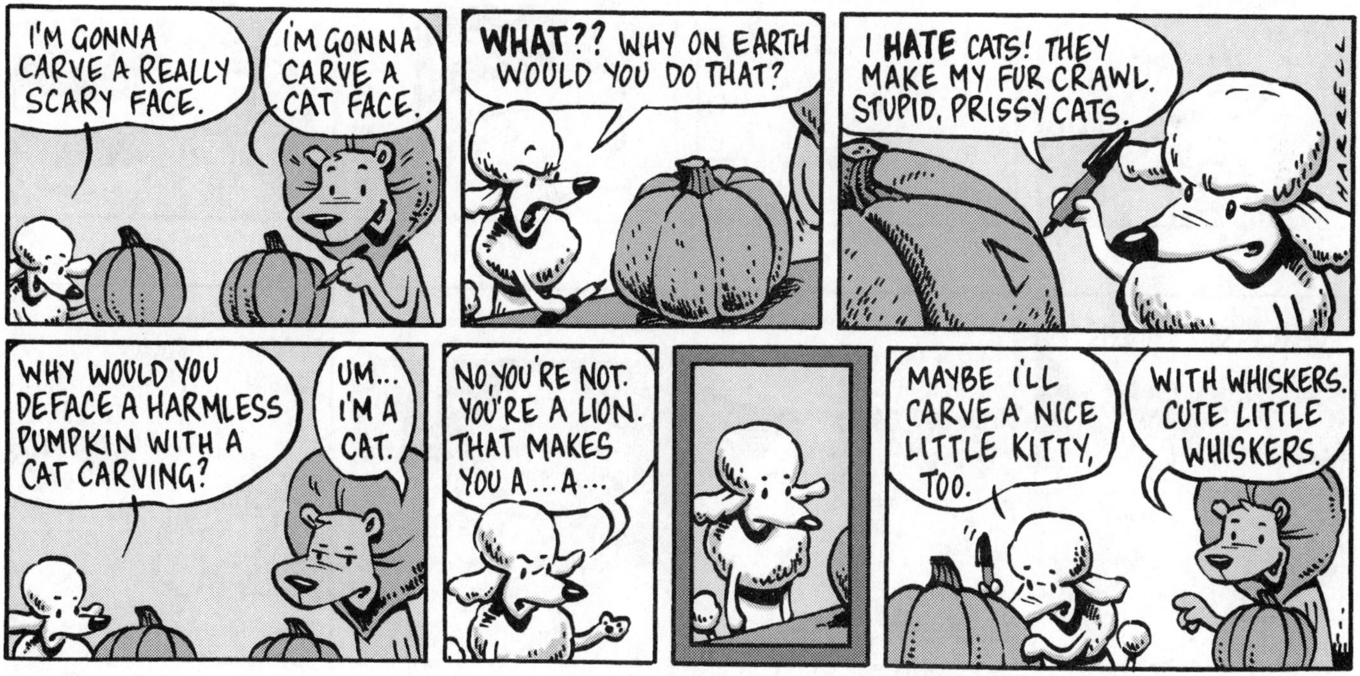
I'M GONNA CARVE A REALLY SCARY FACE.
I'M GONNA CARVE A CAT FACE.
WHAT?? WHY ON EARTH WOULD YOU DO THAT?
I HATE CATS! THEY MAKE MY FUR CRAWL. STUPID, PRISSY CATS.
HARRELL
WHY WOULD YOU DEFACE A HARMLESS PUMPKIN WITH A CAT CARVING?
UM... I'M A CAT.
NO, YOU'RE NOT. YOU'RE A LION. THAT MAKES YOU A...A...
MAYBE I'LL CARVE A NICE LITTLE KITTY, TOO.
WITH WHISKERS. CUTE LITTLE WHISKERS.

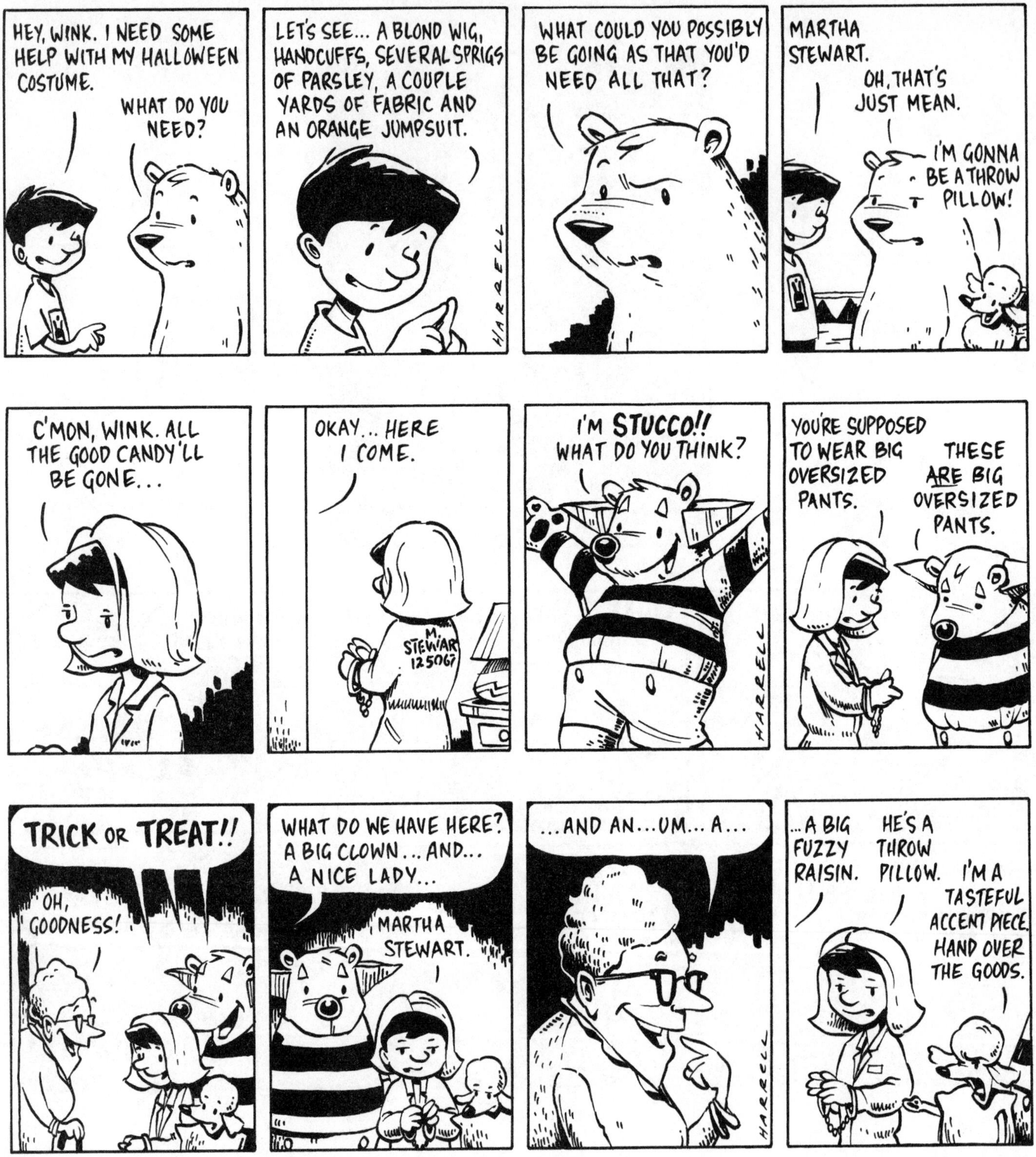
HEY, WINK. I NEED SOME HELP WITH MY HALLOWEEN COSTUME.
WHAT DO YOU NEED?
LET'S SEE... A BLOND WIG, HANDCUFFS, SEVERAL SPRIGS OF PARSLEY, A COUPLE YARDS OF FABRIC AND AN ORANGE JUMPSUIT.
HARRELL
WHAT COULD YOU POSSIBLY BE GOING AS THAT YOU'D NEED ALL THAT?
MARTHA STEWART.
OH, THAT'S JUST MEAN.
I'M GONNA BE A THROW PILLOW!
C'MON, WINK. ALL THE GOOD CANDY'LL BE GONE...
OKAY... HERE I COME.
M. STEWAR 125067
I'M STUCCO!! WHAT DO YOU THINK?
HARRELL
YOU'RE SUPPOSED TO WEAR BIG OVERSIZED PANTS.
THESE ARE BIG OVERSIZED PANTS.
TRICK OR TREAT!!
OH, GOODNESS!
WHAT DO WE HAVE HERE? A BIG CLOWN... AND... A NICE LADY...
MARTHA STEWART.
...AND AN...UM... A...
HARRELL
...A BIG FUZZY RAISIN.
HE'S A THROW PILLOW.
I'M A TASTEFUL ACCENT PIECE. HAND OVER THE GOODS.

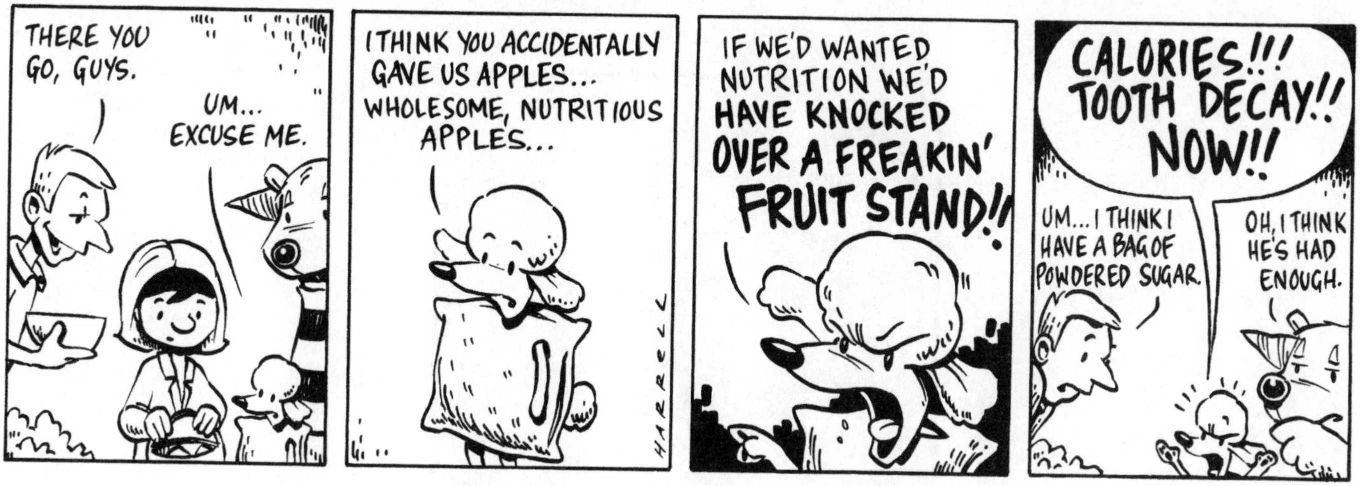
THERE YOU GO, GUYS.
UM... EXCUSE ME.
I THINK YOU ACCIDENTALLY GAVE US APPLES... WHOLESOME, NUTRITIOUS APPLES...
HARRELL
IF WE'D WANTED NUTRITION WE'D HAVE KNOCKED OVER A FREAKIN' FRUIT STAND!!
CALORIES!!! TOOTH DECAY!! NOW!!
UM... I THINK I HAVE A BAG OF POWDERED SUGAR.
OH, I THINK HE'S HAD ENOUGH.

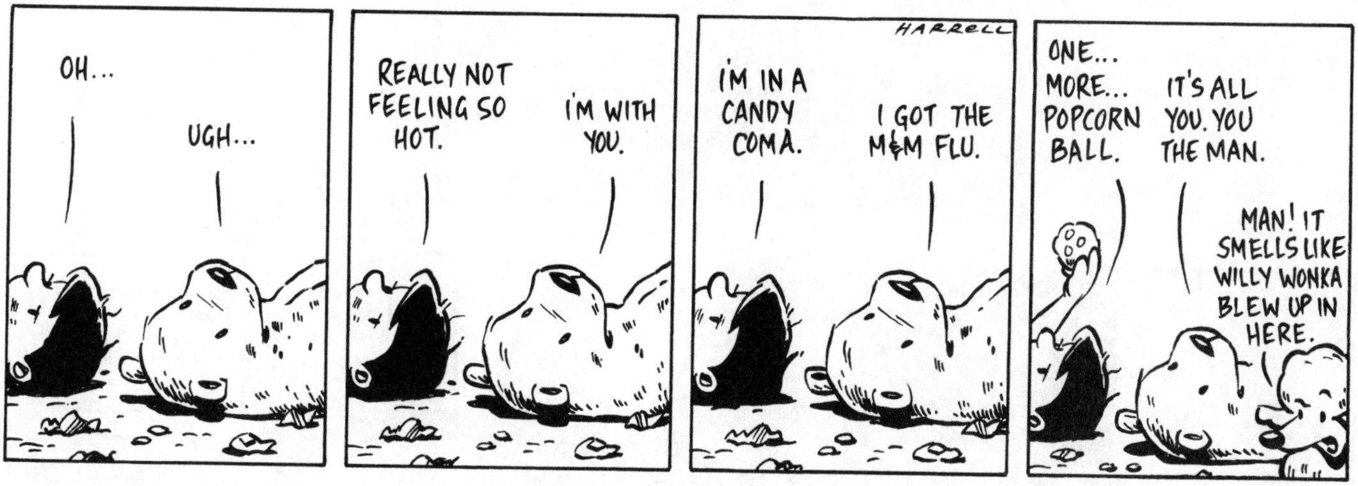
OH...
UGH...
REALLY NOT FEELING SO HOT.
I'M WITH YOU.
HARRELL
I'M IN A CANDY COMA.
I GOT THE M&M FLU.
ONE... MORE... POPCORN BALL.
IT'S ALL YOU. YOU THE MAN.
MAN! IT SMELLS LIKE WILLY WONKA BLEW UP IN HERE.

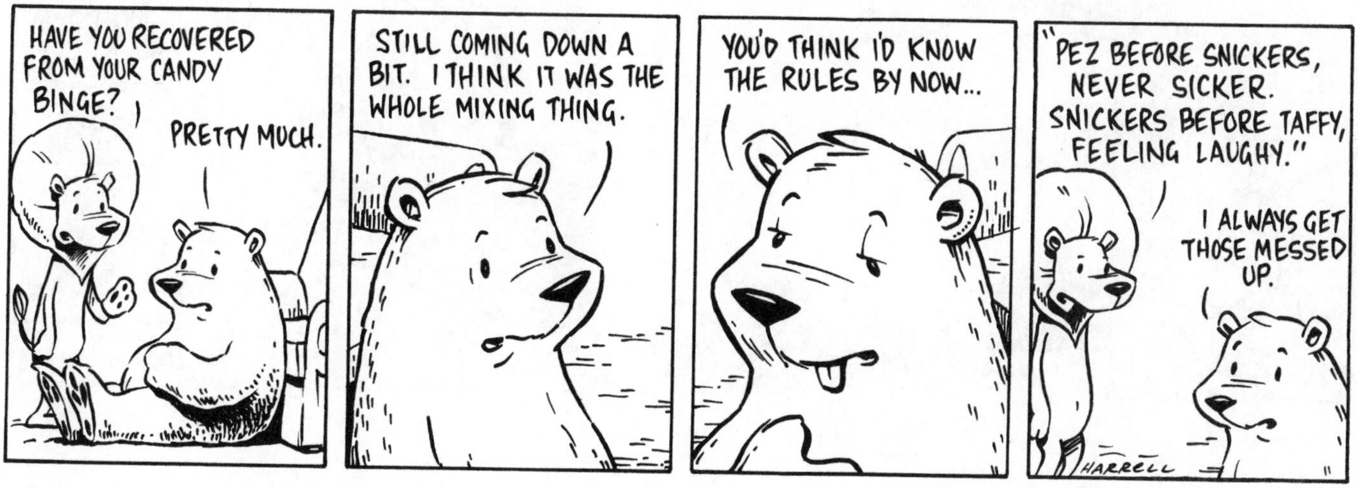
HAVE YOU RECOVERED FROM YOUR CANDY BINGE?
PRETTY MUCH.
STILL COMING DOWN A BIT. I THINK IT WAS THE WHOLE MIXING THING.
YOU'D THINK I'D KNOW THE RULES BY NOW...
"PEZ BEFORE SNICKERS, NEVER SICKER. SNICKERS BEFORE TAFFY, FEELING LAUGHY."
I ALWAYS GET THOSE MESSED UP.
HARRELL

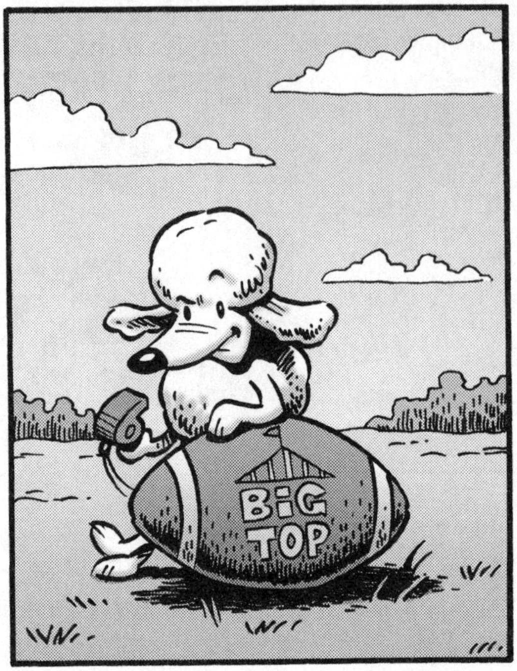
BIG TOP

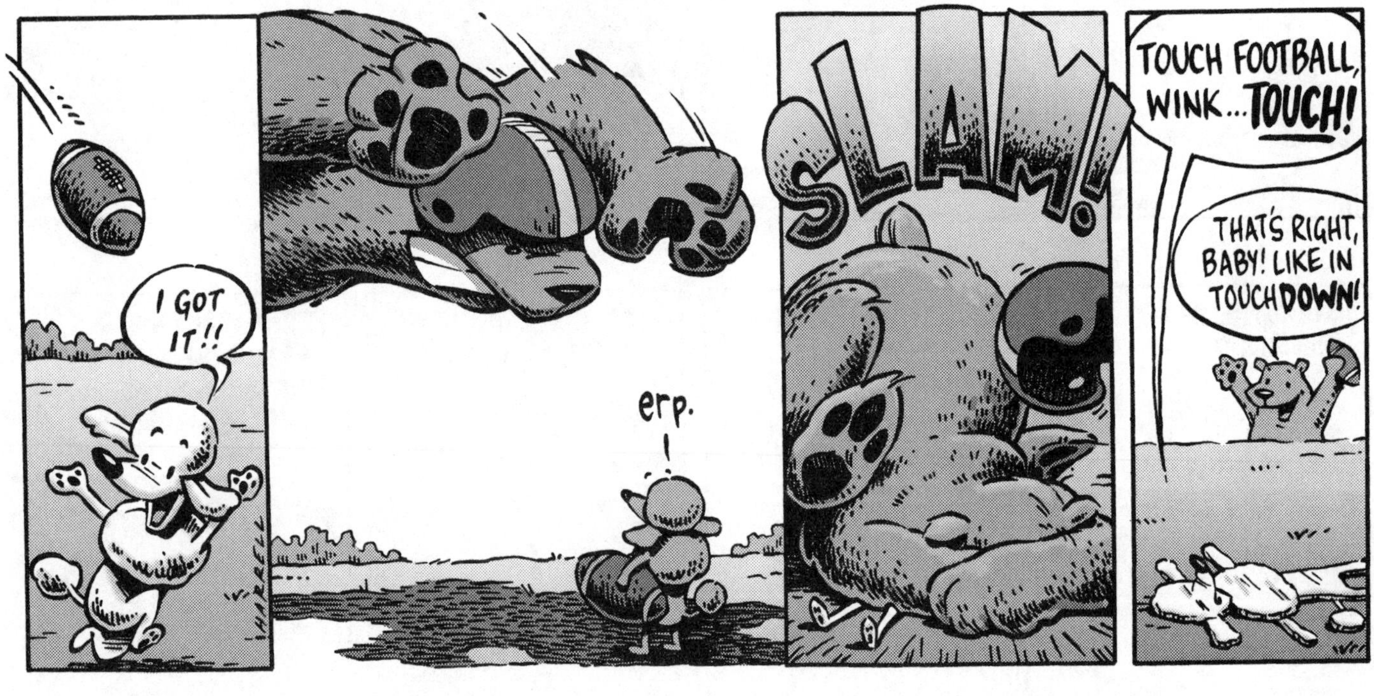
I GOT IT!!
erp.
SLAM!
TOUCH FOOTBALL, WINK...TOUCH!
THAT'S RIGHT, BABY! LIKE IN TOUCHDOWN!

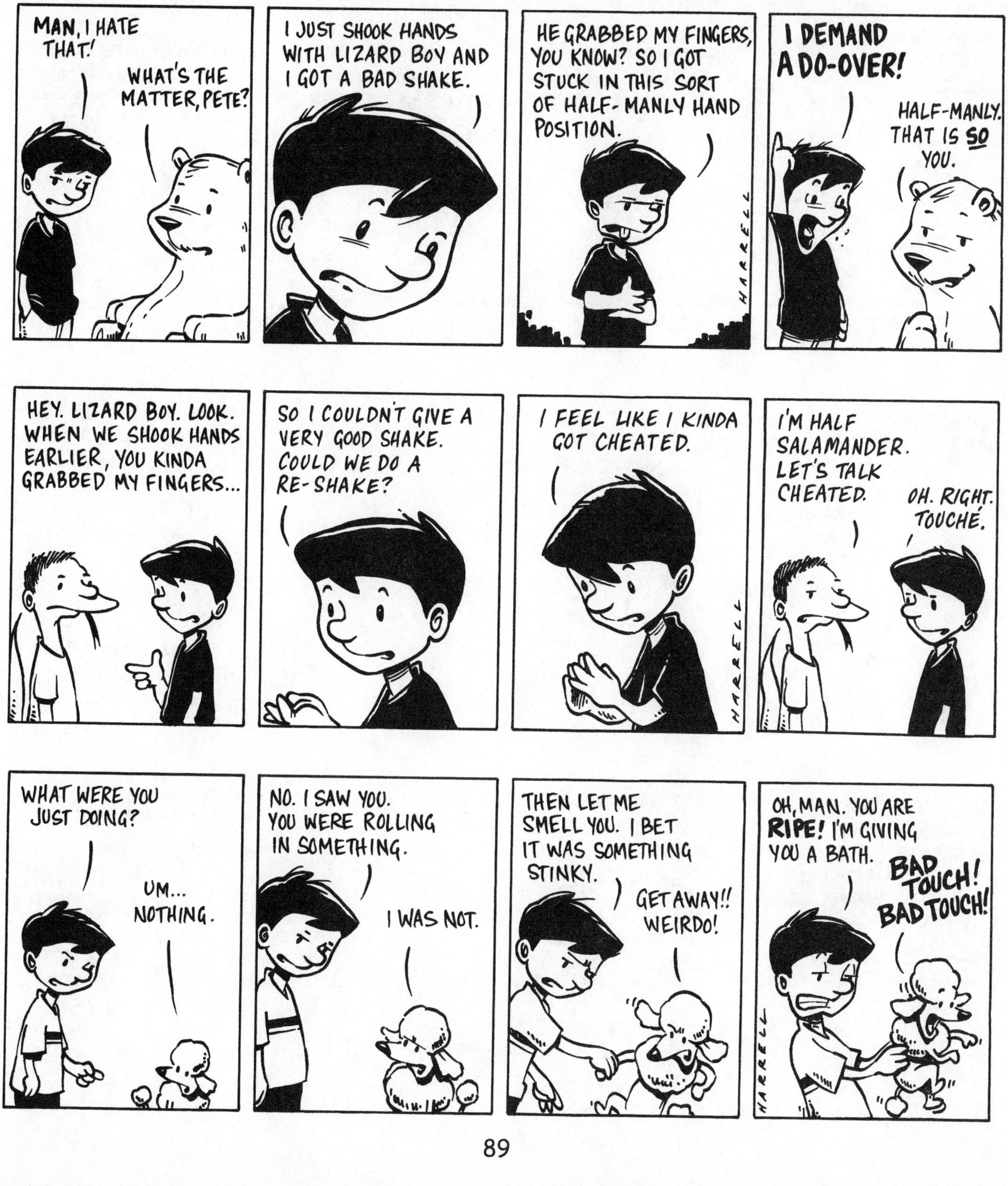
MAN, I HATE THAT!
WHAT'S THE MATTER, PETE?
I JUST SHOOK HANDS WITH LIZARD BOY AND I GOT A BAD SHAKE.
HE GRABBED MY FINGERS, YOU KNOW? SO I GOT STUCK IN THIS SORT OF HALF-MANLY HAND POSITION.
HARRELL
I DEMAND A DO-OVER!
HALF-MANLY. THAT IS SO YOU.
HEY. LIZARD BOY. LOOK. WHEN WE SHOOK HANDS EARLIER, YOU KINDA GRABBED MY FINGERS...
SO I COULDN'T GIVE A VERY GOOD SHAKE. COULD WE DO A RE-SHAKE?
I FEEL LIKE I KINDA GOT CHEATED.
HARRELL
I'M HALF SALAMANDER. LET'S TALK CHEATED.
OH. RIGHT. TOUCHÉ.
WHAT WERE YOU JUST DOING?
UM... NOTHING.
NO. I SAW YOU. YOU WERE ROLLING IN SOMETHING.
I WAS NOT.
THEN LET ME SMELL YOU. I BET IT WAS SOMETHING STINKY.
GET AWAY!! WEIRDO!
OH, MAN. YOU ARE RIPE! I'M GIVING YOU A BATH.
BAD TOUCH! BAD TOUCH!
HARRELL

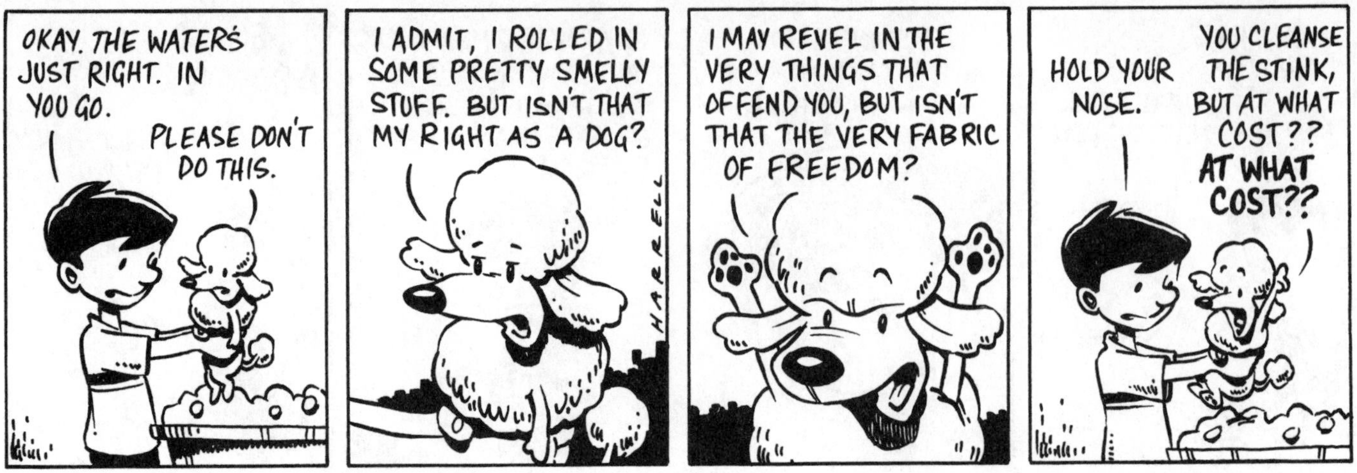
OKAY. THE WATER'S JUST RIGHT. IN YOU GO.
PLEASE DON'T DO THIS.
I ADMIT, I ROLLED IN SOME PRETTY SMELLY STUFF. BUT ISN'T THAT MY RIGHT AS A DOG?
HARRELL
I MAY REVEL IN THE VERY THINGS THAT OFFEND YOU, BUT ISN'T THAT THE VERY FABRIC OF FREEDOM?
HOLD YOUR NOSE.
YOU CLEANSE THE STINK, BUT AT WHAT COST?? AT WHAT COST??

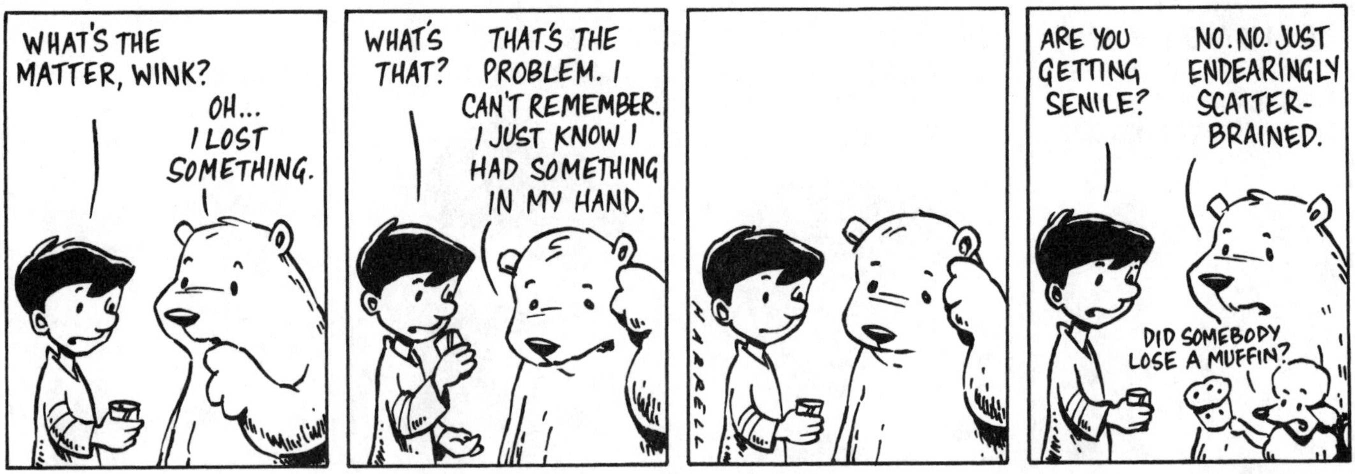
WHAT'S THE MATTER, WINK?
OH... I LOST SOMETHING.
WHAT'S THAT?
THAT'S THE PROBLEM. I CAN'T REMEMBER. I JUST KNOW I HAD SOMETHING IN MY HAND.
HARRELL
ARE YOU GETTING SENILE?
NO. NO. JUST ENDEARINGLY SCATTER-BRAINED.
DID SOMEBODY LOSE A MUFFIN?

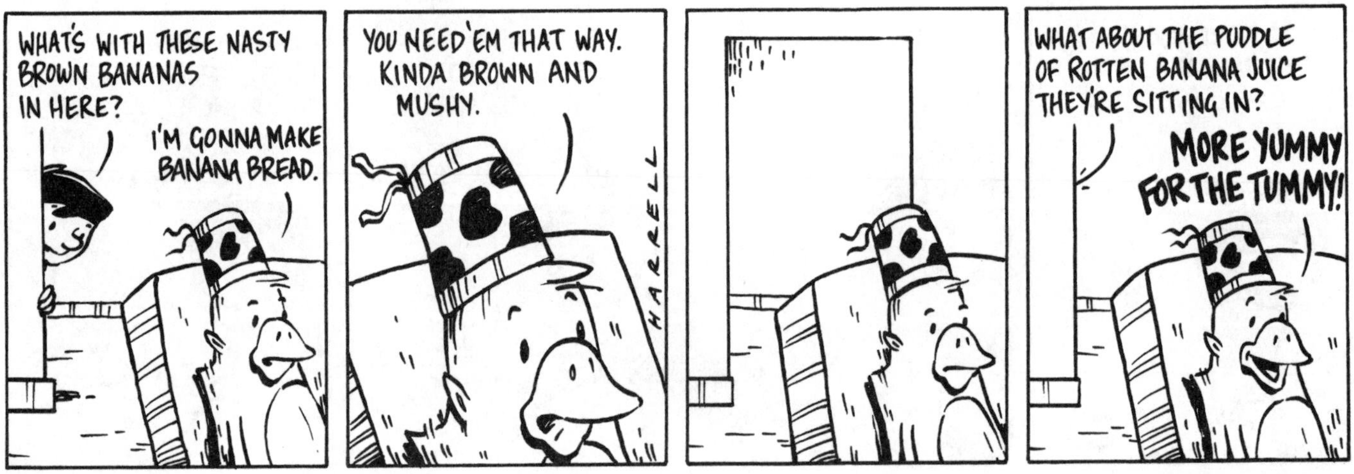
WHAT'S WITH THESE NASTY BROWN BANANAS IN HERE?
I'M GONNA MAKE BANANA BREAD.
YOU NEED 'EM THAT WAY. KINDA BROWN AND MUSHY.
HARRELL
WHAT ABOUT THE PUDDLE OF ROTTEN BANANA JUICE THEY'RE SITTING IN?
MORE YUMMY FOR THE TUMMY!

Big Top

HEY, PETE. TELL ME HOW THIS SOUNDS.

SINGLE, BROWN BEAR SEEKS LADY BEAR, NON SMOKER FOR LONG WALKS ON MIDWAY, UNICYCLE RIDES, SALMON SMOOTHIES AND LOTS OF CUDDLE TIME.

TOO NEEDY?

NO... NO. IT SOUNDS GOOD.

IT MAY BE JUST A LITTLE... LIMITING.

HOW SO?

IT'S JUST SO SPECIFIC. WHAT IF SOMEONE DOESN'T **LIKE** FISH SMOOTHIES?

I COULD NEVER LOVE SOMEONE LIKE THAT.

YOU JUST MAY BE SETTING YOUR STANDARDS A LITTLE HIGH.

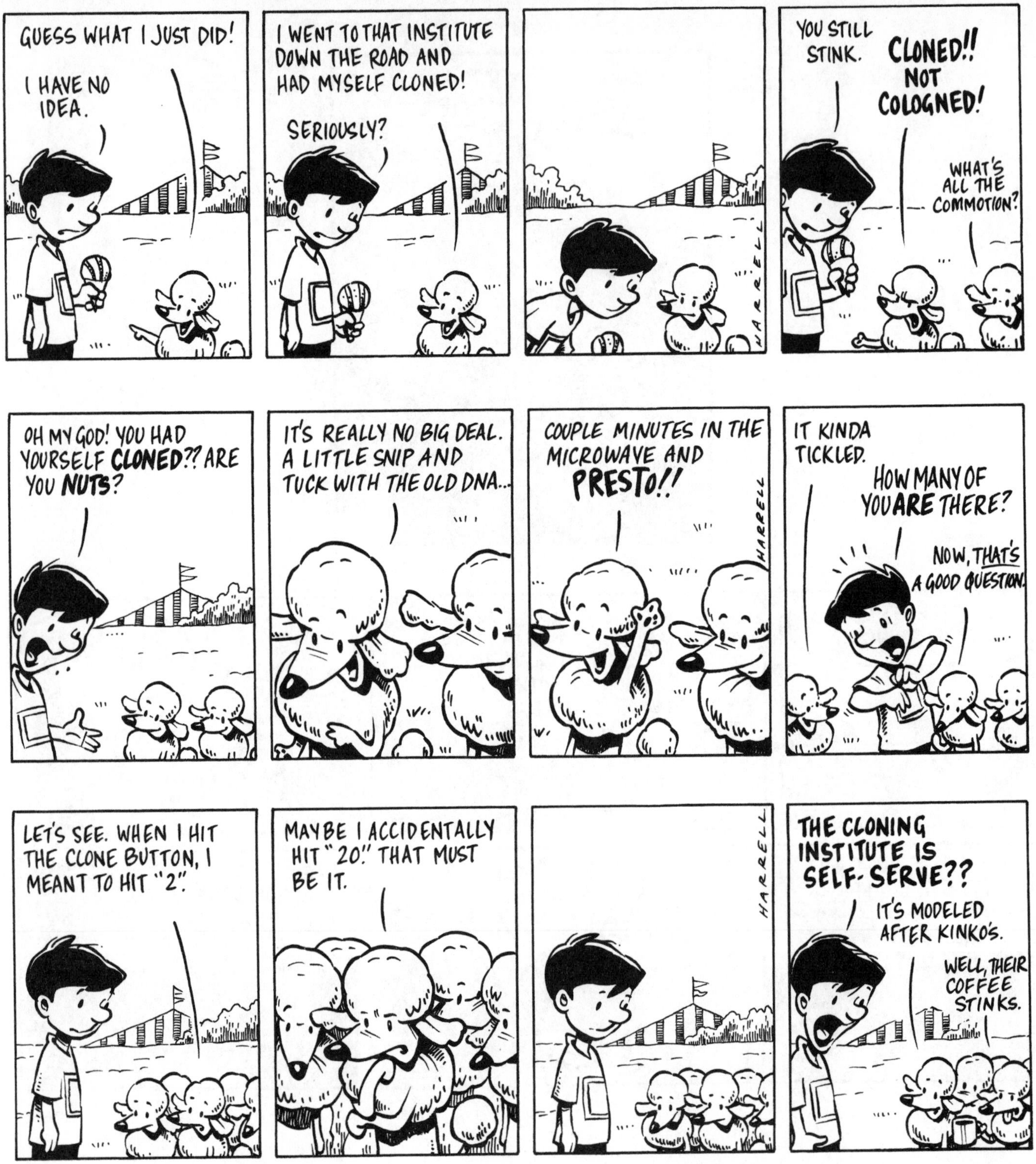
GUESS WHAT I JUST DID!
I HAVE NO IDEA.
I WENT TO THAT INSTITUTE DOWN THE ROAD AND HAD MYSELF CLONED!
SERIOUSLY?
HARRELL
YOU STILL STINK.
CLONED!! NOT COLOGNED!
WHAT'S ALL THE COMMOTION?
OH MY GOD! YOU HAD YOURSELF CLONED?? ARE YOU NUTS?
IT'S REALLY NO BIG DEAL. A LITTLE SNIP AND TUCK WITH THE OLD DNA...
COUPLE MINUTES IN THE MICROWAVE AND PRESTO!!
HARRELL
IT KINDA TICKLED.
HOW MANY OF YOU ARE THERE?
NOW, THAT'S A GOOD QUESTION.
LET'S SEE. WHEN I HIT THE CLONE BUTTON, I MEANT TO HIT "2."
MAYBE I ACCIDENTALLY HIT "20." THAT MUST BE IT.
HARRELL
THE CLONING INSTITUTE IS SELF-SERVE??
IT'S MODELED AFTER KINKO'S.
WELL, THEIR COFFEE STINKS.

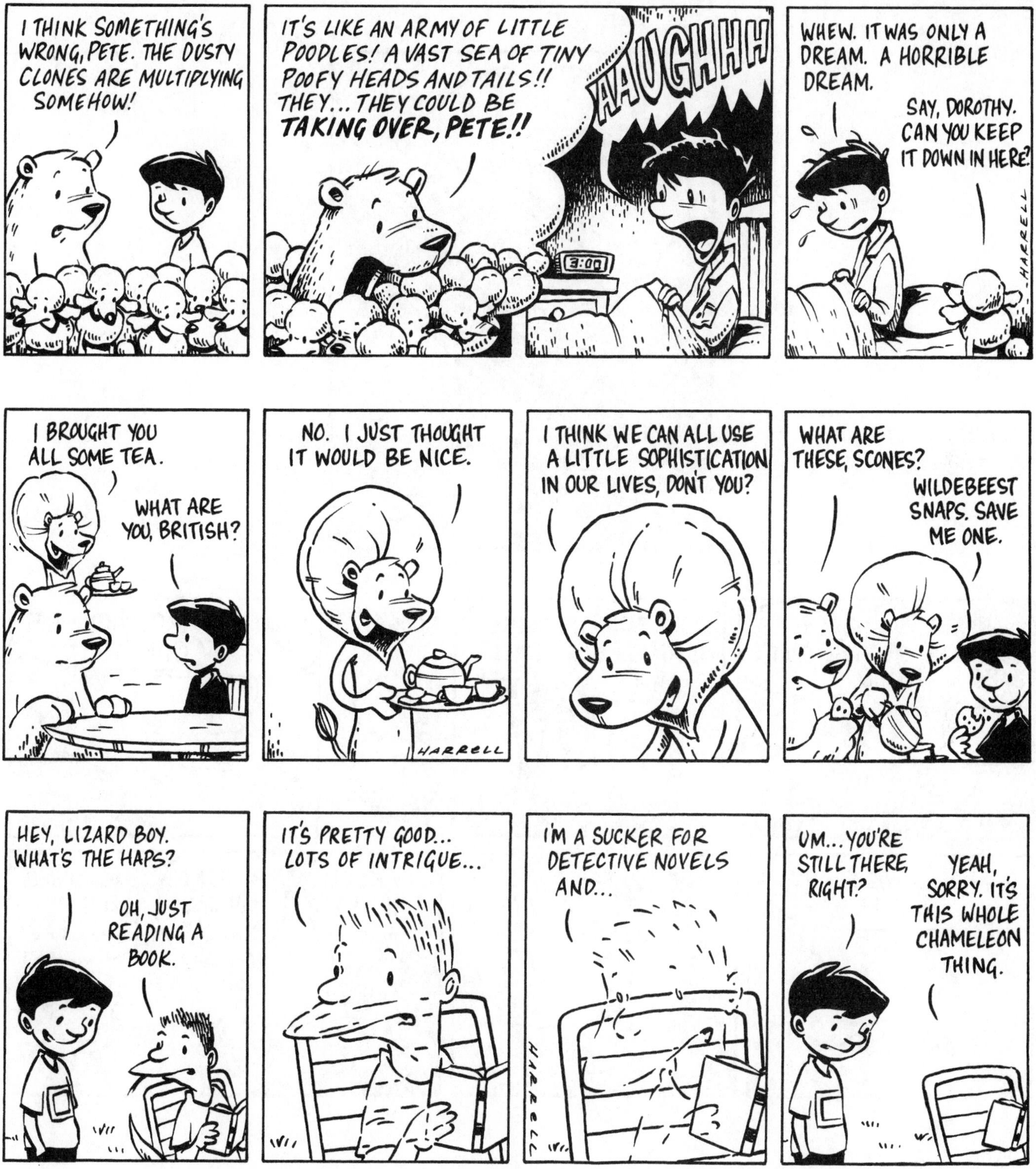
I THINK SOMETHING'S WRONG, PETE. THE DUSTY CLONES ARE MULTIPLYING SOMEHOW!
IT'S LIKE AN ARMY OF LITTLE POODLES! A VAST SEA OF TINY POOFY HEADS AND TAILS!! THEY... THEY COULD BE TAKING OVER, PETE!!
AAUGHHH
3:00
WHEW. IT WAS ONLY A DREAM. A HORRIBLE DREAM.
SAY, DOROTHY. CAN YOU KEEP IT DOWN IN HERE?
HARRELL
I BROUGHT YOU ALL SOME TEA.
WHAT ARE YOU, BRITISH?
NO. I JUST THOUGHT IT WOULD BE NICE.
HARRELL
I THINK WE CAN ALL USE A LITTLE SOPHISTICATION IN OUR LIVES, DON'T YOU?
WHAT ARE THESE, SCONES?
WILDEBEEST SNAPS. SAVE ME ONE.
HEY, LIZARD BOY. WHAT'S THE HAPS?
OH, JUST READING A BOOK.
IT'S PRETTY GOOD... LOTS OF INTRIGUE...
HARRELL
I'M A SUCKER FOR DETECTIVE NOVELS AND...
UM... YOU'RE STILL THERE, RIGHT?
YEAH, SORRY. IT'S THIS WHOLE CHAMELEON THING.

 MANFRED, I'VE NEVER SEEN ONE OF THOSE CANDY BARS. WHAT'S IN IT?

 CARAMEL...PEANUTS... NOUGAT... IT'S REALLY GOOD.

 NOUGAT... I

 WHAT A WEIRD WORD. WHAT **IS** NOUGAT, ANYWAY?

 IT JUST SOUNDS FUNNY... NOUGAT.

 "HAVE YOU TRIED THE NOUGAT?"..."OH, THIS IS LOVELY NOUGAT."

 YOU NEED A HOBBY. NOUGAT. NOUGAT. NOUGAT. HAS ANYONE SEEN MY CANDY BAR?

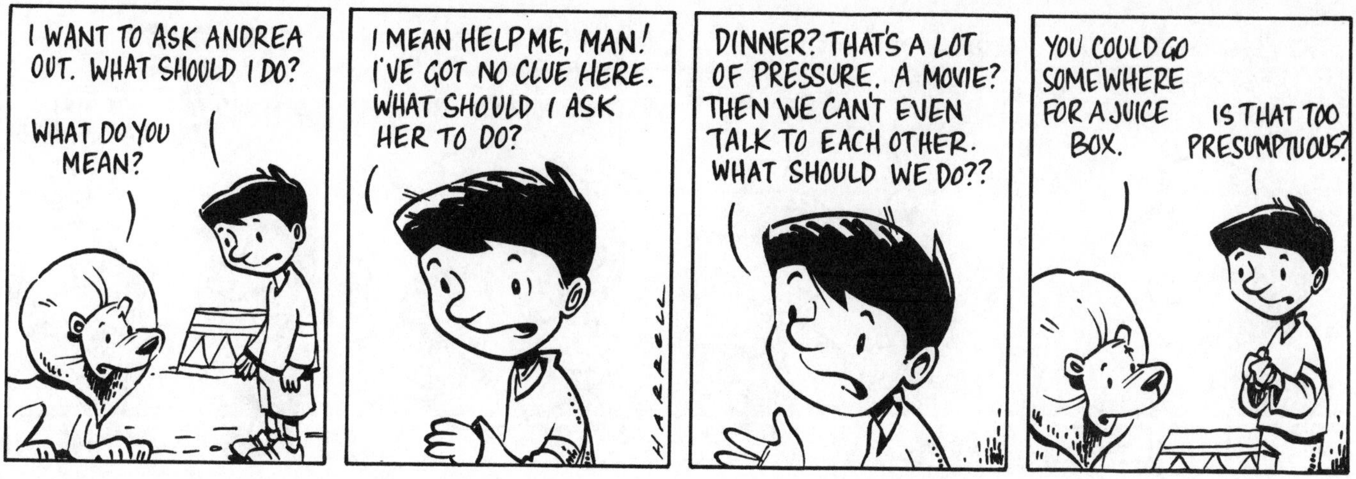
I WANT TO ASK ANDREA OUT. WHAT SHOULD I DO?
WHAT DO YOU MEAN?
I MEAN HELP ME, MAN! I'VE GOT NO CLUE HERE. WHAT SHOULD I ASK HER TO DO?
HARRELL
DINNER? THAT'S A LOT OF PRESSURE. A MOVIE? THEN WE CAN'T EVEN TALK TO EACH OTHER. WHAT SHOULD WE DO??
YOU COULD GO SOMEWHERE FOR A JUICE BOX.
IS THAT TOO PRESUMPTUOUS?

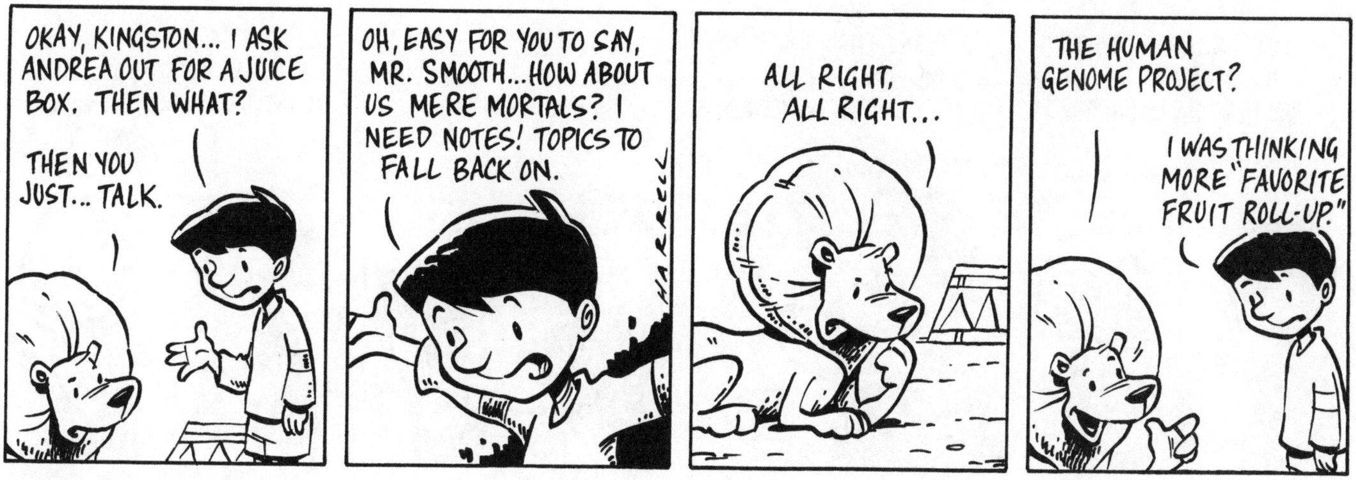
OKAY, KINGSTON... I ASK ANDREA OUT FOR A JUICE BOX. THEN WHAT?
THEN YOU JUST... TALK.
OH, EASY FOR YOU TO SAY, MR. SMOOTH...HOW ABOUT US MERE MORTALS? I NEED NOTES! TOPICS TO FALL BACK ON.
HARRELL
ALL RIGHT, ALL RIGHT...
THE HUMAN GENOME PROJECT?
I WAS THINKING MORE "FAVORITE FRUIT ROLL-UP."

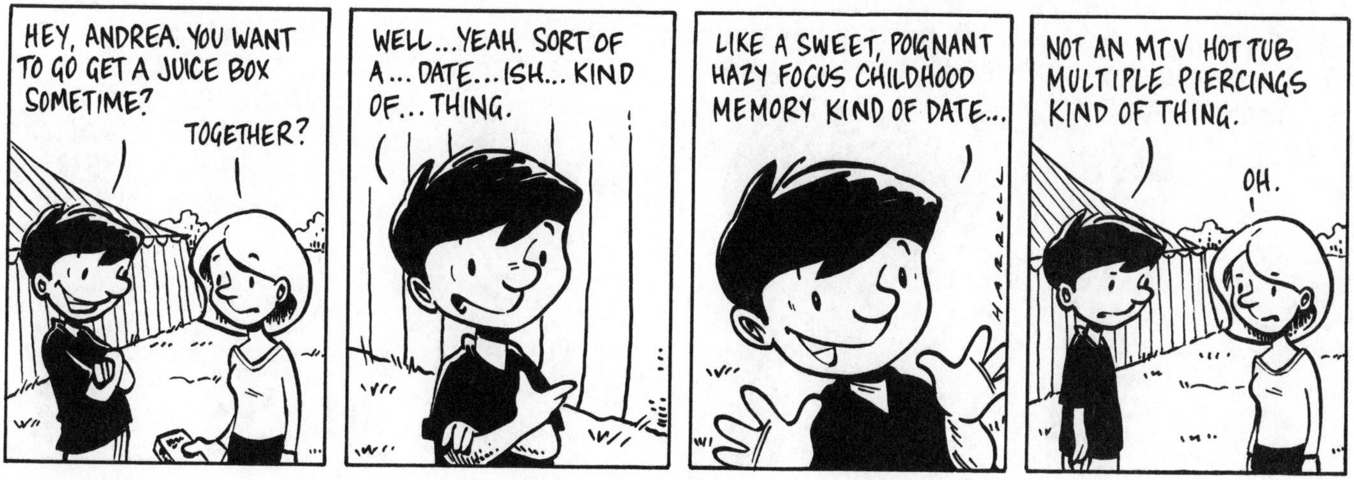
HEY, ANDREA. YOU WANT TO GO GET A JUICE BOX SOMETIME?
TOGETHER?
WELL...YEAH. SORT OF A... DATE...ISH... KIND OF... THING.
LIKE A SWEET, POIGNANT HAZY FOCUS CHILDHOOD MEMORY KIND OF DATE...
HARRELL
NOT AN MTV HOT TUB MULTIPLE PIERCINGS KIND OF THING.
OH.

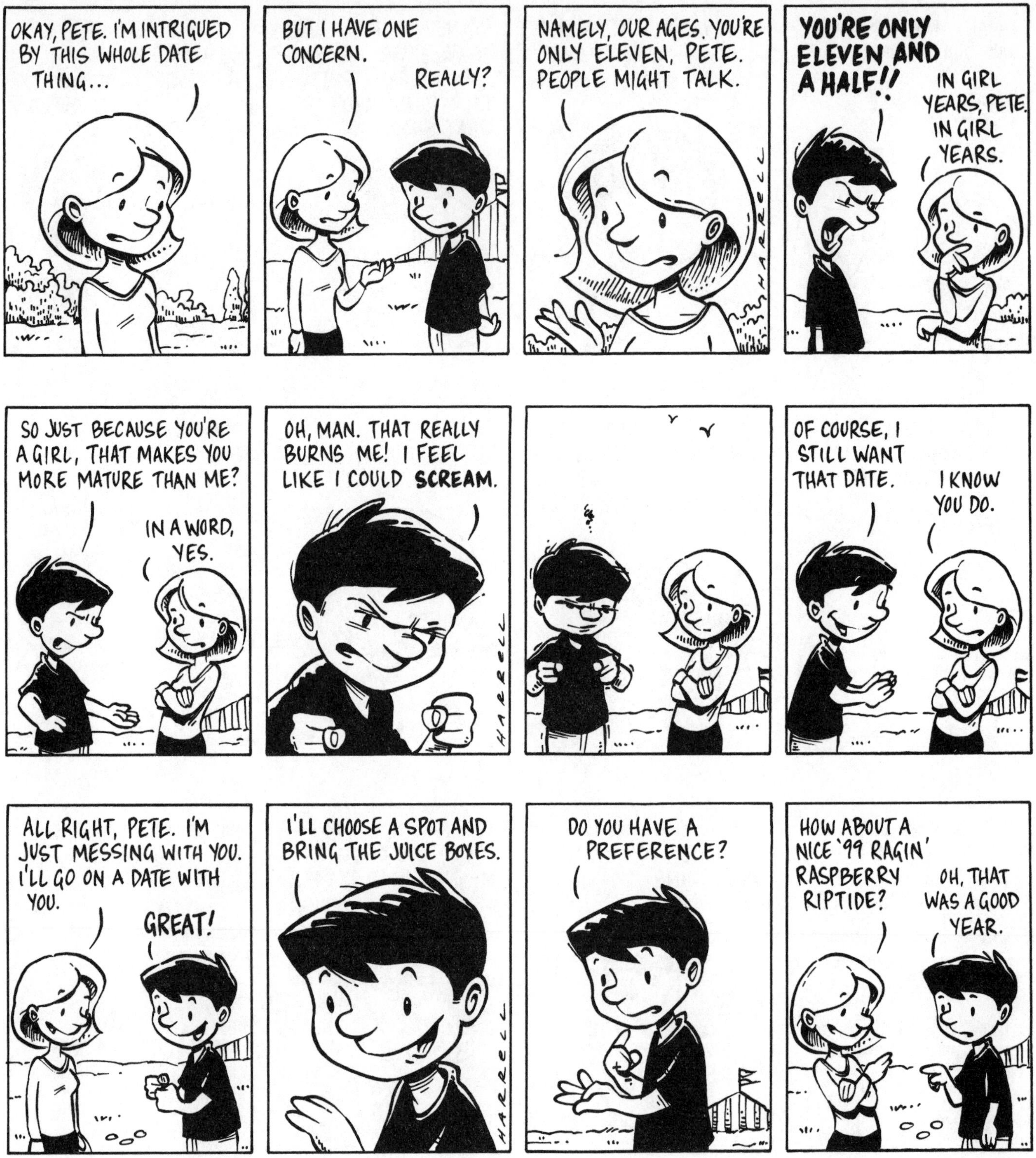
OKAY, PETE. I'M INTRIGUED BY THIS WHOLE DATE THING...
BUT I HAVE ONE CONCERN.
REALLY?
NAMELY, OUR AGES. YOU'RE ONLY ELEVEN, PETE. PEOPLE MIGHT TALK.
YOU'RE ONLY ELEVEN AND A HALF!!
IN GIRL YEARS, PETE. IN GIRL YEARS.
SO JUST BECAUSE YOU'RE A GIRL, THAT MAKES YOU MORE MATURE THAN ME?
IN A WORD, YES.
OH, MAN. THAT REALLY BURNS ME! I FEEL LIKE I COULD SCREAM.
OF COURSE, I STILL WANT THAT DATE.
I KNOW YOU DO.
ALL RIGHT, PETE. I'M JUST MESSING WITH YOU. I'LL GO ON A DATE WITH YOU.
GREAT!
I'LL CHOOSE A SPOT AND BRING THE JUICE BOXES.
DO YOU HAVE A PREFERENCE?
HOW ABOUT A NICE '99 RAGIN' RASPBERRY RIPTIDE?
OH, THAT WAS A GOOD YEAR.
HARRELL

SMELL THAT?

YEAH...
GOOD STUFF.

THE CHILL IN THE AIR...
THE SMELL OF BURNING
LEAVES...THE FIRST TIME
YOU THROW ON YOUR
FAVORITE OLD HEAVY
COAT...

THE MELTED HALF A
SNICKERS YOU LEFT
IN THE POCKET...

DIBS.

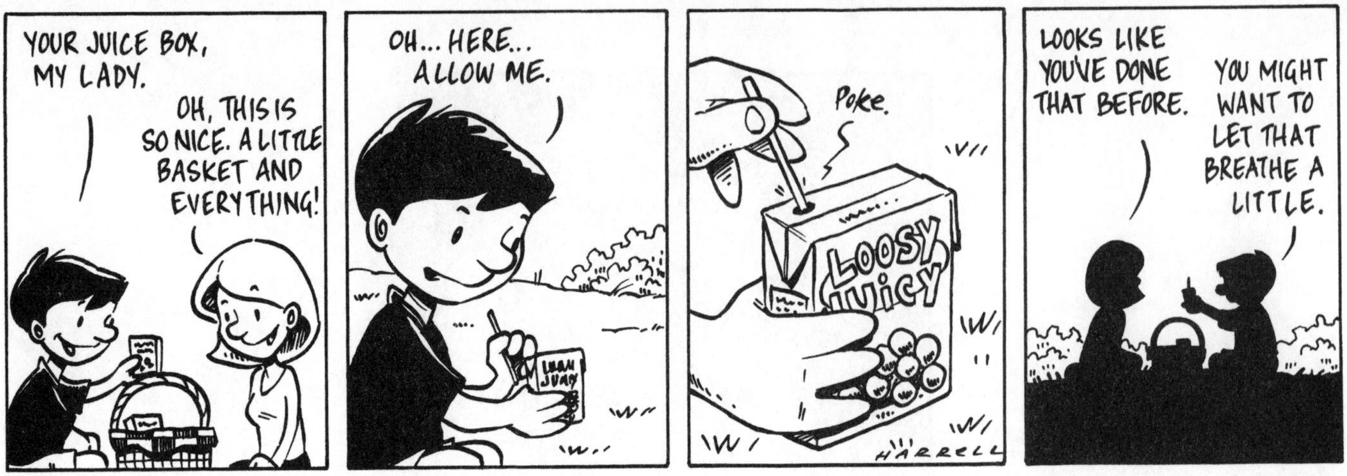
YOUR JUICE BOX, MY LADY.
OH, THIS IS SO NICE. A LITTLE BASKET AND EVERYTHING!
OH... HERE... ALLOW ME.
Poke.
LOOSY JUICY
HARRELL
LOOKS LIKE YOU'VE DONE THAT BEFORE.
YOU MIGHT WANT TO LET THAT BREATHE A LITTLE.

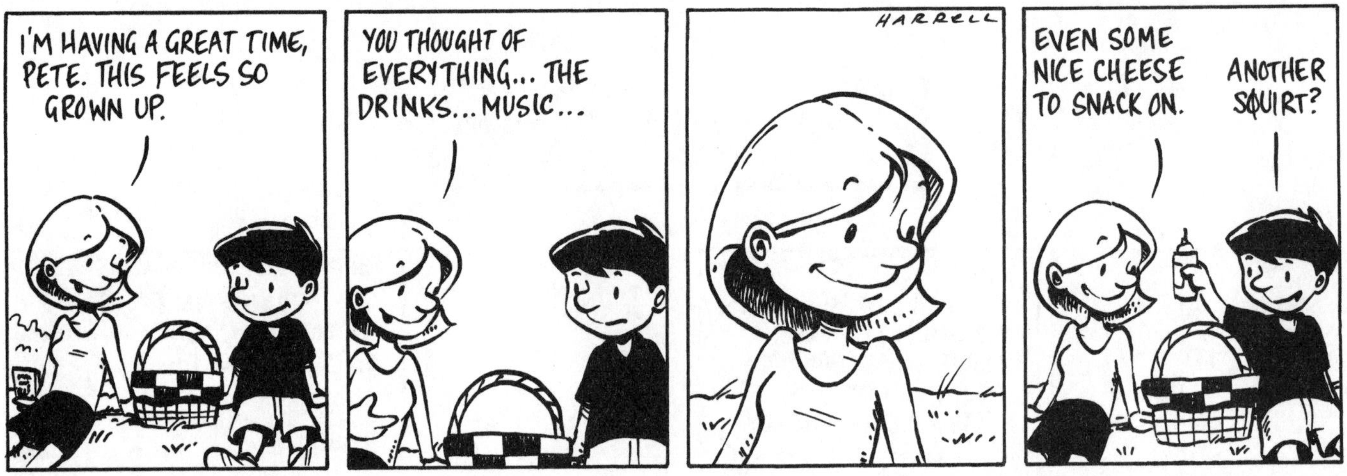
I'M HAVING A GREAT TIME, PETE. THIS FEELS SO GROWN UP.
YOU THOUGHT OF EVERYTHING... THE DRINKS... MUSIC...
HARRELL
EVEN SOME NICE CHEESE TO SNACK ON.
ANOTHER SQUIRT?

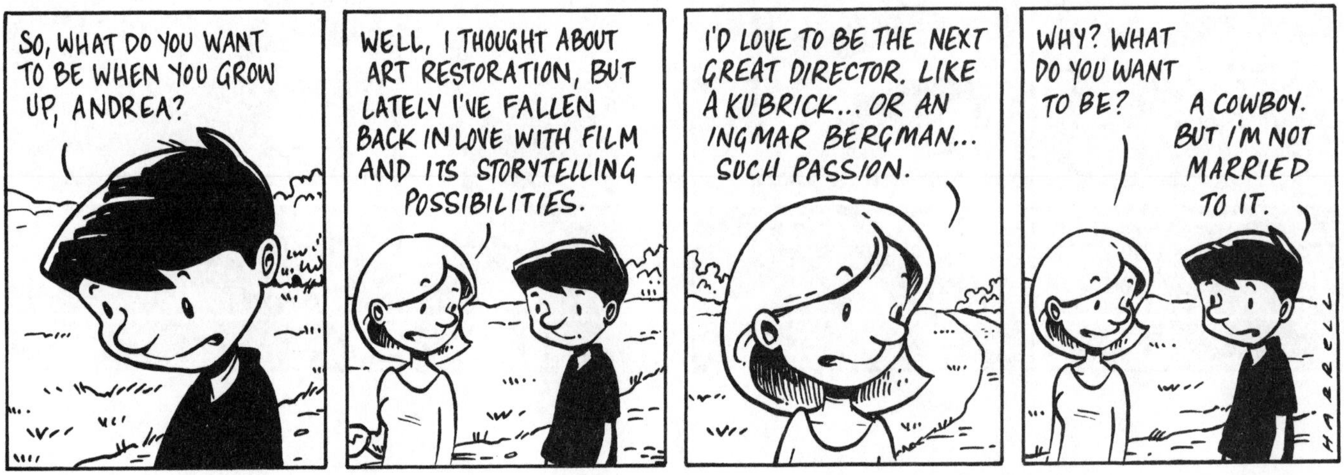
SO, WHAT DO YOU WANT TO BE WHEN YOU GROW UP, ANDREA?
WELL, I THOUGHT ABOUT ART RESTORATION, BUT LATELY I'VE FALLEN BACK IN LOVE WITH FILM AND ITS STORYTELLING POSSIBILITIES.
I'D LOVE TO BE THE NEXT GREAT DIRECTOR. LIKE A KUBRICK... OR AN INGMAR BERGMAN... SUCH PASSION.
WHY? WHAT DO YOU WANT TO BE?
A COWBOY. BUT I'M NOT MARRIED TO IT.
HARRELL

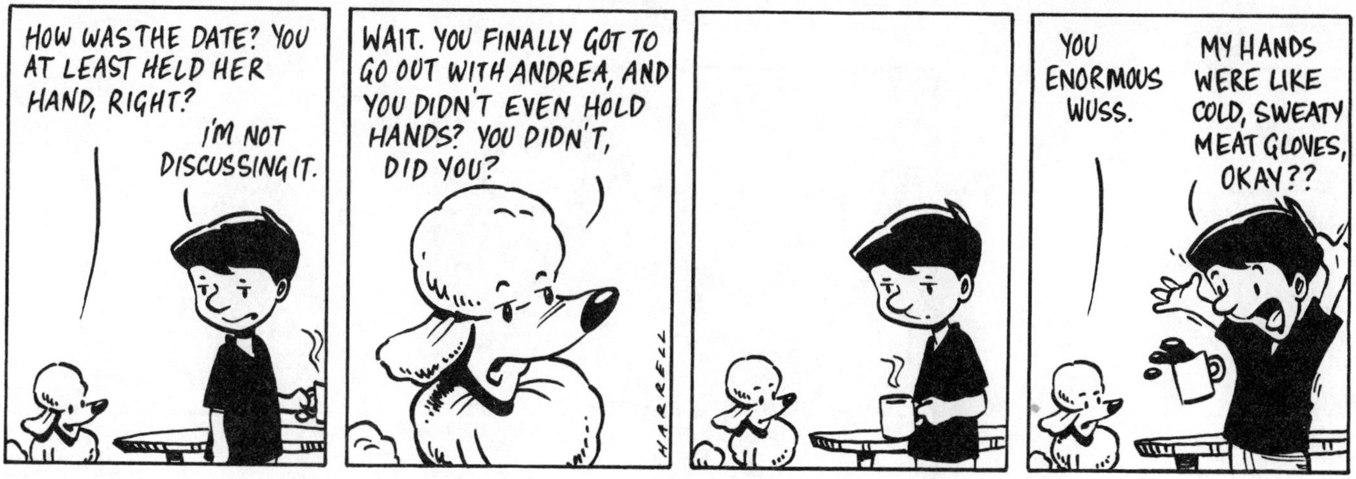
HOW WAS THE DATE? YOU AT LEAST HELD HER HAND, RIGHT?
I'M NOT DISCUSSING IT.
WAIT. YOU FINALLY GOT TO GO OUT WITH ANDREA, AND YOU DIDN'T EVEN HOLD HANDS? YOU DIDN'T, DID YOU?
HARRELL
YOU ENORMOUS WUSS.
MY HANDS WERE LIKE COLD, SWEATY MEAT GLOVES, OKAY??

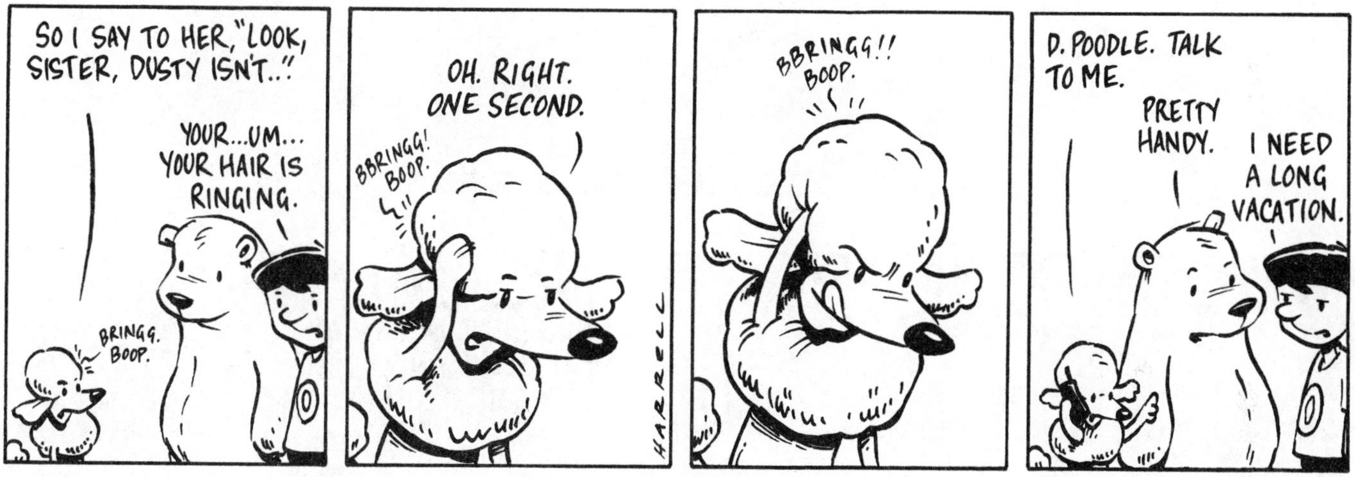
SO I SAY TO HER, "LOOK, SISTER, DUSTY ISN'T..."
YOUR...UM... YOUR HAIR IS RINGING.
BRINGG. BOOP.
OH. RIGHT. ONE SECOND.
BBRINGG! BOOP.
HARRELL
BBRINGG!! BOOP.
D. POODLE. TALK TO ME.
PRETTY HANDY.
I NEED A LONG VACATION.

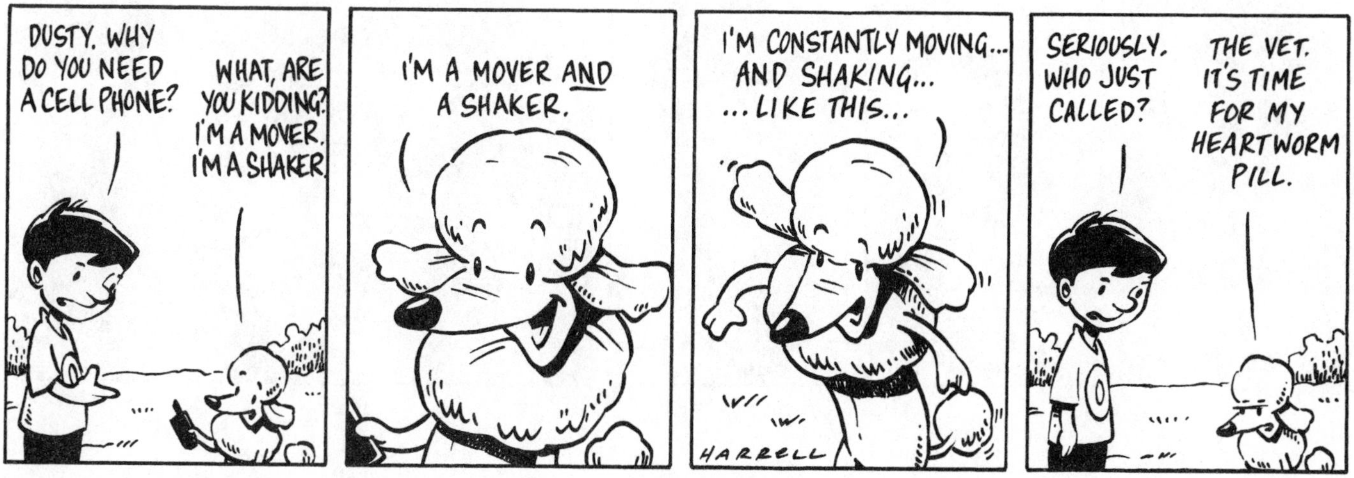
DUSTY. WHY DO YOU NEED A CELL PHONE?
WHAT, ARE YOU KIDDING? I'M A MOVER. I'M A SHAKER.
I'M A MOVER AND A SHAKER.
I'M CONSTANTLY MOVING... AND SHAKING... ...LIKE THIS...
HARRELL
SERIOUSLY. WHO JUST CALLED?
THE VET. IT'S TIME FOR MY HEARTWORM PILL.

BiG TOP

PAFFF
SPLOT
POiNK
COME ON!! KEEP YOUR EYE ON THE PIE AND FOLLOW THROUGH!!
CAN I TAKE A LITTLE BREATHER HERE?

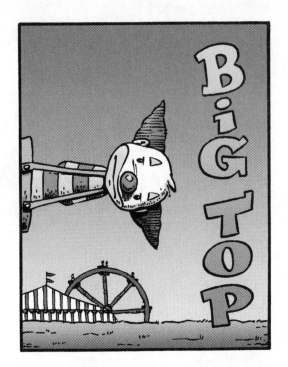

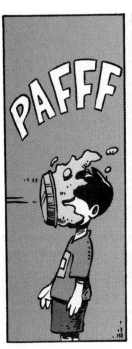

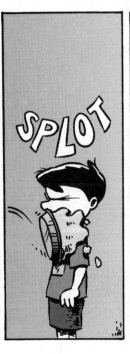

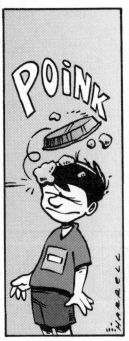

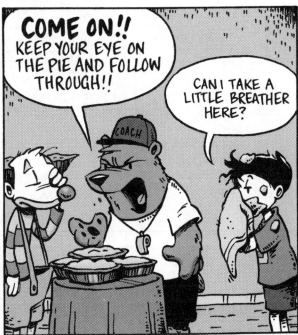

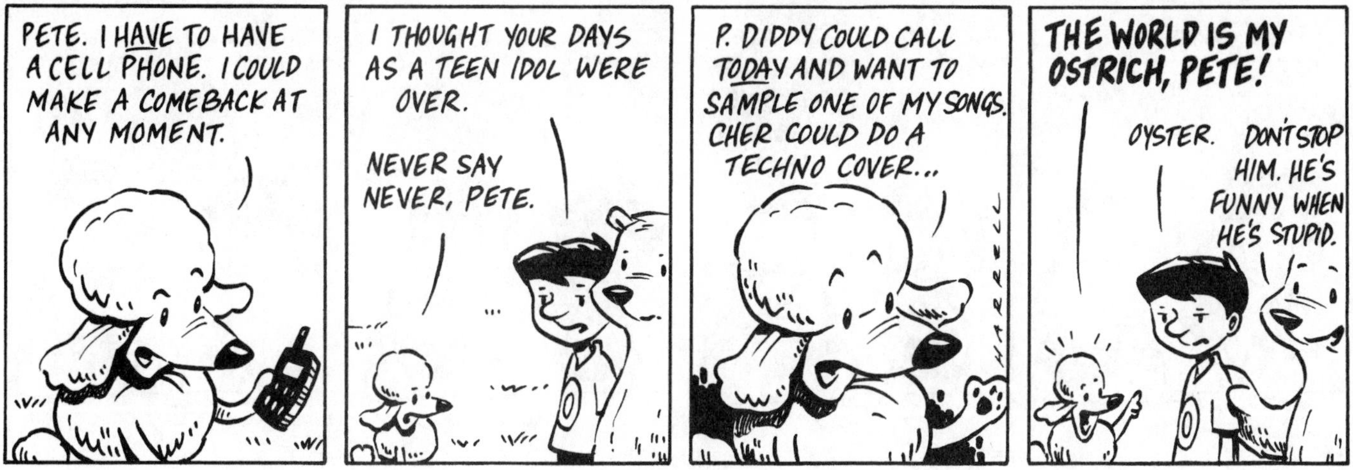
PETE. I HAVE TO HAVE A CELL PHONE. I COULD MAKE A COMEBACK AT ANY MOMENT.
I THOUGHT YOUR DAYS AS A TEEN IDOL WERE OVER.
NEVER SAY NEVER, PETE.
P. DIDDY COULD CALL TODAY AND WANT TO SAMPLE ONE OF MY SONGS. CHER COULD DO A TECHNO COVER...
HARRELL
THE WORLD IS MY OSTRICH, PETE!
OYSTER.
DON'T STOP HIM. HE'S FUNNY WHEN HE'S STUPID.

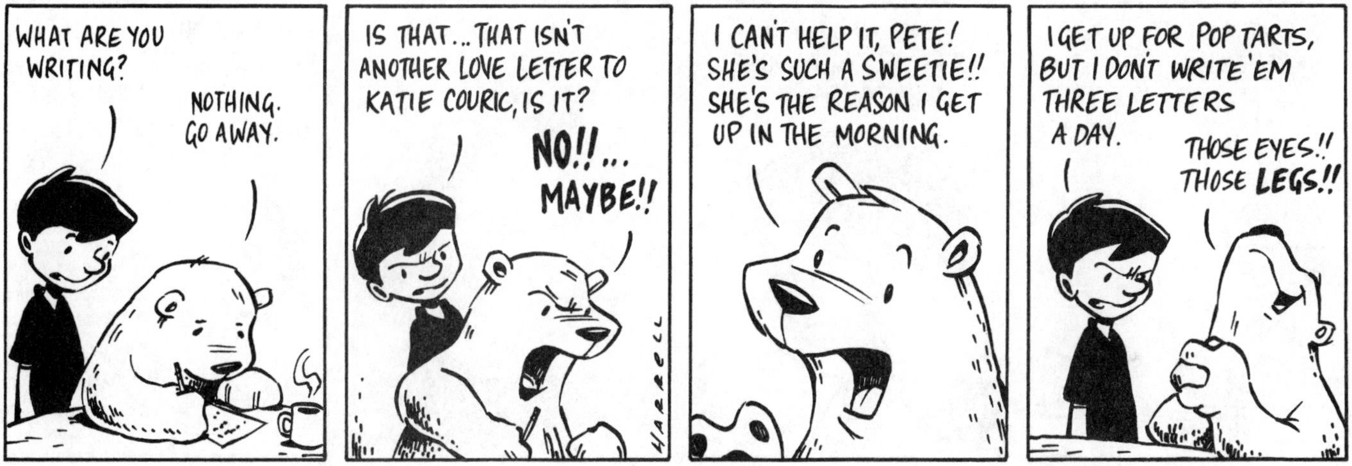
WHAT ARE YOU WRITING?
NOTHING. GO AWAY.
IS THAT... THAT ISN'T ANOTHER LOVE LETTER TO KATIE COURIC, IS IT?
NO!!... MAYBE!!
HARRELL
I CAN'T HELP IT, PETE! SHE'S SUCH A SWEETIE!! SHE'S THE REASON I GET UP IN THE MORNING.
I GET UP FOR POP TARTS, BUT I DON'T WRITE 'EM THREE LETTERS A DAY.
THOSE EYES!! THOSE LEGS!!

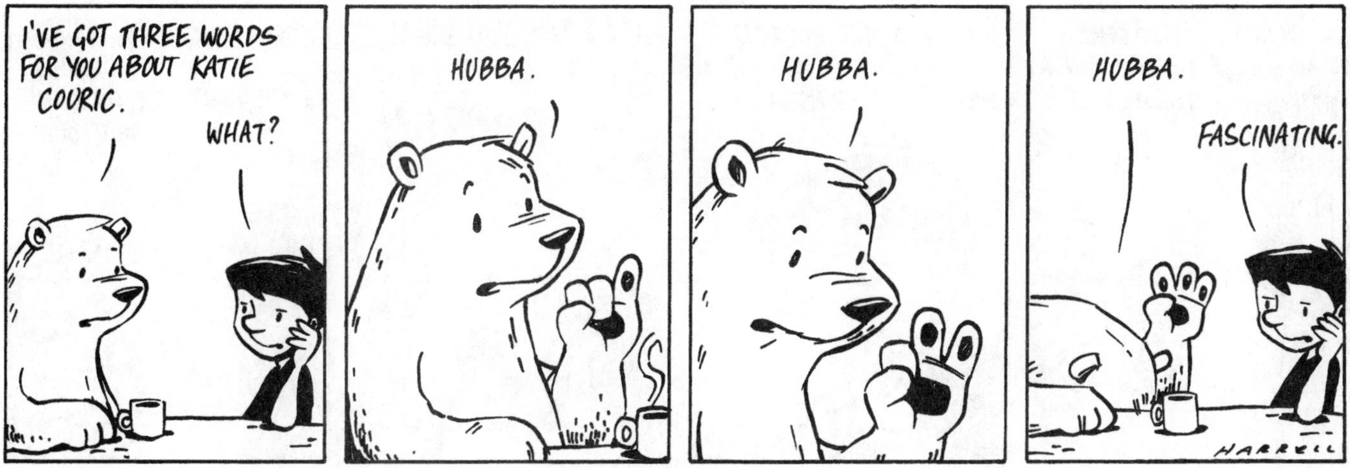
I'VE GOT THREE WORDS FOR YOU ABOUT KATIE COURIC.
WHAT?
HUBBA.
HUBBA.
HUBBA.
FASCINATING.
HARRELL

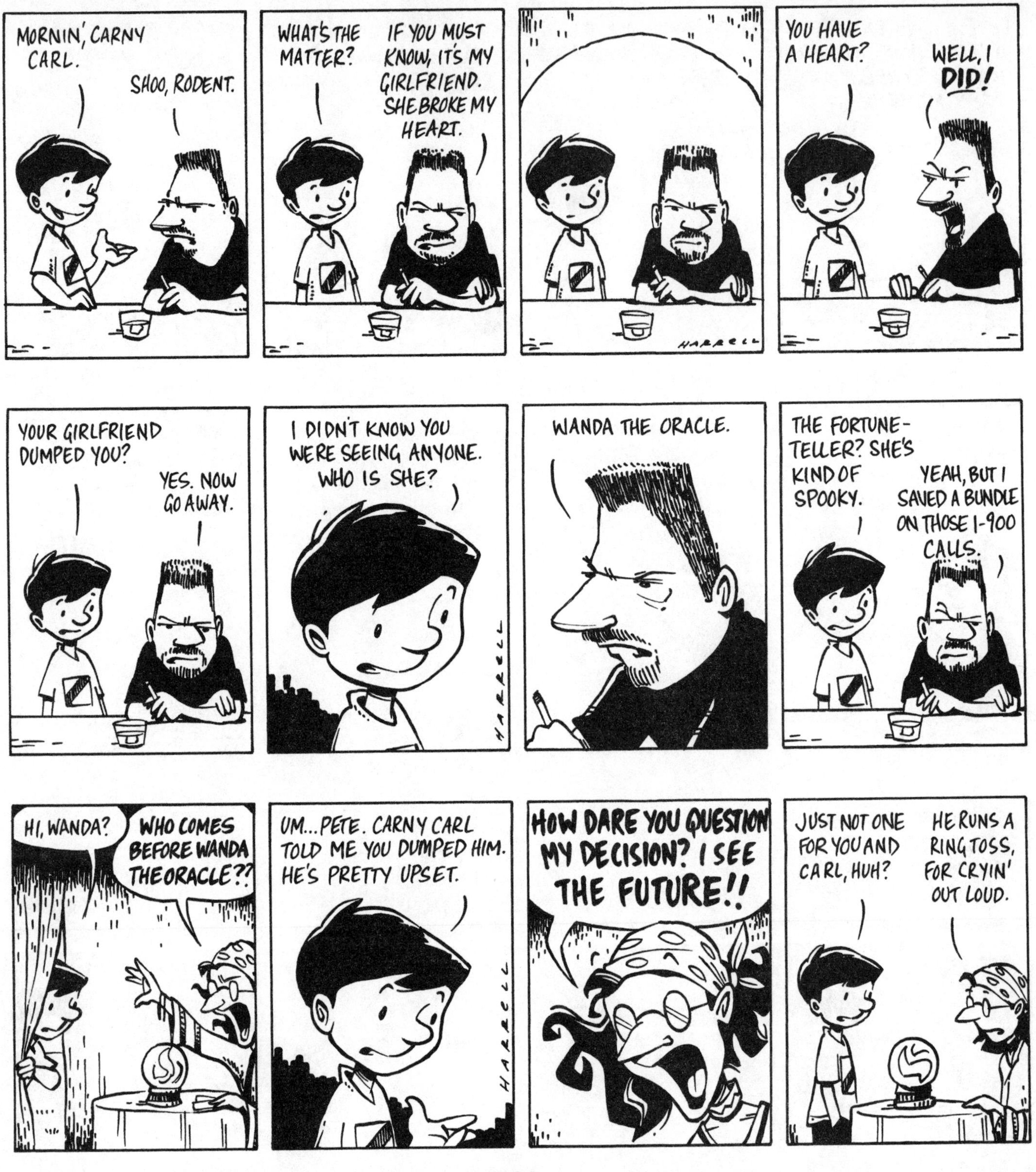
MORNIN', CARNY CARL.
SHOO, RODENT.
WHAT'S THE MATTER?
IF YOU MUST KNOW, IT'S MY GIRLFRIEND. SHE BROKE MY HEART.
YOU HAVE A HEART?
WELL, I DID!
HARRELL
YOUR GIRLFRIEND DUMPED YOU?
YES. NOW GO AWAY.
I DIDN'T KNOW YOU WERE SEEING ANYONE. WHO IS SHE?
HARRELL
WANDA THE ORACLE.
THE FORTUNE-TELLER? SHE'S KIND OF SPOOKY.
YEAH, BUT I SAVED A BUNDLE ON THOSE 1-900 CALLS.
HI, WANDA?
WHO COMES BEFORE WANDA THE ORACLE??
UM... PETE. CARNY CARL TOLD ME YOU DUMPED HIM. HE'S PRETTY UPSET.
HARRELL
HOW DARE YOU QUESTION MY DECISION? I SEE THE FUTURE!!
JUST NOT ONE FOR YOU AND CARL, HUH?
HE RUNS A RING TOSS, FOR CRYIN' OUT LOUD.

WE SHOULD BUILD A FIRE. IT'S A PERFECT NIGHT FOR IT.

YEAH! GO BRING IN SOME FIREWOOD, MANFRED!

NO, NO... I'LL GET THE FLUE OPEN AND **YOU** GRAB SOME WOOD!

NO, WAIT. **I'LL** HEAT UP SOME HOT CHOCOLATE WHILE **YOU** GET THE WOOD!

...I'LL THROW IN THE LITTLE MARSHMALLOWS.

ALL RIGHT! ALL RIGHT! I'LL DO IT.

WHAT'S THE PROBLEM?

TOO COLD?

SPIDERS IN THE WOODPILE.

COVER ME. I'M GOING IN.

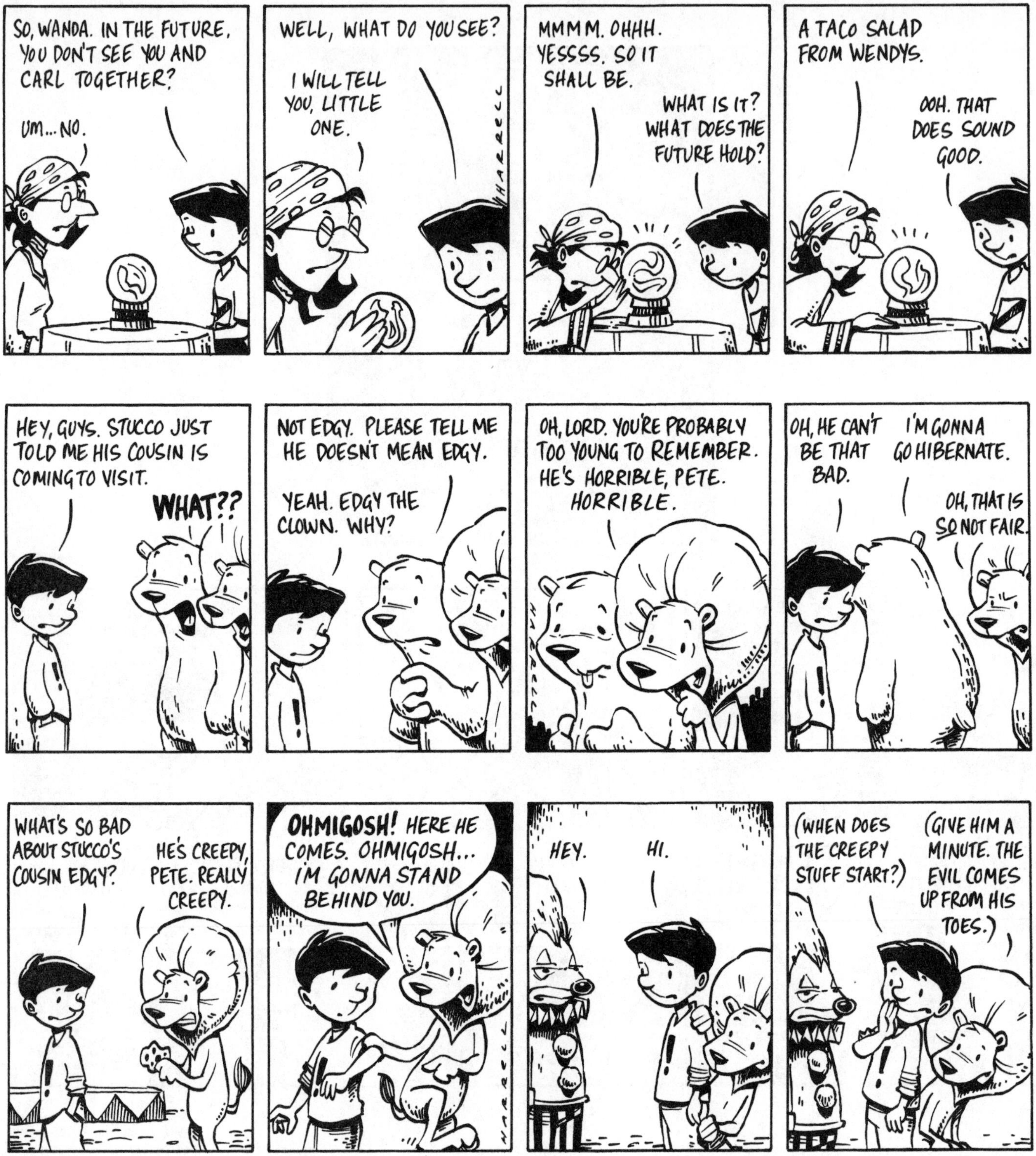
SO, WANDA. IN THE FUTURE, YOU DON'T SEE YOU AND CARL TOGETHER?
UM... NO.
WELL, WHAT DO YOU SEE?
I WILL TELL YOU, LITTLE ONE.
MMMM. OHHH. YESSSS. SO IT SHALL BE.
WHAT IS IT? WHAT DOES THE FUTURE HOLD?
A TACO SALAD FROM WENDYS.
OOH. THAT DOES SOUND GOOD.
HEY, GUYS. STUCCO JUST TOLD ME HIS COUSIN IS COMING TO VISIT.
WHAT??
NOT EDGY. PLEASE TELL ME HE DOESN'T MEAN EDGY.
YEAH. EDGY THE CLOWN. WHY?
OH, LORD. YOU'RE PROBABLY TOO YOUNG TO REMEMBER. HE'S HORRIBLE, PETE. HORRIBLE.
OH, HE CAN'T BE THAT BAD.
I'M GONNA GO HIBERNATE.
OH, THAT IS SO NOT FAIR.
WHAT'S SO BAD ABOUT STUCCO'S COUSIN EDGY?
HE'S CREEPY, PETE. REALLY CREEPY.
OHMIGOSH! HERE HE COMES. OHMIGOSH... I'M GONNA STAND BEHIND YOU.
HEY.
HI.
(WHEN DOES THE CREEPY STUFF START?)
(GIVE HIM A MINUTE. THE EVIL COMES UP FROM HIS TOES.)

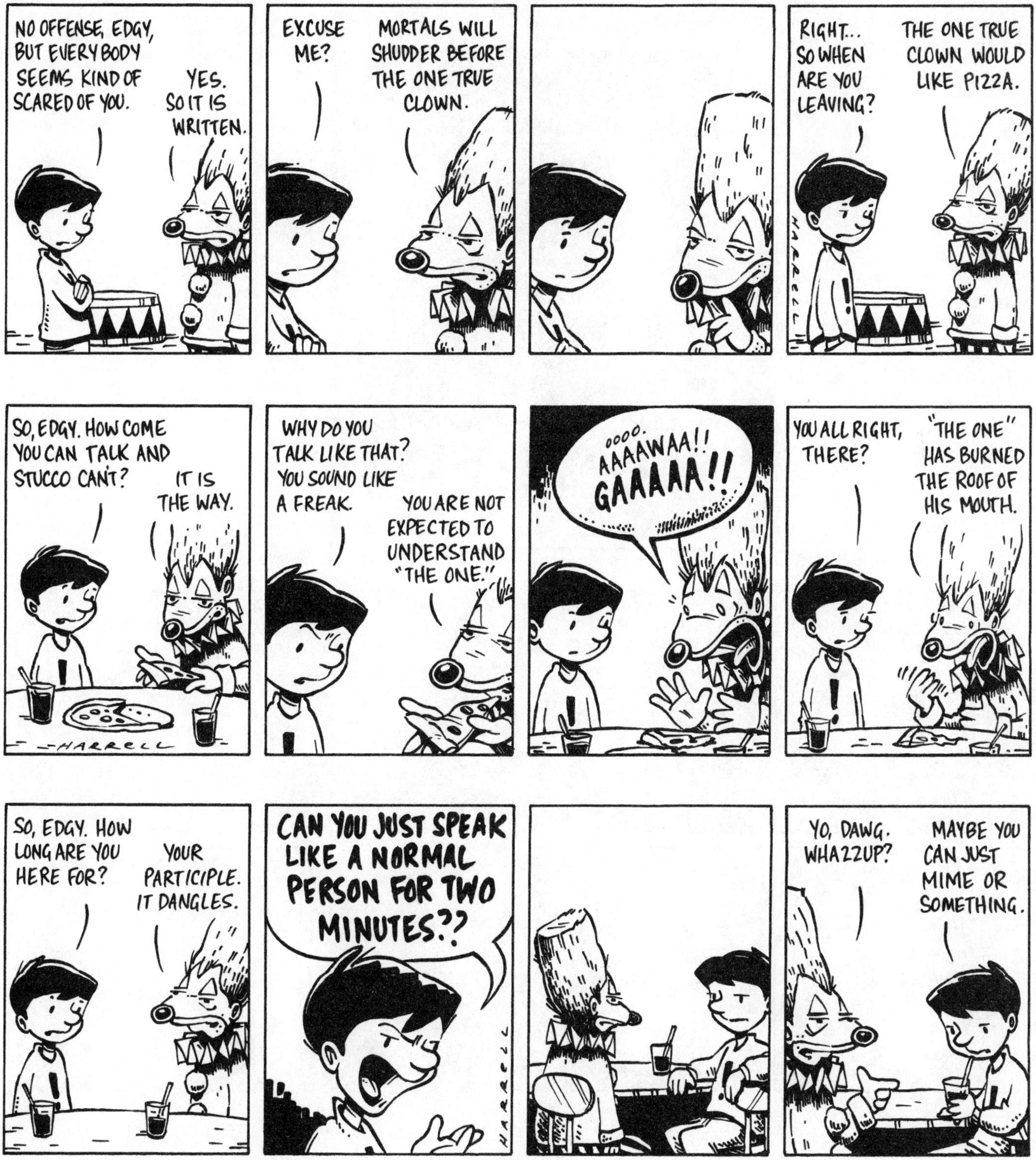
NO OFFENSE, EDGY, BUT EVERYBODY SEEMS KIND OF SCARED OF YOU.
YES. SO IT IS WRITTEN.
EXCUSE ME?
MORTALS WILL SHUDDER BEFORE THE ONE TRUE CLOWN.
RIGHT... SO WHEN ARE YOU LEAVING?
THE ONE TRUE CLOWN WOULD LIKE PIZZA.
HARRELL
SO, EDGY. HOW COME YOU CAN TALK AND STUCCO CAN'T?
IT IS THE WAY.
HARRELL
WHY DO YOU TALK LIKE THAT? YOU SOUND LIKE A FREAK.
YOU ARE NOT EXPECTED TO UNDERSTAND "THE ONE."
OOOO. AAAAWAA!! GAAAAA!!
YOU ALL RIGHT, THERE?
"THE ONE" HAS BURNED THE ROOF OF HIS MOUTH.
SO, EDGY. HOW LONG ARE YOU HERE FOR?
YOUR PARTICIPLE. IT DANGLES.
CAN YOU JUST SPEAK LIKE A NORMAL PERSON FOR TWO MINUTES??
HARRELL
YO, DAWG. WHAZZUP?
MAYBE YOU CAN JUST MIME OR SOMETHING.

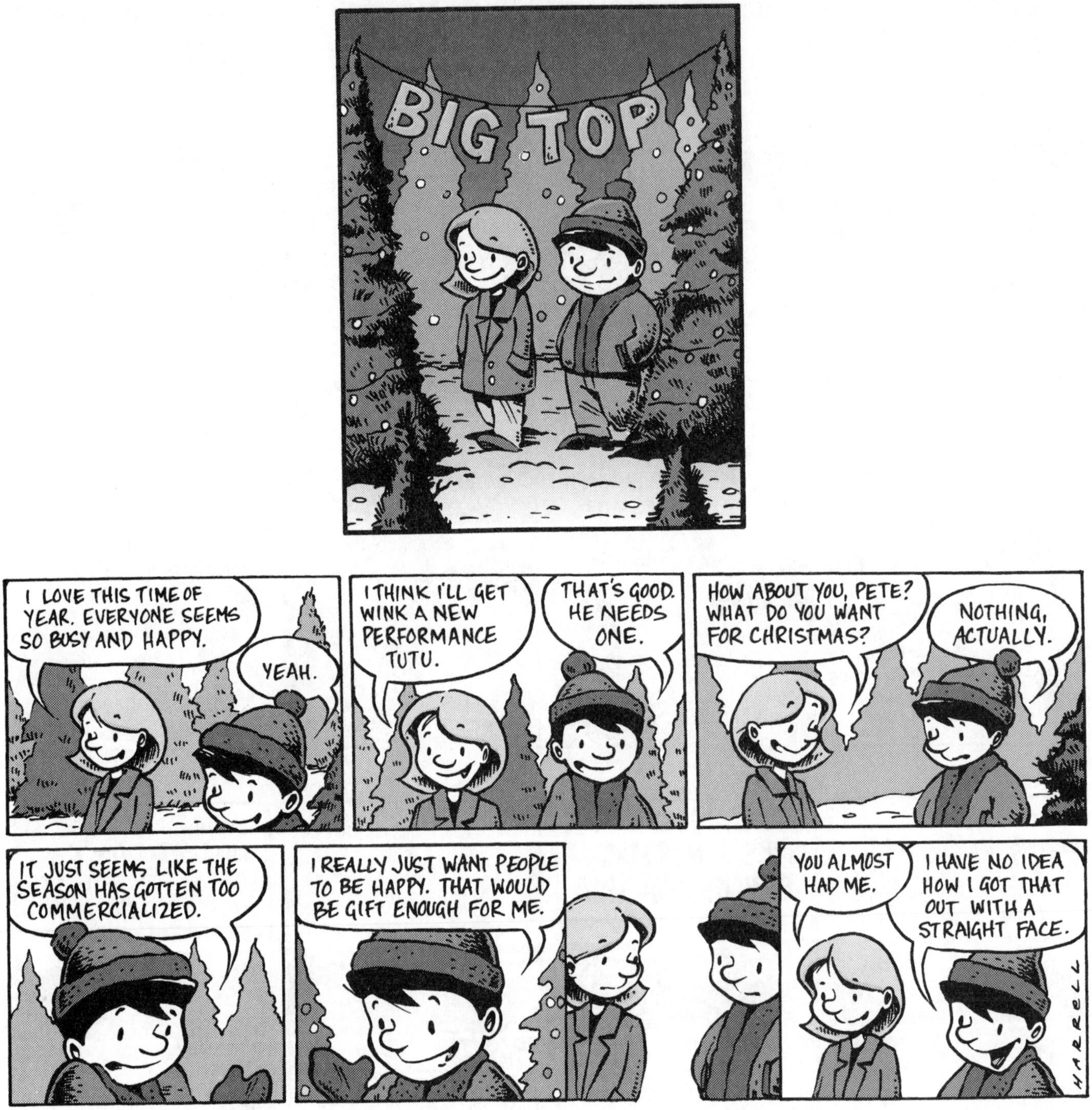
BIG TOP
I LOVE THIS TIME OF YEAR. EVERYONE SEEMS SO BUSY AND HAPPY.
YEAH.
I THINK I'LL GET WINK A NEW PERFORMANCE TUTU.
THAT'S GOOD. HE NEEDS ONE.
HOW ABOUT YOU, PETE? WHAT DO YOU WANT FOR CHRISTMAS?
NOTHING, ACTUALLY.
IT JUST SEEMS LIKE THE SEASON HAS GOTTEN TOO COMMERCIALIZED.
I REALLY JUST WANT PEOPLE TO BE HAPPY. THAT WOULD BE GIFT ENOUGH FOR ME.
YOU ALMOST HAD ME.
I HAVE NO IDEA HOW I GOT THAT OUT WITH A STRAIGHT FACE.
HARRELL

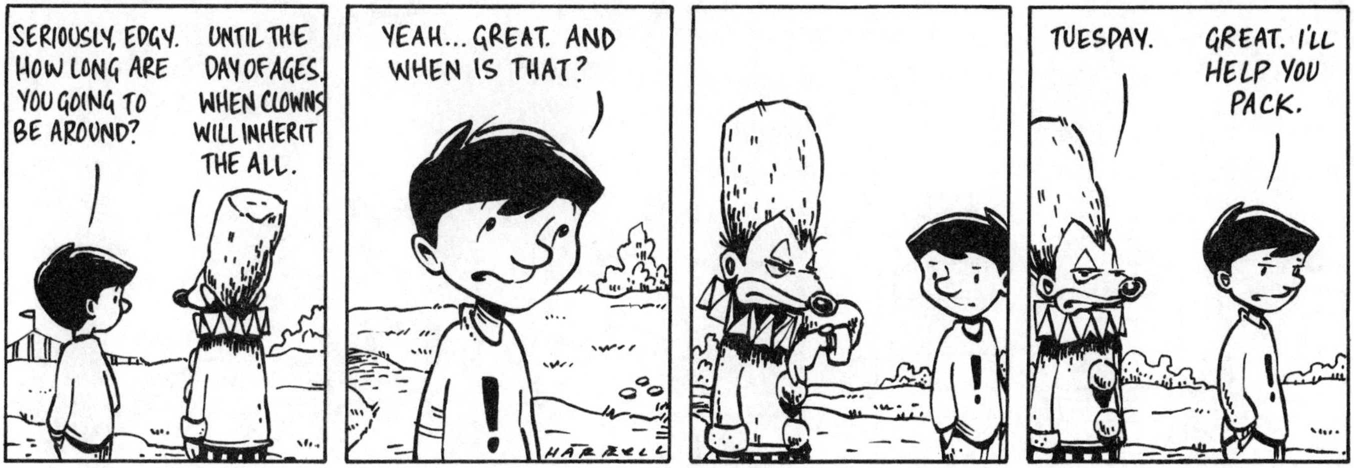
SERIOUSLY, EDGY. HOW LONG ARE YOU GOING TO BE AROUND?
UNTIL THE DAY OF AGES. WHEN CLOWNS WILL INHERIT THE ALL.
YEAH... GREAT. AND WHEN IS THAT?
TUESDAY.
GREAT. I'LL HELP YOU PACK.

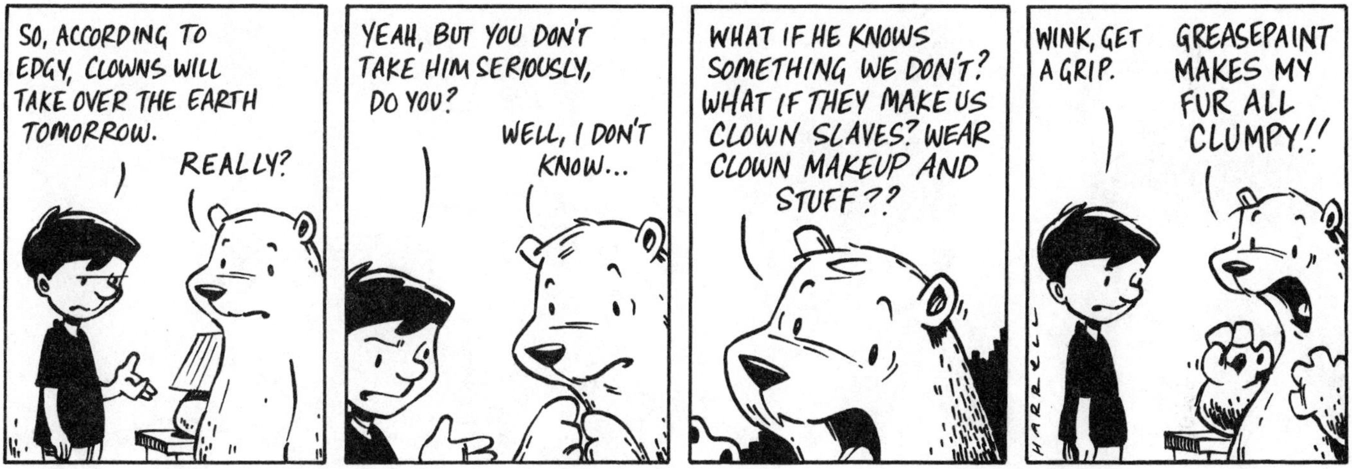
SO, ACCORDING TO EDGY, CLOWNS WILL TAKE OVER THE EARTH TOMORROW.
REALLY?
YEAH, BUT YOU DON'T TAKE HIM SERIOUSLY, DO YOU?
WELL, I DON'T KNOW...
WHAT IF HE KNOWS SOMETHING WE DON'T? WHAT IF THEY MAKE US CLOWN SLAVES? WEAR CLOWN MAKEUP AND STUFF??
WINK, GET A GRIP.
GREASEPAINT MAKES MY FUR ALL CLUMPY!!

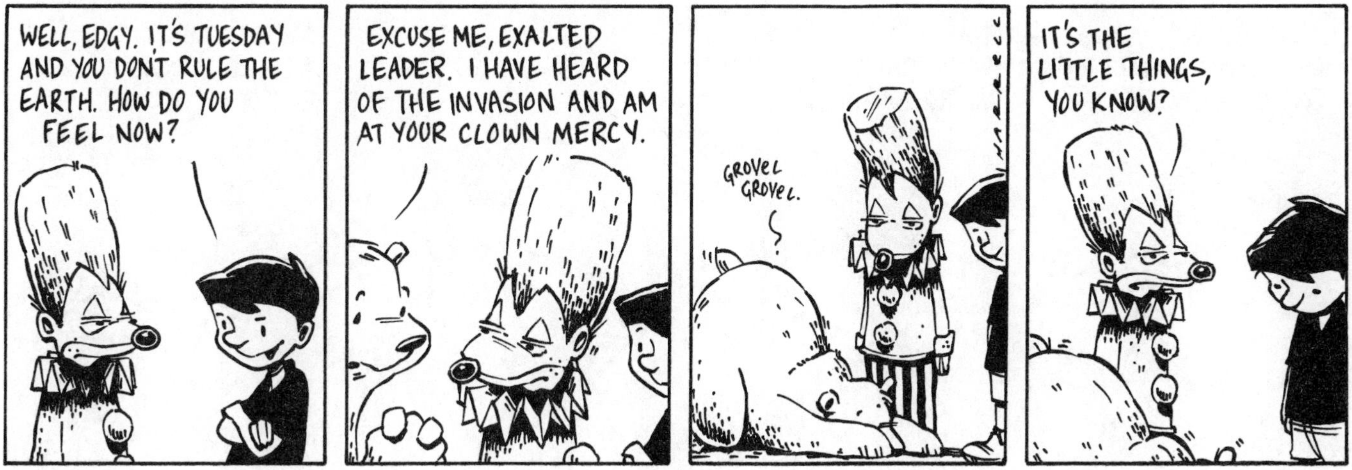
WELL, EDGY. IT'S TUESDAY AND YOU DON'T RULE THE EARTH. HOW DO YOU FEEL NOW?
EXCUSE ME, EXALTED LEADER. I HAVE HEARD OF THE INVASION AND AM AT YOUR CLOWN MERCY.
GROVEL GROVEL.
IT'S THE LITTLE THINGS, YOU KNOW?

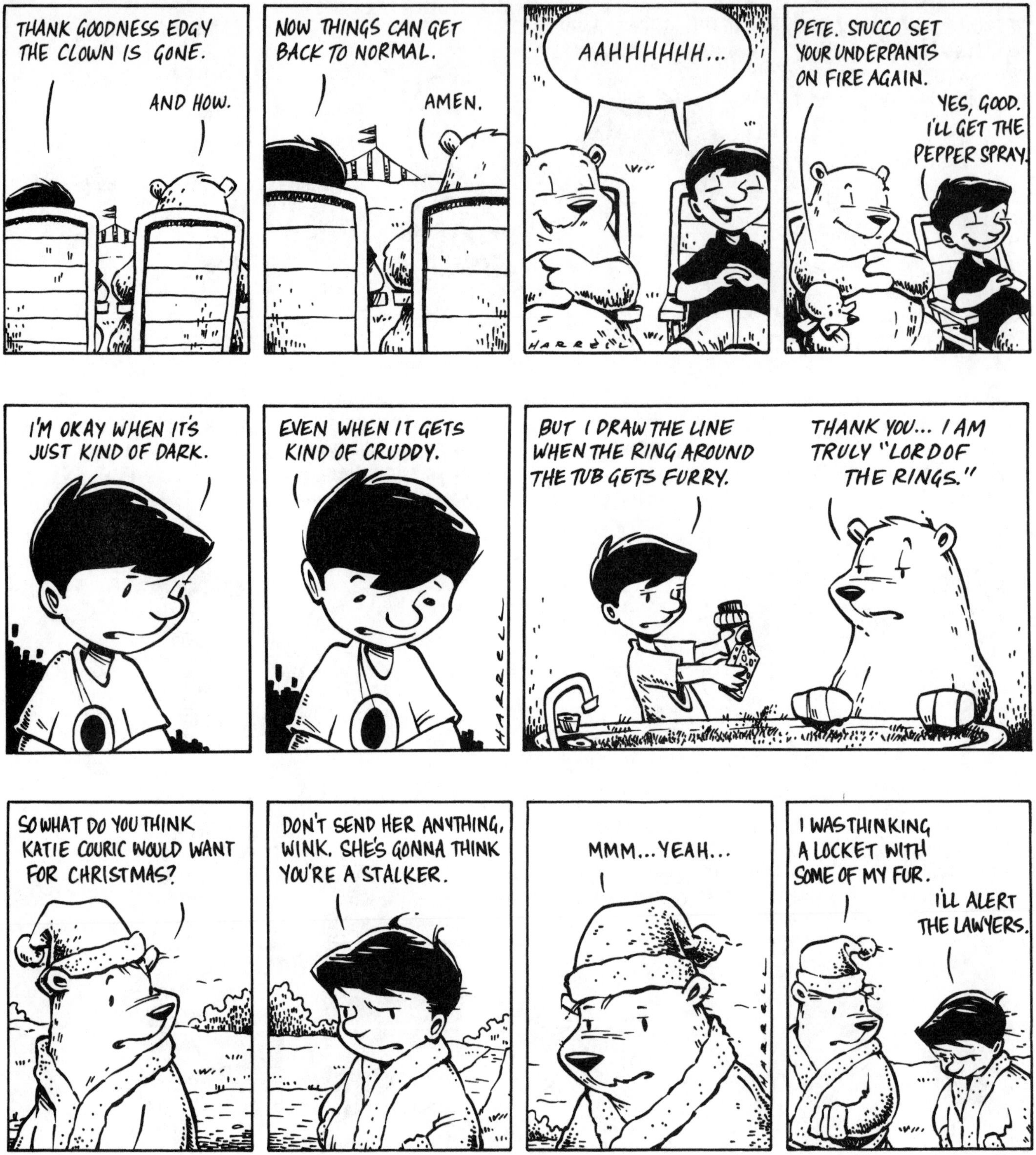
THANK GOODNESS EDGY THE CLOWN IS GONE.
AND HOW.
NOW THINGS CAN GET BACK TO NORMAL.
AMEN.
AAHHHHHH...
PETE. STUCCO SET YOUR UNDERPANTS ON FIRE AGAIN.
YES, GOOD. I'LL GET THE PEPPER SPRAY.
HARRELL
I'M OKAY WHEN IT'S JUST KIND OF DARK.
EVEN WHEN IT GETS KIND OF CRUDDY.
HARRELL
BUT I DRAW THE LINE WHEN THE RING AROUND THE TUB GETS FURRY.
THANK YOU... I AM TRULY "LORD OF THE RINGS."
SO WHAT DO YOU THINK KATIE COURIC WOULD WANT FOR CHRISTMAS?
DON'T SEND HER ANYTHING, WINK. SHE'S GONNA THINK YOU'RE A STALKER.
MMM... YEAH...
HARRELL
I WAS THINKING A LOCKET WITH SOME OF MY FUR.
I'LL ALERT THE LAWYERS.

BIG TOP
FOR: SANTA

I LOVE THIS TIME OF YEAR. ALL THE PARTIES. EVERYONE IN A GOOD MOOD...
WELL, ALMOST EVERYONE, LIZARD BOY.
WHAT ARE YOU TALKING ABOUT?
OH, WINK'S HAVING A LITTLE HOLIDAY-RELATED STRESS.
©HARRELL
YOU KNOW HOW SOME PEOPLE HATE SWIMSUIT SEASON?
YEAH?
MAN, I HATE SANTA SUIT SEASON.
C'MON. SUCK IT IN.
I KNEW WE SHOULD'VE GONE WITH THE QUADRUPLE XL.
XXXL SANTA SUIT

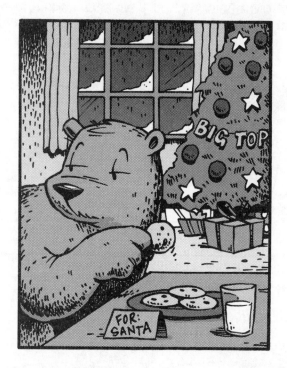

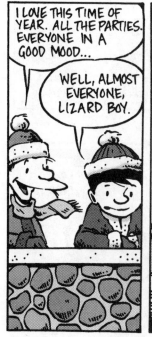

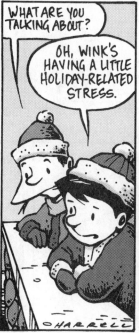

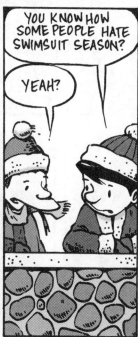

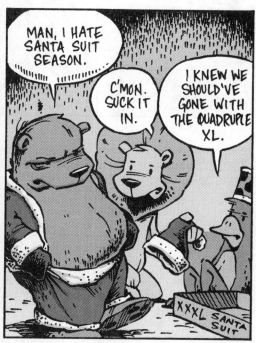

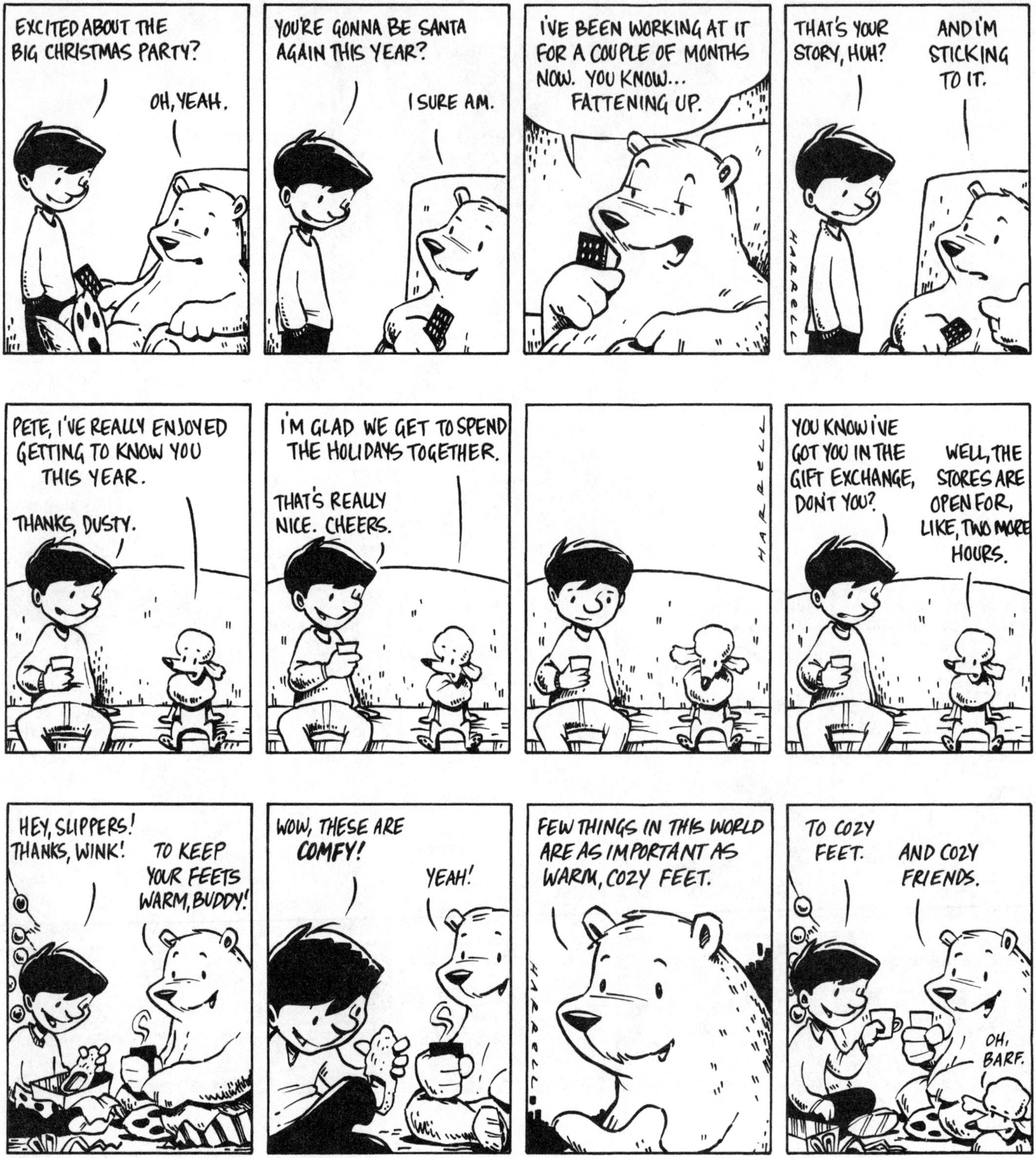
EXCITED ABOUT THE BIG CHRISTMAS PARTY?
OH, YEAH.
YOU'RE GONNA BE SANTA AGAIN THIS YEAR?
I SURE AM.
I'VE BEEN WORKING AT IT FOR A COUPLE OF MONTHS NOW. YOU KNOW... FATTENING UP.
THAT'S YOUR STORY, HUH?
AND I'M STICKING TO IT.
HARRELL
PETE, I'VE REALLY ENJOYED GETTING TO KNOW YOU THIS YEAR.
THANKS, DUSTY.
I'M GLAD WE GET TO SPEND THE HOLIDAYS TOGETHER.
THAT'S REALLY NICE. CHEERS.
HARRELL
YOU KNOW I'VE GOT YOU IN THE GIFT EXCHANGE, DON'T YOU?
WELL, THE STORES ARE OPEN FOR, LIKE, TWO MORE HOURS.
HEY, SLIPPERS! THANKS, WINK!
TO KEEP YOUR FEETS WARM, BUDDY!
WOW, THESE ARE COMFY!
YEAH!
FEW THINGS IN THIS WORLD ARE AS IMPORTANT AS WARM, COZY FEET.
HARRELL
TO COZY FEET.
AND COZY FRIENDS.
OH, BARF.

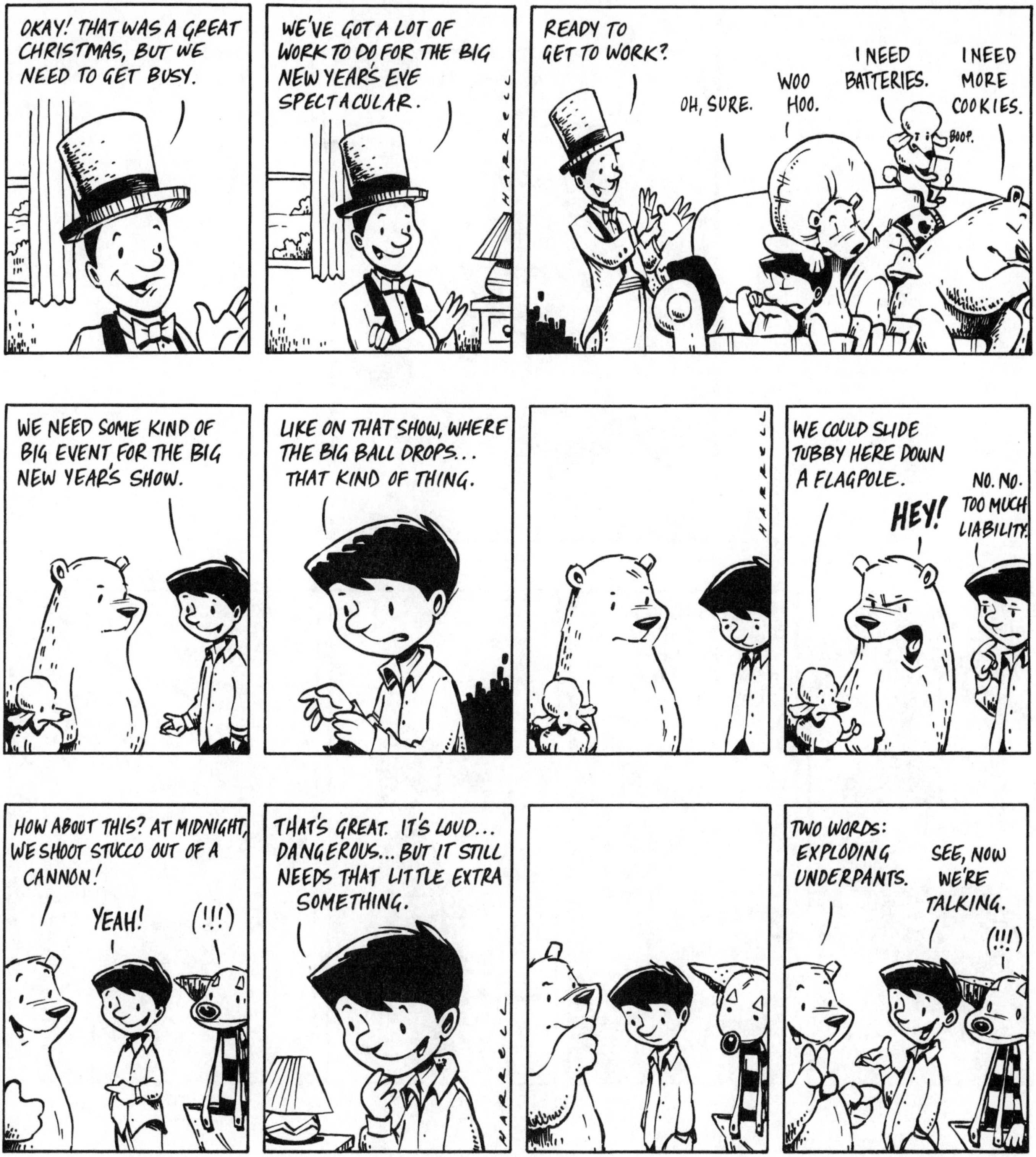
OKAY! THAT WAS A GREAT CHRISTMAS, BUT WE NEED TO GET BUSY.
WE'VE GOT A LOT OF WORK TO DO FOR THE BIG NEW YEAR'S EVE SPECTACULAR.
HARRELL
READY TO GET TO WORK?
OH, SURE.
WOO HOO.
I NEED BATTERIES.
BOOP.
I NEED MORE COOKIES.
WE NEED SOME KIND OF BIG EVENT FOR THE BIG NEW YEAR'S SHOW.
LIKE ON THAT SHOW, WHERE THE BIG BALL DROPS... THAT KIND OF THING.
HARRELL
WE COULD SLIDE TUBBY HERE DOWN A FLAGPOLE.
HEY!
NO. NO. TOO MUCH LIABILITY.
HOW ABOUT THIS? AT MIDNIGHT, WE SHOOT STUCCO OUT OF A CANNON!
YEAH!
(!!!)
THAT'S GREAT. IT'S LOUD... DANGEROUS... BUT IT STILL NEEDS THAT LITTLE EXTRA SOMETHING.
HARRELL
TWO WORDS: EXPLODING UNDERPANTS.
SEE, NOW WE'RE TALKING.
(!!!)

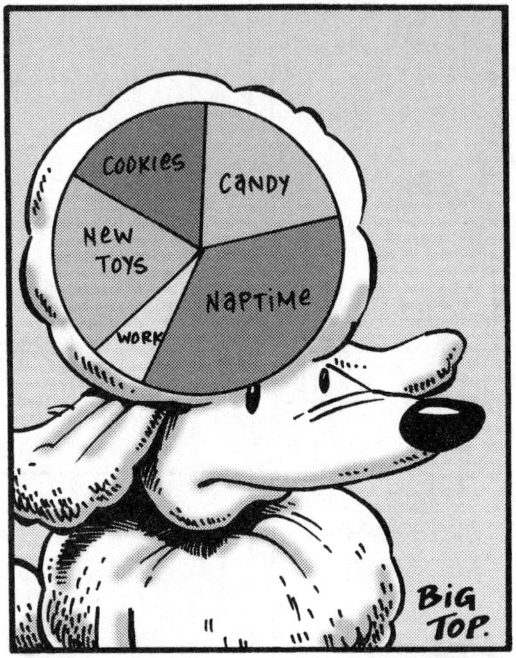
Cookies
Candy
New Toys
Naptime
WORK
BIG TOP.

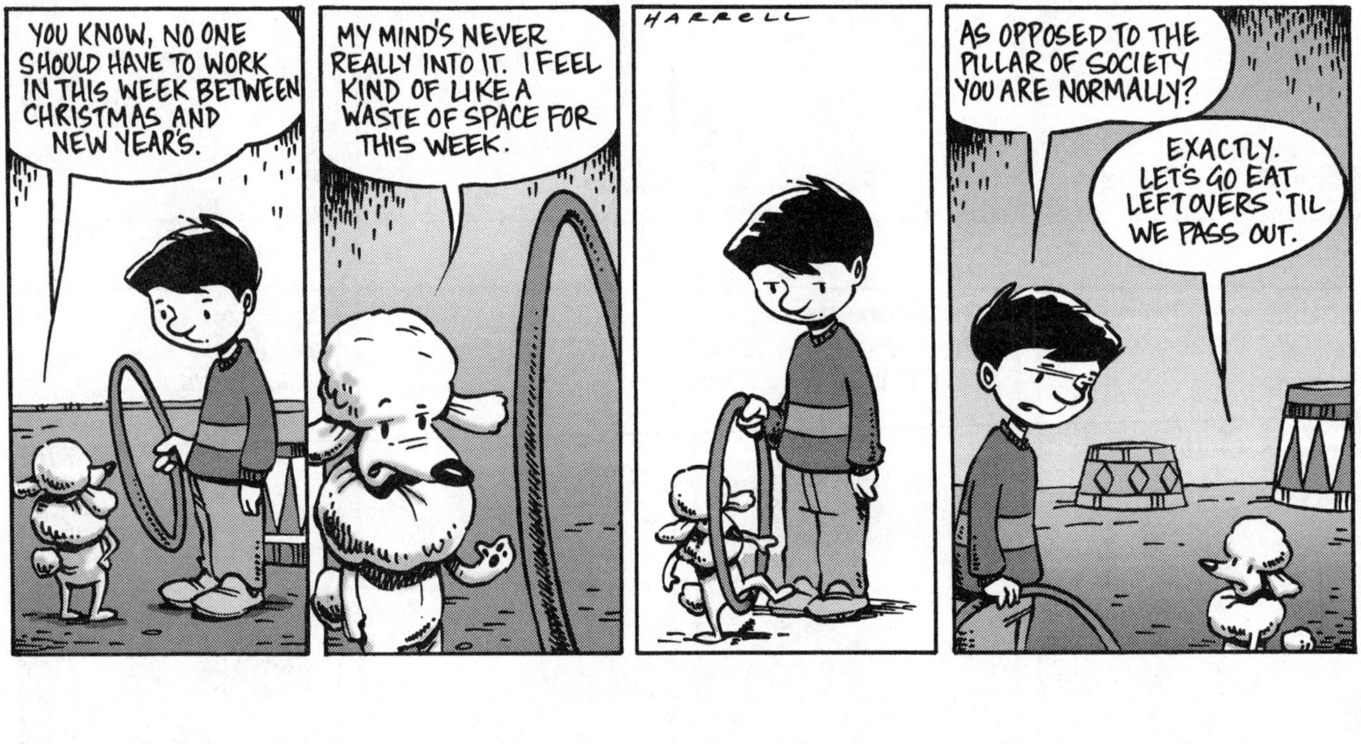
YOU KNOW, NO ONE SHOULD HAVE TO WORK IN THIS WEEK BETWEEN CHRISTMAS AND NEW YEAR'S.
MY MIND'S NEVER REALLY INTO IT. I FEEL KIND OF LIKE A WASTE OF SPACE FOR THIS WEEK.
HARRELL
AS OPPOSED TO THE PILLAR OF SOCIETY YOU ARE NORMALLY?
EXACTLY. LET'S GO EAT LEFTOVERS 'TIL WE PASS OUT.

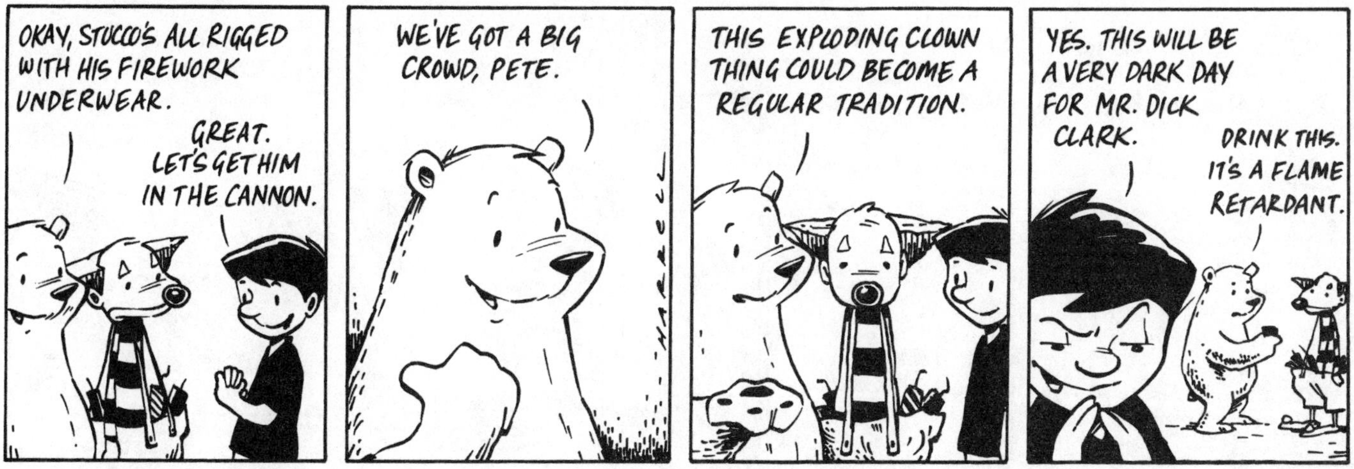
OKAY, STUCCO'S ALL RIGGED WITH HIS FIREWORK UNDERWEAR.
GREAT. LET'S GET HIM IN THE CANNON.
WE'VE GOT A BIG CROWD, PETE.
THIS EXPLODING CLOWN THING COULD BECOME A REGULAR TRADITION.
YES. THIS WILL BE A VERY DARK DAY FOR MR. DICK CLARK.
DRINK THIS. IT'S A FLAME RETARDANT.

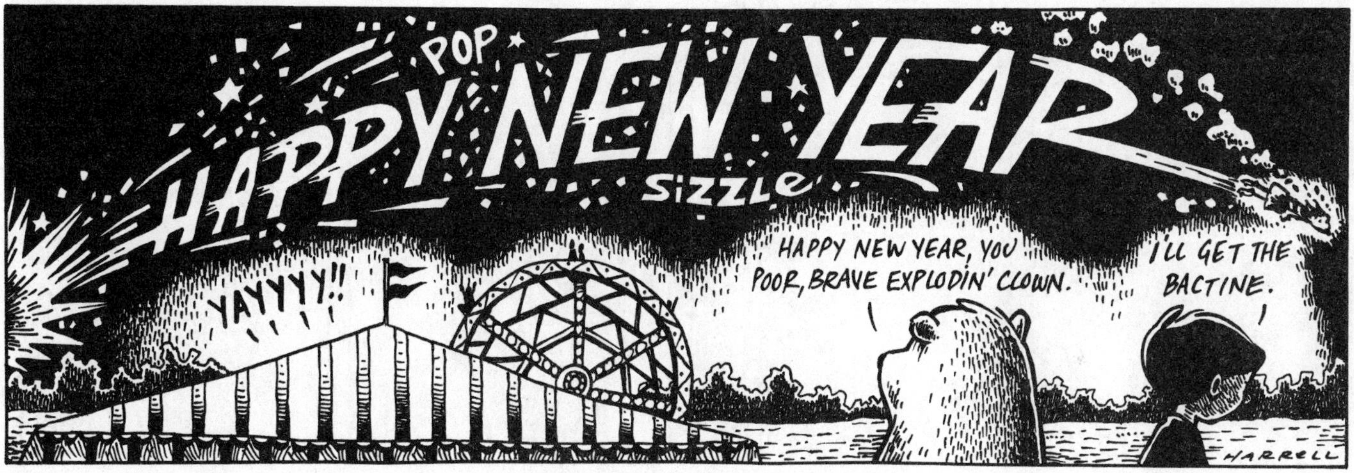
POP
HAPPY NEW YEAR
SIZZLE
YAYYYY!!
HAPPY NEW YEAR, YOU POOR, BRAVE EXPLODIN' CLOWN.
I'LL GET THE BACTINE.
HARRELL

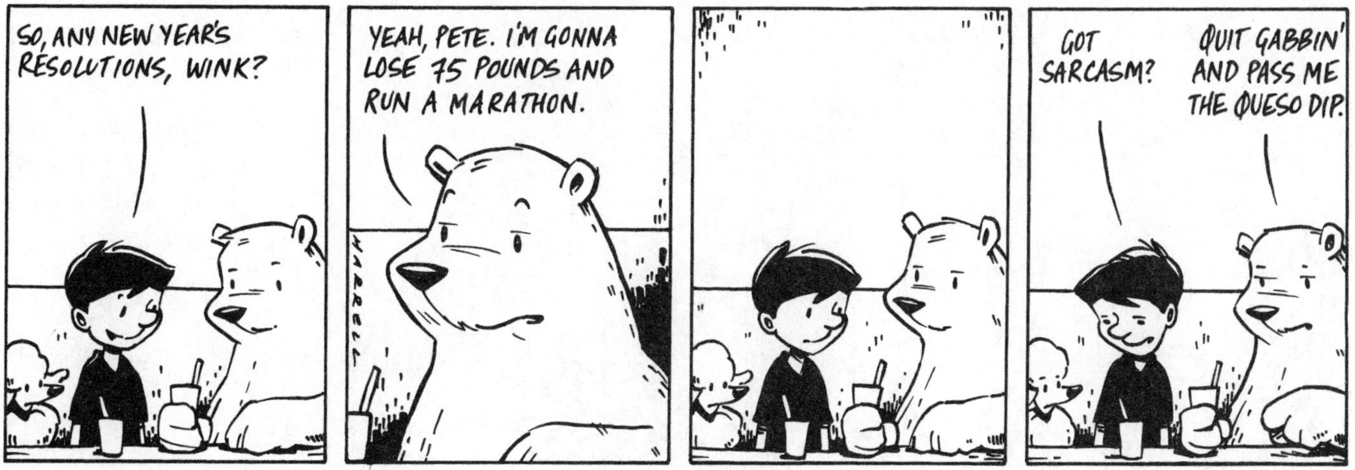
SO, ANY NEW YEAR'S RESOLUTIONS, WINK?
YEAH, PETE. I'M GONNA LOSE 75 POUNDS AND RUN A MARATHON.
GOT SARCASM?
QUIT GABBIN' AND PASS ME THE QUESO DIP.

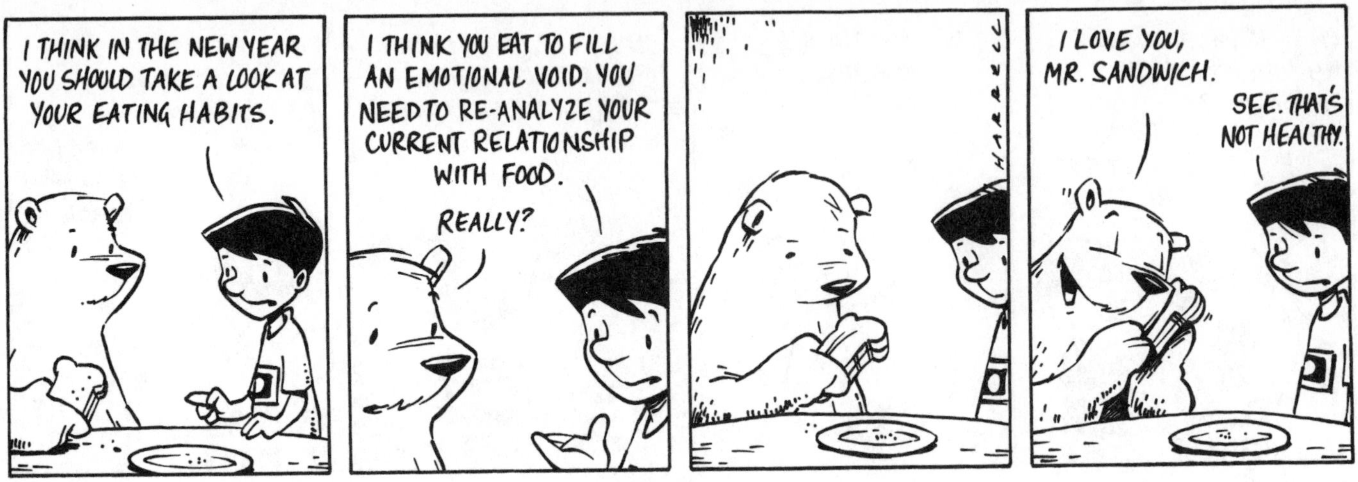
I THINK IN THE NEW YEAR YOU SHOULD TAKE A LOOK AT YOUR EATING HABITS.
I THINK YOU EAT TO FILL AN EMOTIONAL VOID. YOU NEED TO RE-ANALYZE YOUR CURRENT RELATIONSHIP WITH FOOD.
REALLY?
HARRELL
I LOVE YOU, MR. SANDWICH.
SEE. THAT'S NOT HEALTHY.

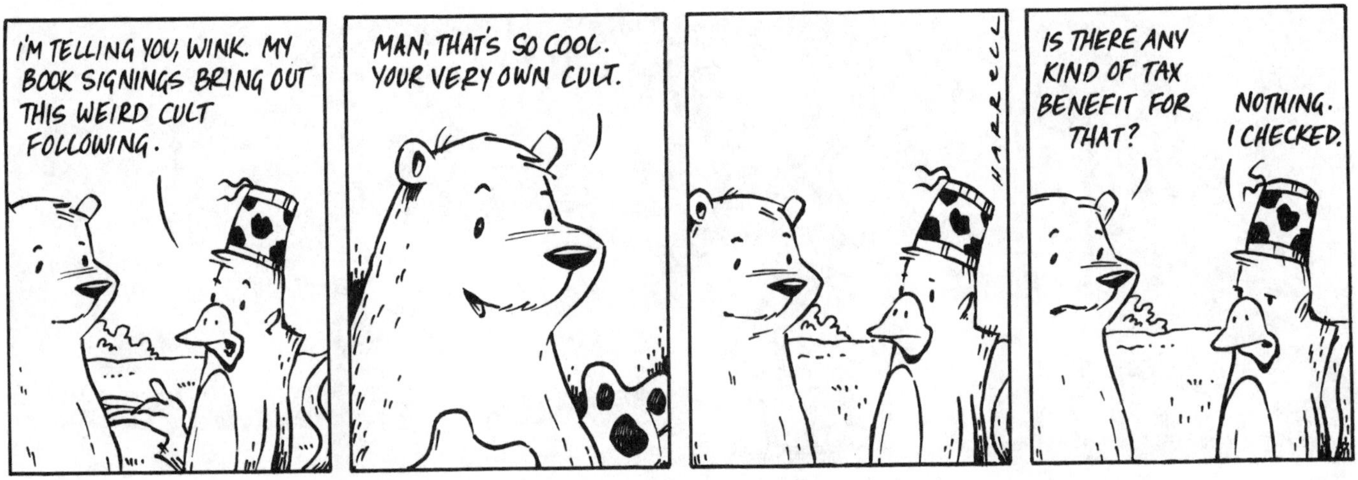
I'M TELLING YOU, WINK. MY BOOK SIGNINGS BRING OUT THIS WEIRD CULT FOLLOWING.
MAN, THAT'S SO COOL. YOUR VERY OWN CULT.
HARRELL
IS THERE ANY KIND OF TAX BENEFIT FOR THAT?
NOTHING. I CHECKED.

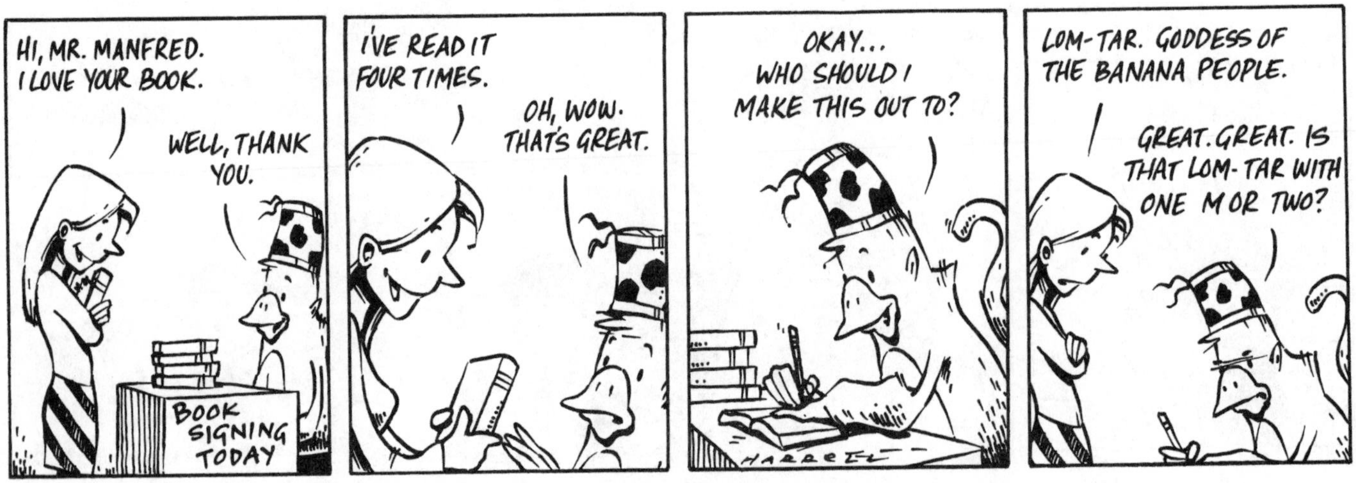
HI, MR. MANFRED. I LOVE YOUR BOOK.
WELL, THANK YOU.
BOOK SIGNING TODAY
I'VE READ IT FOUR TIMES.
OH, WOW. THAT'S GREAT.
OKAY... WHO SHOULD I MAKE THIS OUT TO?
HARRELL
LOM-TAR. GODDESS OF THE BANANA PEOPLE.
GREAT. GREAT. IS THAT LOM-TAR WITH ONE M OR TWO?

TONIGHT: BIG TOP POETRY JAM
SNAP.

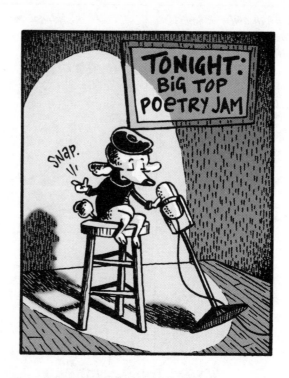

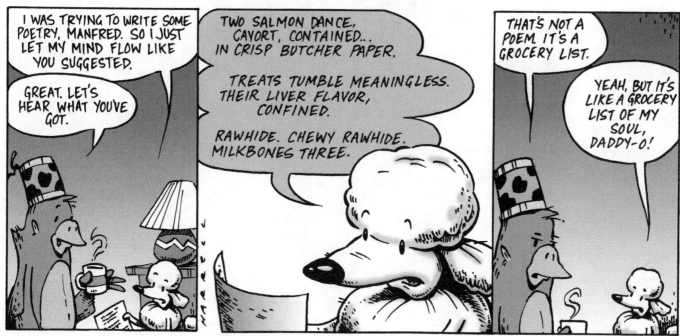

I WAS TRYING TO WRITE SOME POETRY, MANFRED. SO I JUST LET MY MIND FLOW LIKE YOU SUGGESTED.
GREAT. LET'S HEAR WHAT YOU'VE GOT.
TWO SALMON DANCE, CAVORT, CONTAINED... IN CRISP BUTCHER PAPER.
TREATS TUMBLE MEANINGLESS. THEIR LIVER FLAVOR, CONFINED.
RAWHIDE. CHEWY RAWHIDE. MILKBONES THREE.
THAT'S NOT A POEM. IT'S A GROCERY LIST.
YEAH, BUT IT'S LIKE A GROCERY LIST OF MY SOUL, DADDY-O!
HARRELL

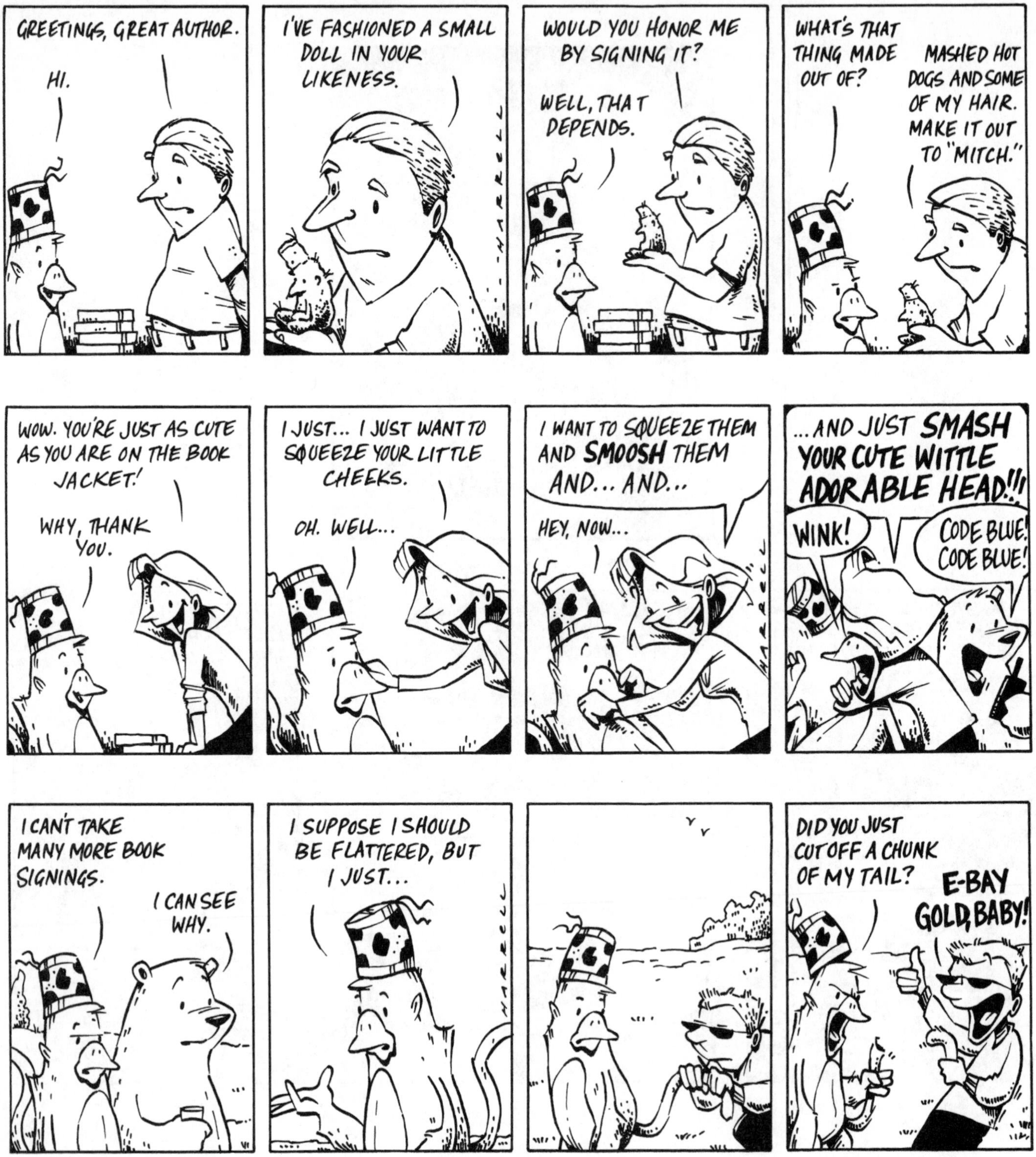
GREETINGS, GREAT AUTHOR.
HI.
I'VE FASHIONED A SMALL DOLL IN YOUR LIKENESS.
WOULD YOU HONOR ME BY SIGNING IT?
WELL, THAT DEPENDS.
WHAT'S THAT THING MADE OUT OF?
MASHED HOT DOGS AND SOME OF MY HAIR. MAKE IT OUT TO "MITCH."
WOW. YOU'RE JUST AS CUTE AS YOU ARE ON THE BOOK JACKET!
WHY, THANK YOU.
I JUST... I JUST WANT TO SQUEEZE YOUR LITTLE CHEEKS.
OH. WELL...
I WANT TO SQUEEZE THEM AND SMOOSH THEM AND... AND...
HEY, NOW...
...AND JUST SMASH YOUR CUTE WITTLE ADORABLE HEAD!!!
WINK!
CODE BLUE! CODE BLUE!
I CAN'T TAKE MANY MORE BOOK SIGNINGS.
I CAN SEE WHY.
I SUPPOSE I SHOULD BE FLATTERED, BUT I JUST...
DID YOU JUST CUT OFF A CHUNK OF MY TAIL?
E-BAY GOLD, BABY!

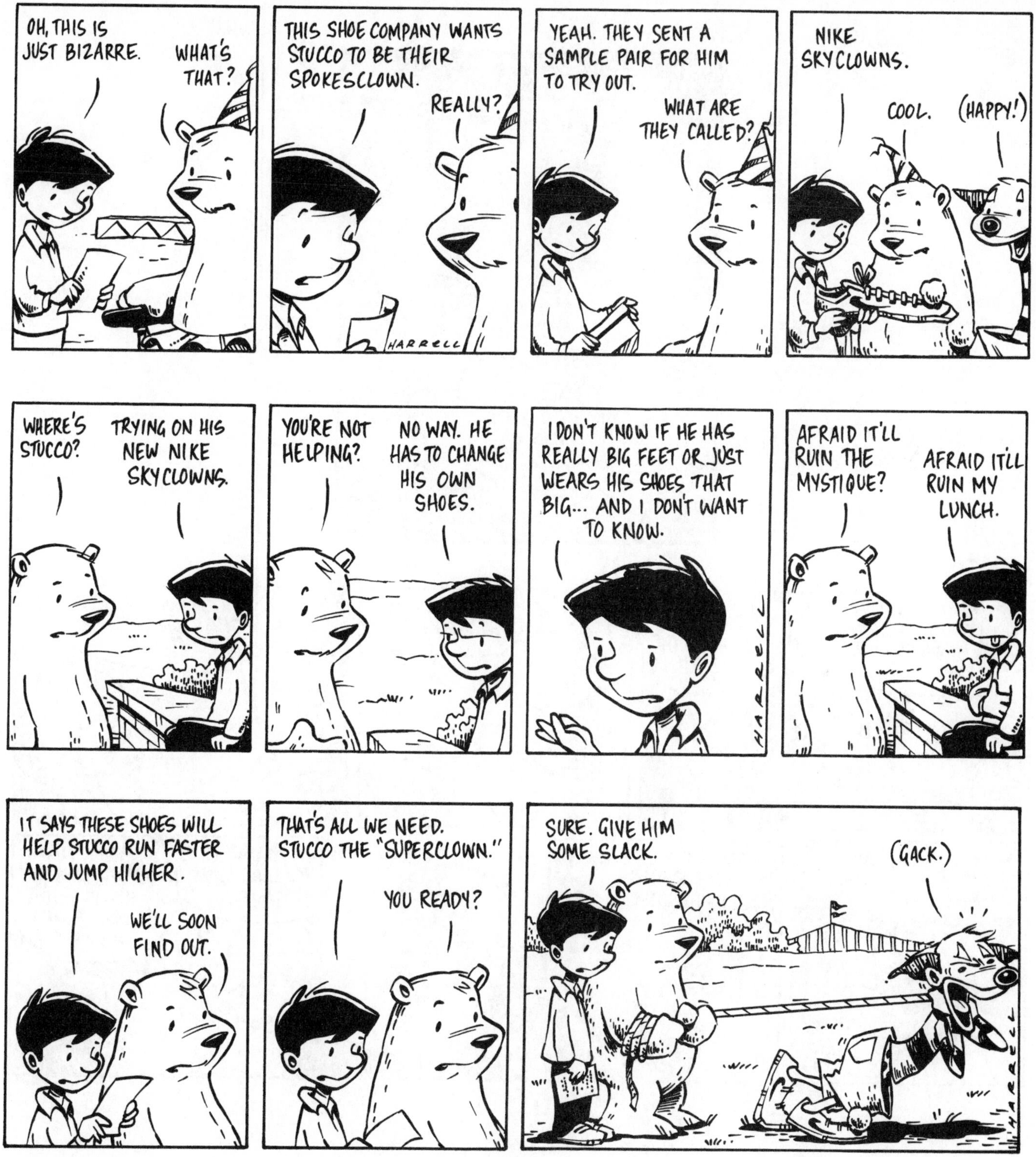
OH, THIS IS JUST BIZARRE.
WHAT'S THAT?
THIS SHOE COMPANY WANTS STUCCO TO BE THEIR SPOKESCLOWN.
REALLY?
HARRELL
YEAH. THEY SENT A SAMPLE PAIR FOR HIM TO TRY OUT.
WHAT ARE THEY CALLED?
NIKE SKYCLOWNS.
COOL.
(HAPPY!)
WHERE'S STUCCO?
TRYING ON HIS NEW NIKE SKYCLOWNS.
YOU'RE NOT HELPING?
NO WAY. HE HAS TO CHANGE HIS OWN SHOES.
I DON'T KNOW IF HE HAS REALLY BIG FEET OR JUST WEARS HIS SHOES THAT BIG... AND I DON'T WANT TO KNOW.
HARRELL
AFRAID IT'LL RUIN THE MYSTIQUE?
AFRAID IT'LL RUIN MY LUNCH.
IT SAYS THESE SHOES WILL HELP STUCCO RUN FASTER AND JUMP HIGHER.
WE'LL SOON FIND OUT.
THAT'S ALL WE NEED. STUCCO THE "SUPERCLOWN."
YOU READY?
SURE. GIVE HIM SOME SLACK.
(GACK.)
HARRELL

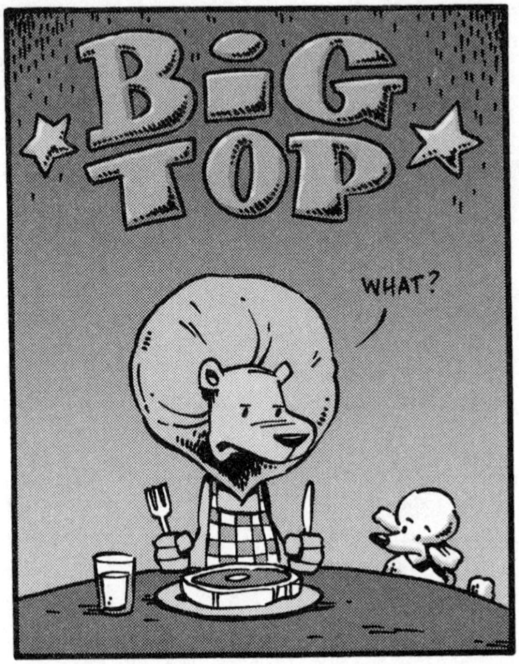
BIG TOP
WHAT?

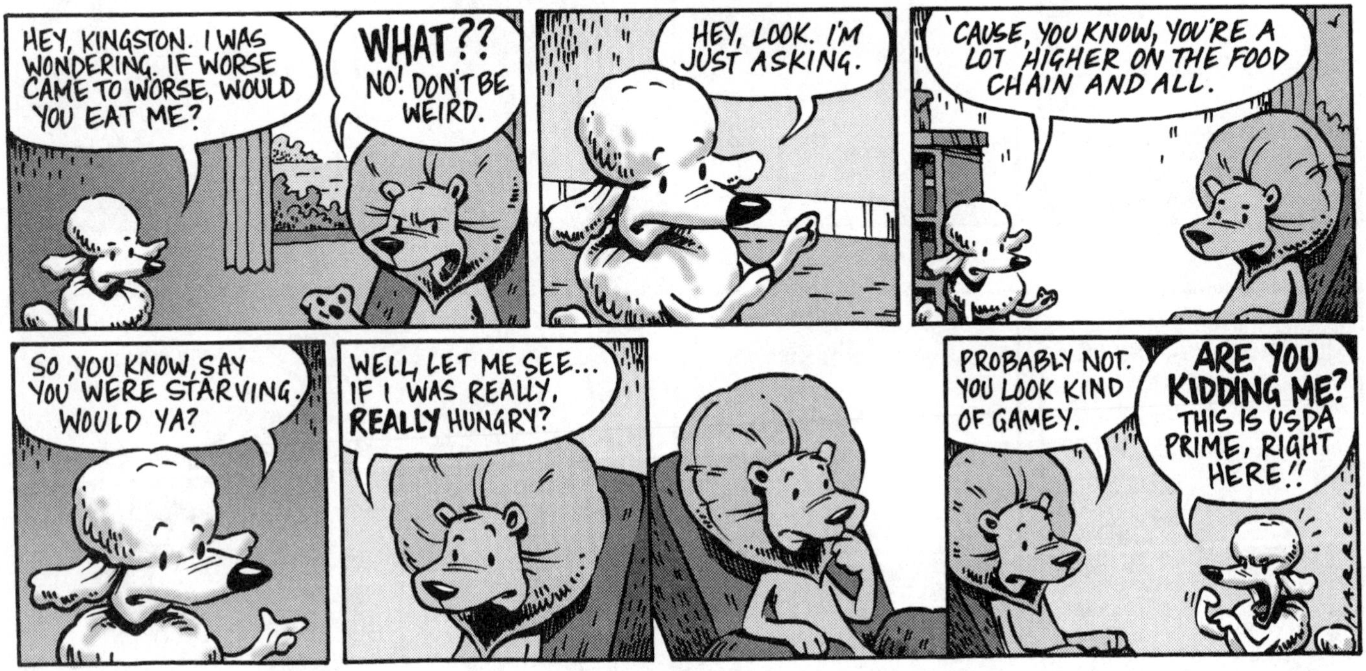
HEY, KINGSTON. I WAS WONDERING. IF WORSE CAME TO WORSE, WOULD YOU EAT ME?
WHAT?? NO! DON'T BE WEIRD.
HEY, LOOK. I'M JUST ASKING.
'CAUSE, YOU KNOW, YOU'RE A LOT HIGHER ON THE FOOD CHAIN AND ALL.
SO, YOU KNOW, SAY YOU WERE STARVING. WOULD YA?
WELL, LET ME SEE... IF I WAS REALLY, REALLY HUNGRY?
PROBABLY NOT. YOU LOOK KIND OF GAMEY.
ARE YOU KIDDING ME? THIS IS USDA PRIME, RIGHT HERE!!
HARRELL

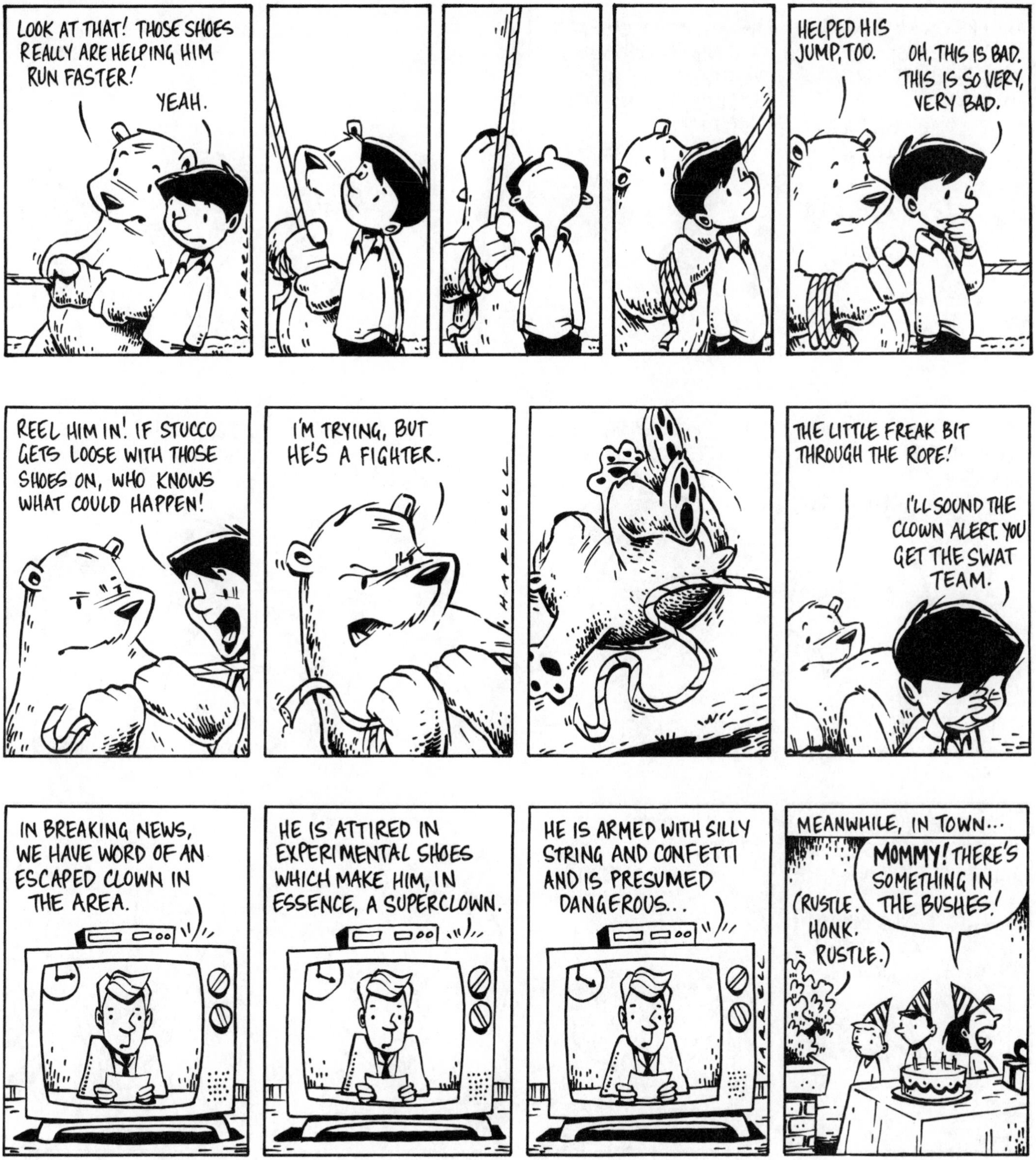
LOOK AT THAT! THOSE SHOES REALLY ARE HELPING HIM RUN FASTER!
YEAH.
HELPED HIS JUMP, TOO.
OH, THIS IS BAD. THIS IS SO VERY, VERY BAD.
REEL HIM IN! IF STUCCO GETS LOOSE WITH THOSE SHOES ON, WHO KNOWS WHAT COULD HAPPEN!
I'M TRYING, BUT HE'S A FIGHTER.
THE LITTLE FREAK BIT THROUGH THE ROPE!
I'LL SOUND THE CLOWN ALERT. YOU GET THE SWAT TEAM.
IN BREAKING NEWS, WE HAVE WORD OF AN ESCAPED CLOWN IN THE AREA.
HE IS ATTIRED IN EXPERIMENTAL SHOES WHICH MAKE HIM, IN ESSENCE, A SUPERCLOWN.
HE IS ARMED WITH SILLY STRING AND CONFETTI AND IS PRESUMED DANGEROUS...
MEANWHILE, IN TOWN...
(RUSTLE. HONK. RUSTLE.)
MOMMY! THERE'S SOMETHING IN THE BUSHES!

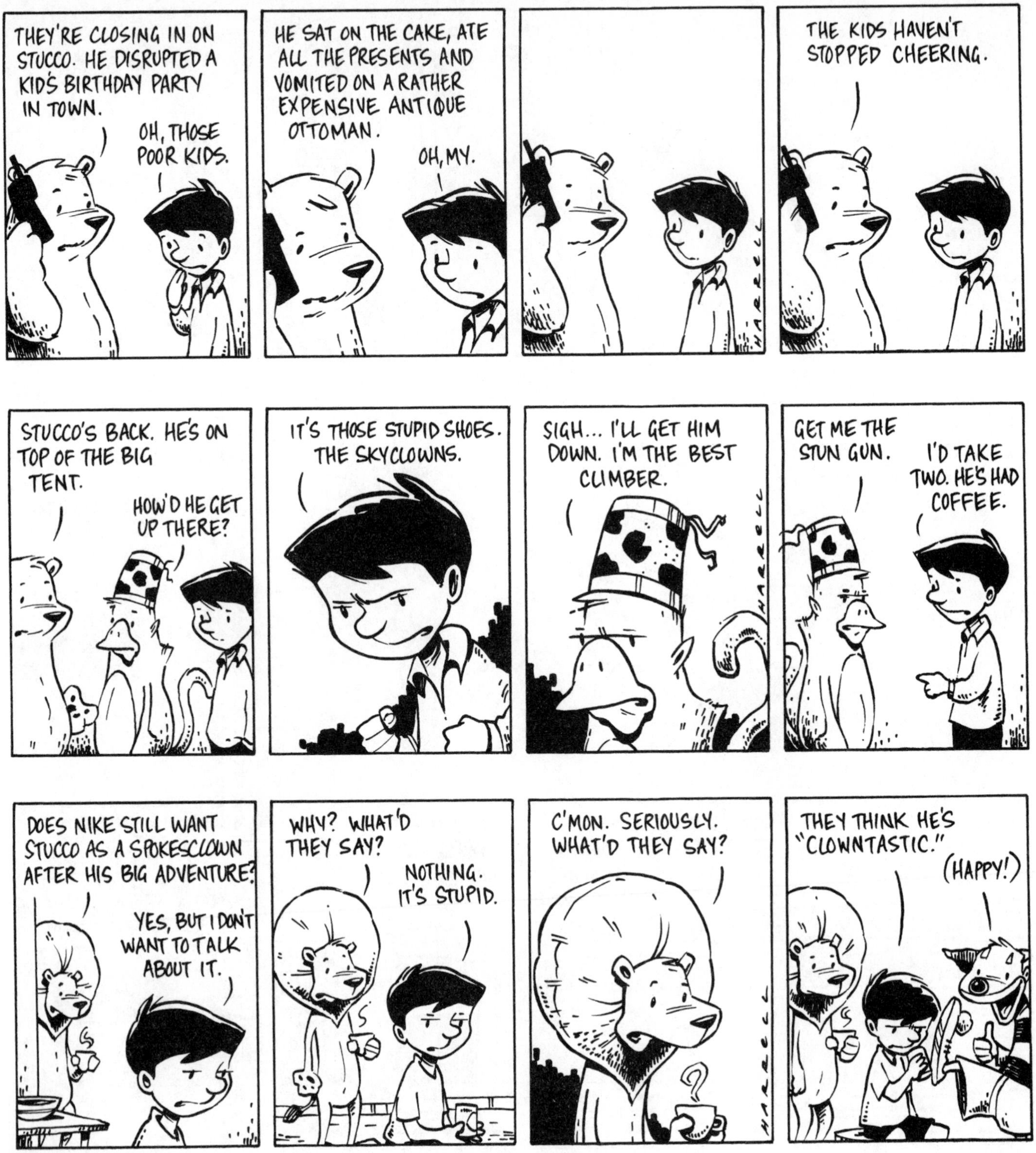
THEY'RE CLOSING IN ON STUCCO. HE DISRUPTED A KID'S BIRTHDAY PARTY IN TOWN.
OH, THOSE POOR KIDS.
HE SAT ON THE CAKE, ATE ALL THE PRESENTS AND VOMITED ON A RATHER EXPENSIVE ANTIQUE OTTOMAN.
OH, MY.
HARRELL
THE KIDS HAVEN'T STOPPED CHEERING.
STUCCO'S BACK. HE'S ON TOP OF THE BIG TENT.
HOW'D HE GET UP THERE?
IT'S THOSE STUPID SHOES. THE SKYCLOWNS.
SIGH... I'LL GET HIM DOWN. I'M THE BEST CLIMBER.
HARRELL
GET ME THE STUN GUN.
I'D TAKE TWO. HE'S HAD COFFEE.
DOES NIKE STILL WANT STUCCO AS A SPOKESCLOWN AFTER HIS BIG ADVENTURE?
YES, BUT I DON'T WANT TO TALK ABOUT IT.
WHY? WHAT'D THEY SAY?
NOTHING. IT'S STUPID.
C'MON. SERIOUSLY. WHAT'D THEY SAY?
?
HARRELL
THEY THINK HE'S "CLOWNTASTIC."
(HAPPY!)

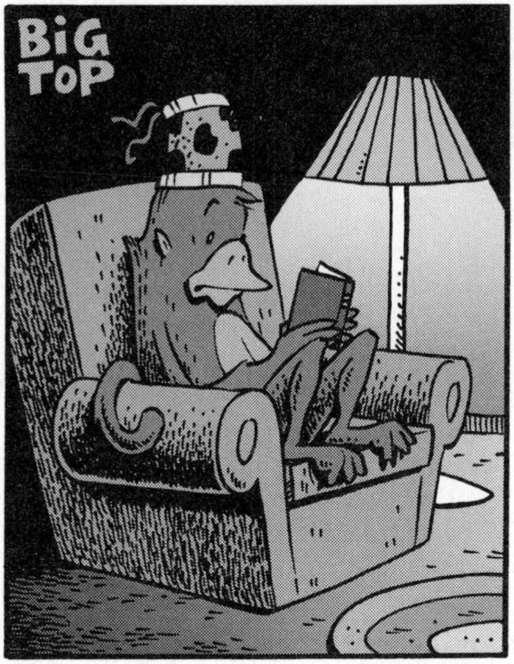
BIG TOP

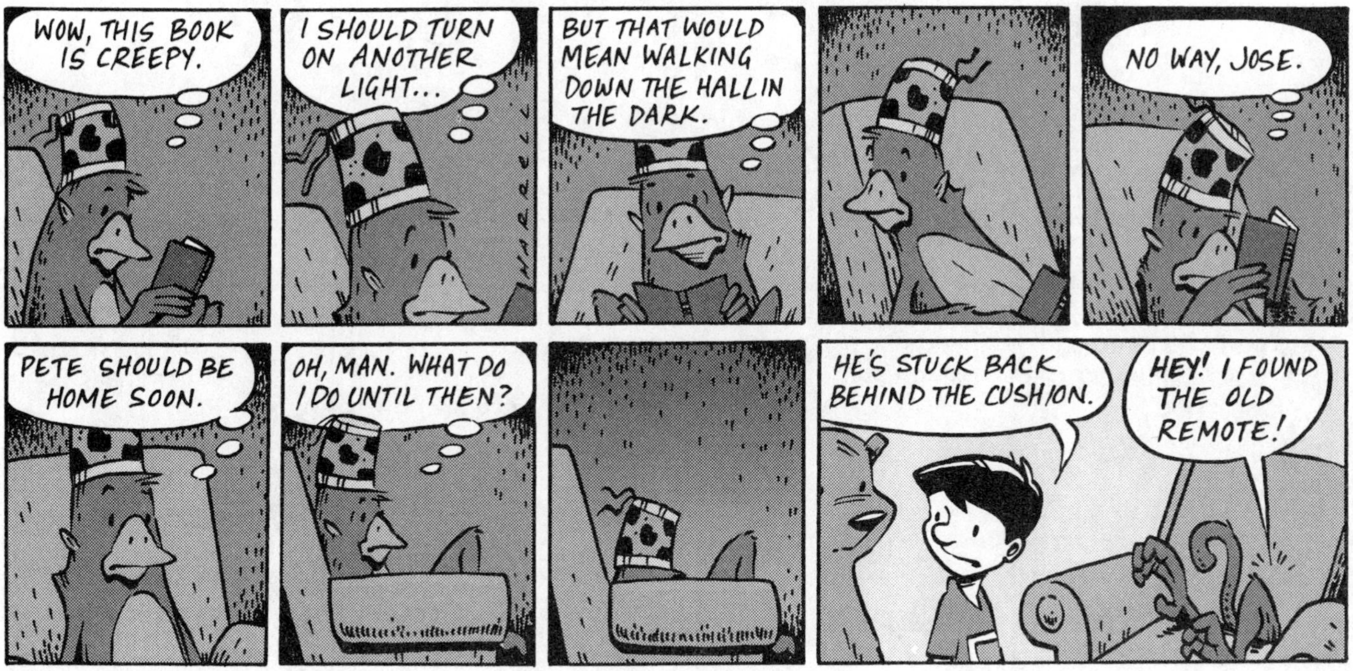
WOW, THIS BOOK IS CREEPY.
I SHOULD TURN ON ANOTHER LIGHT...
BUT THAT WOULD MEAN WALKING DOWN THE HALL IN THE DARK.
NO WAY, JOSE.
PETE SHOULD BE HOME SOON.
OH, MAN. WHAT DO I DO UNTIL THEN?
HE'S STUCK BACK BEHIND THE CUSHION.
HEY! I FOUND THE OLD REMOTE!

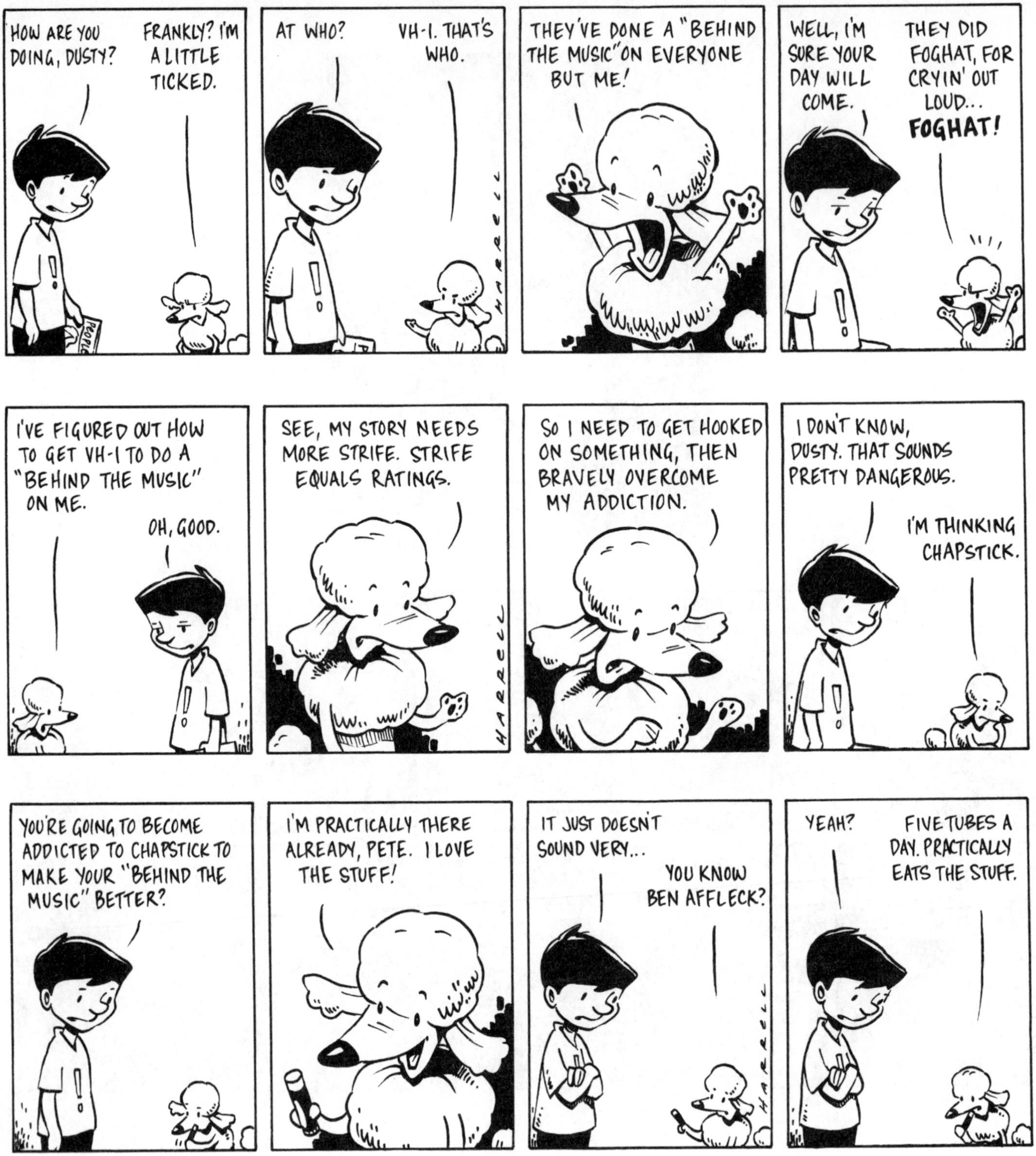
HOW ARE YOU DOING, DUSTY?
FRANKLY? I'M A LITTLE TICKED.
AT WHO?
VH-1. THAT'S WHO.
THEY'VE DONE A "BEHIND THE MUSIC" ON EVERYONE BUT ME!
WELL, I'M SURE YOUR DAY WILL COME.
THEY DID FOGHAT, FOR CRYIN' OUT LOUD... **FOGHAT!**
HARRELL
I'VE FIGURED OUT HOW TO GET VH-1 TO DO A "BEHIND THE MUSIC" ON ME.
OH, GOOD.
SEE, MY STORY NEEDS MORE STRIFE. STRIFE EQUALS RATINGS.
SO I NEED TO GET HOOKED ON SOMETHING, THEN BRAVELY OVERCOME MY ADDICTION.
I DON'T KNOW, DUSTY. THAT SOUNDS PRETTY DANGEROUS.
I'M THINKING CHAPSTICK.
HARRELL
YOU'RE GOING TO BECOME ADDICTED TO CHAPSTICK TO MAKE YOUR "BEHIND THE MUSIC" BETTER?
I'M PRACTICALLY THERE ALREADY, PETE. I LOVE THE STUFF!
IT JUST DOESN'T SOUND VERY...
YOU KNOW BEN AFFLECK?
YEAH?
FIVE TUBES A DAY. PRACTICALLY EATS THE STUFF.
HARRELL

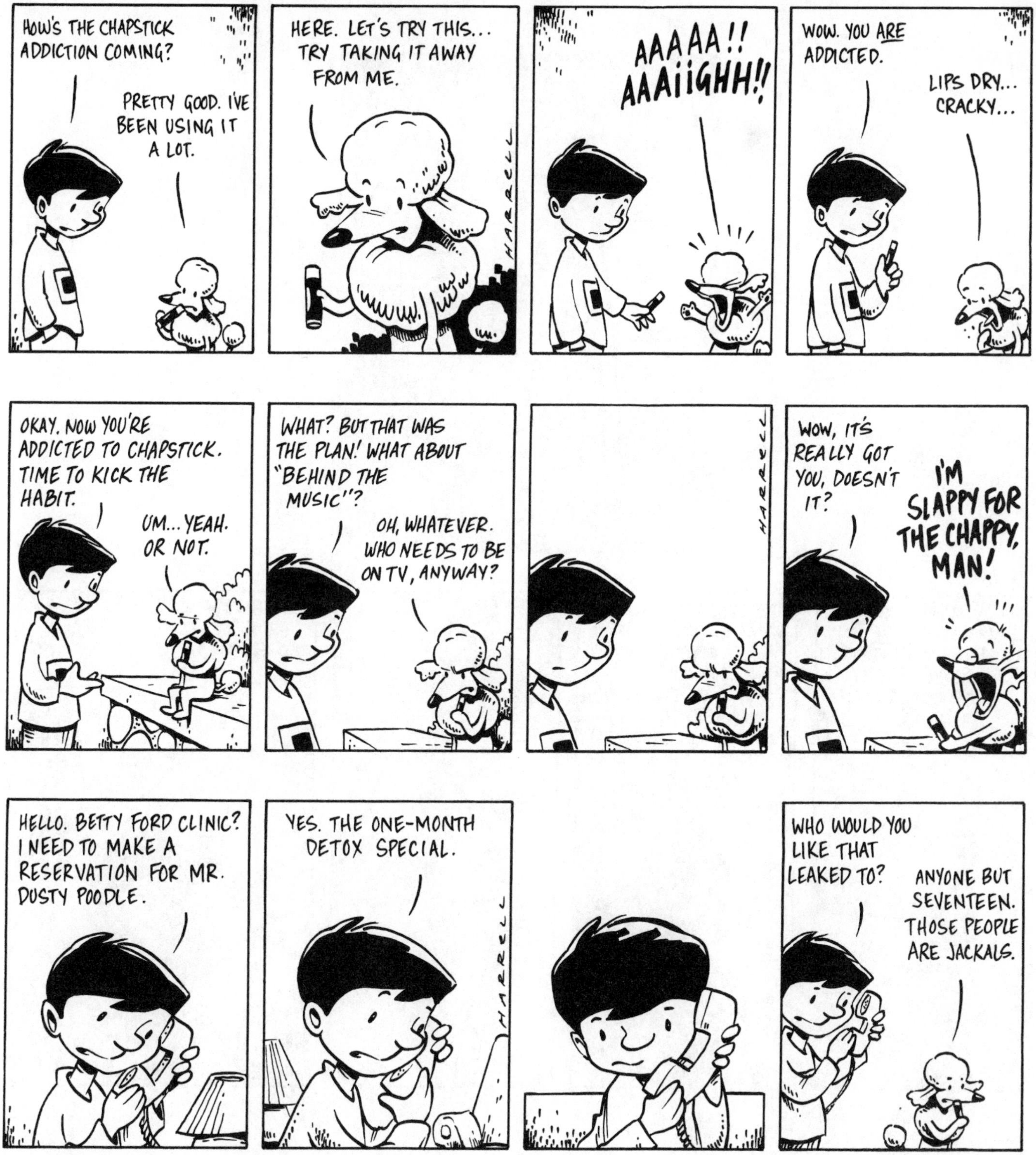
HOW'S THE CHAPSTICK ADDICTION COMING?
PRETTY GOOD. I'VE BEEN USING IT A LOT.
HERE. LET'S TRY THIS... TRY TAKING IT AWAY FROM ME.
HARRELL
AAAAA!! AAAiiGHH!!
WOW. YOU ARE ADDICTED.
LIPS DRY... CRACKY...
OKAY. NOW YOU'RE ADDICTED TO CHAPSTICK. TIME TO KICK THE HABIT.
UM... YEAH. OR NOT.
WHAT? BUT THAT WAS THE PLAN! WHAT ABOUT "BEHIND THE MUSIC"?
OH, WHATEVER. WHO NEEDS TO BE ON TV, ANYWAY?
HARRELL
WOW, IT'S REALLY GOT YOU, DOESN'T IT?
I'M SLAPPY FOR THE CHAPPY, MAN!
HELLO. BETTY FORD CLINIC? I NEED TO MAKE A RESERVATION FOR MR. DUSTY POODLE.
YES. THE ONE-MONTH DETOX SPECIAL.
HARRELL
WHO WOULD YOU LIKE THAT LEAKED TO?
ANYONE BUT SEVENTEEN. THOSE PEOPLE ARE JACKALS.

BIG TOP
LOTION
NEW

OOH. YOUR SKIN LOOKS REALLY DRY, PETE. IN THESE COLD WINTER MONTHS, YOU MIGHT WANT TO USE A LITTLE LOTION.
OFF MY BACK, BEAR. WHAT DO YOU KNOW ABOUT LOTION? YOU HAVE FUR. YOU COULDN'T USE LOTION IF YOU WANTED TO.
OKAY. OKAY.
MAYBE **YOU** COULD USE A LITTLE **CONDITIONER.**
WOW, PETE. YOU COULD GRATE CHEESE ON THESE ELBOWS.
HARRELL

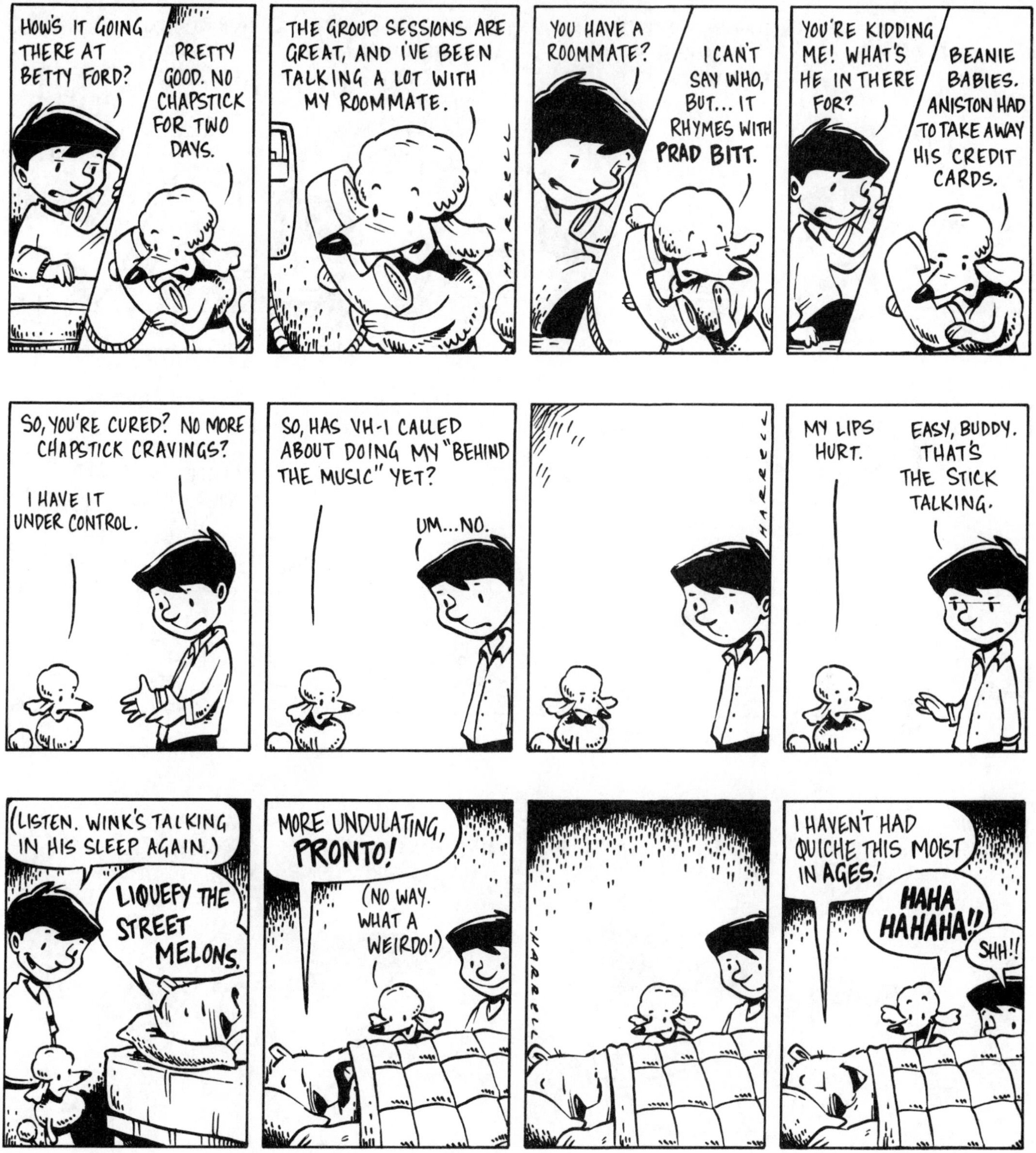
HOW'S IT GOING THERE AT BETTY FORD?
PRETTY GOOD. NO CHAPSTICK FOR TWO DAYS.
THE GROUP SESSIONS ARE GREAT, AND I'VE BEEN TALKING A LOT WITH MY ROOMMATE.
HARRELL
YOU HAVE A ROOMMATE?
I CAN'T SAY WHO, BUT... IT RHYMES WITH PRAD BITT.
YOU'RE KIDDING ME! WHAT'S HE IN THERE FOR?
BEANIE BABIES. ANISTON HAD TO TAKE AWAY HIS CREDIT CARDS.
SO, YOU'RE CURED? NO MORE CHAPSTICK CRAVINGS?
I HAVE IT UNDER CONTROL.
SO, HAS VH-1 CALLED ABOUT DOING MY "BEHIND THE MUSIC" YET?
UM...NO.
HARRELL
MY LIPS HURT.
EASY, BUDDY. THAT'S THE STICK TALKING.
(LISTEN. WINK'S TALKING IN HIS SLEEP AGAIN.)
LIQUEFY THE STREET MELONS.
MORE UNDULATING, PRONTO!
(NO WAY. WHAT A WEIRDO!)
HARRELL
I HAVEN'T HAD QUICHE THIS MOIST IN AGES!
HAHA HAHAHA!!
SHH!!

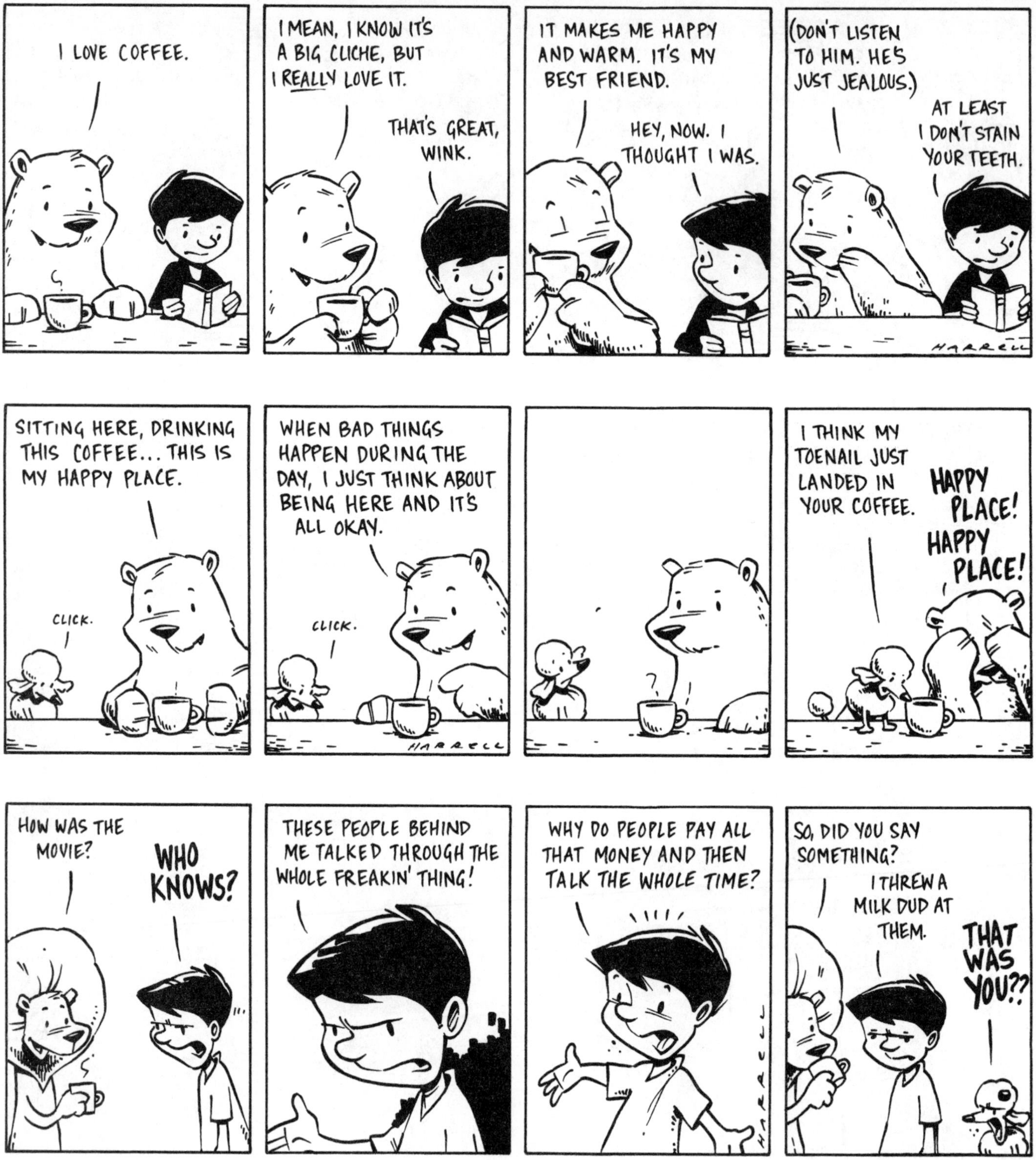
I LOVE COFFEE.
I MEAN, I KNOW IT'S A BIG CLICHE, BUT I REALLY LOVE IT.
THAT'S GREAT, WINK.
IT MAKES ME HAPPY AND WARM. IT'S MY BEST FRIEND.
HEY, NOW. I THOUGHT I WAS.
(DON'T LISTEN TO HIM. HE'S JUST JEALOUS.)
AT LEAST I DON'T STAIN YOUR TEETH.
HARRELL
SITTING HERE, DRINKING THIS COFFEE... THIS IS MY HAPPY PLACE.
CLICK.
WHEN BAD THINGS HAPPEN DURING THE DAY, I JUST THINK ABOUT BEING HERE AND IT'S ALL OKAY.
CLICK.
HARRELL
I THINK MY TOENAIL JUST LANDED IN YOUR COFFEE.
HAPPY PLACE! HAPPY PLACE!
HOW WAS THE MOVIE?
WHO KNOWS?
THESE PEOPLE BEHIND ME TALKED THROUGH THE WHOLE FREAKIN' THING!
WHY DO PEOPLE PAY ALL THAT MONEY AND THEN TALK THE WHOLE TIME?
HARRELL
SO, DID YOU SAY SOMETHING?
I THREW A MILK DUD AT THEM.
THAT WAS YOU??

Special Feature *Never-Before-Seen* Big Top *Outtakes!*

YOU. YOU'RE GOING TO HEADLINE THIS "PUBERTY ROCKS" TOUR?
THAT'S CORRECT.
TWENTY-FIVE CITIES. ME...BRIT...JUSTIN AND THE BOYS...A FEW OTHERS.
SPITNEY BREARS?
SNICKER
OH, HA HA! I WAS UP 'TIL, LIKE, FOUR THIS MORNING.
AHH! HA HA!
OKAY! TAKE THREE!

C'MON, WINK. ALL THE GOOD CANDY'LL BE GONE...
OKAY... HERE I COME.
I'M ... WHOOPS!
RIPPP
CUT!
WARDROBE MALFUNCTION! NOTHIN' TO SEE HERE!

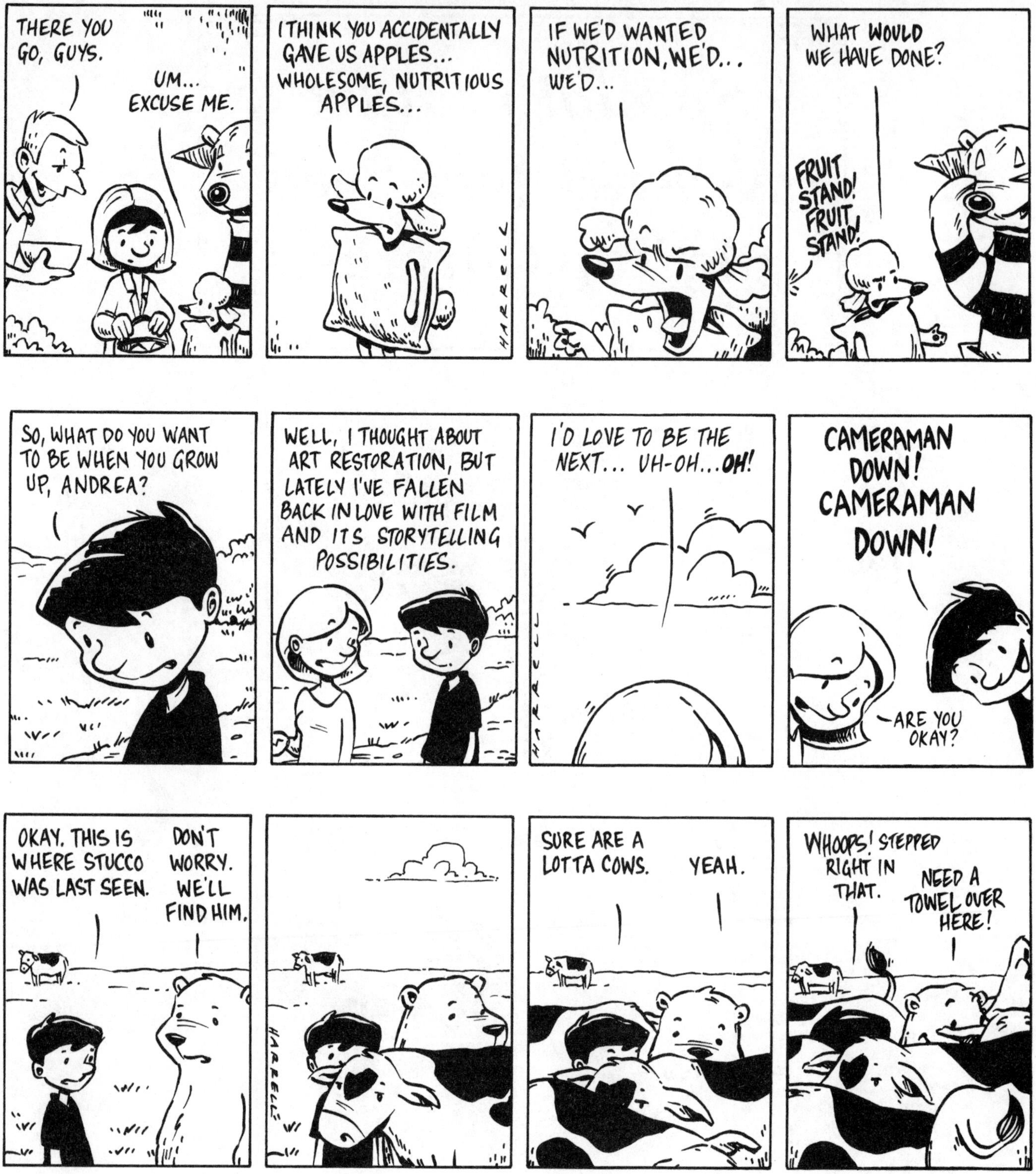
THERE YOU GO, GUYS.
UM... EXCUSE ME.
I THINK YOU ACCIDENTALLY GAVE US APPLES... WHOLESOME, NUTRITIOUS APPLES...
IF WE'D WANTED NUTRITION, WE'D... WE'D...
WHAT WOULD WE HAVE DONE?
FRUIT STAND! FRUIT STAND!
HARRELL
SO, WHAT DO YOU WANT TO BE WHEN YOU GROW UP, ANDREA?
WELL, I THOUGHT ABOUT ART RESTORATION, BUT LATELY I'VE FALLEN BACK IN LOVE WITH FILM AND ITS STORYTELLING POSSIBILITIES.
I'D LOVE TO BE THE NEXT... UH-OH... OH!
CAMERAMAN DOWN! CAMERAMAN DOWN!
ARE YOU OKAY?
HARRELL
OKAY. THIS IS WHERE STUCCO WAS LAST SEEN.
DON'T WORRY. WE'LL FIND HIM.
HARRELL
SURE ARE A LOTTA COWS.
YEAH.
WHOOPS! STEPPED RIGHT IN THAT.
NEED A TOWEL OVER HERE!